FAMILY TIES IN VICTORIAN ENGLAND

FAMILY TIES IN VICTORIAN ENGLAND

Claudia Nelson

VICTORIAN LIFE AND TIMES
Sally Mitchell, Series Editor

PRAEGER

Westport, Connecticut
London

Library of Congress Cataloging-in-Publication Data

Nelson, Claudia.
 Family ties in Victorian England / Claudia Nelson.
     p.   cm.—(Victorian life and times, ISSN 1932–944X)
   Includes bibliographical references and index.
   ISBN 0–275–98697–7 (alk. paper)
   1. Family—England—History—19th century.   2. Family in literature   I. Title.
HQ615.N45   2007
306.870942'09034–dc22   2006038660

British Library Cataloguing in Publication Data is available.

Library of Congress Catalog Card Number: 2006038660
ISBN-10: 0–275–98697–7
ISBN-13: 978–0–275–98697–1
ISSN: 1932–944X

First published in 2007

Praeger Publishers, 88 Post Road West, Westport, CT 06881
An imprint of Greenwood Publishing Group, Inc.
www.praeger.com

Printed in the United States of America

The paper used in this book complies with the
Permanent Paper Standard issued by the National
Information Standards Organization (Z39.48–1984).

10 9 8 7 6 5 4 3 2 1

To my family, most especially Anne and Mary Isabel

CONTENTS

SERIES FOREWORD

Although the nineteenth century has now almost faded from living memory—most people who heard first-hand stories from grandparents who grew up before 1900 have adult grandchildren by now—impressions of the Victorian world continue to influence both popular culture and public debates. These impressions may well be vivid yet contradictory. Many people, for example, believe that Victorian society was safe, family-centered, and stable because women could not work outside the home, although every census taken during the period records hundreds of thousands of female laborers in fields, factories, shops, and schools as well as more than a million domestic servants—often girls of fourteen or fifteen—whose long and unregulated workdays created the comfortable leisured world we see in Merchant and Ivory films. Yet it is also true that there were women who had no household duties and desperately wished for some purpose in life but found that social expectations and family pressure absolutely prohibited their presence in the workplace.

The goal of books in the Victorian Life and Times series is to explain and enrich the simple pictures that show only a partial truth. Although the Victorian period in Great Britain is often portrayed as peaceful, comfortable, and traditional, it was actually a time of truly breathtaking change. In 1837, when eighteen-year-old Victoria became queen, relatively few of England's people had ever traveled more than ten miles from the place where they were born. Little more than half the population could read and write, children as young as five worked in factories and mines, and political power was entirely in the hands of a small minority of men who held property. By the time Queen Victoria died in 1901, railways provided fast and cheap transportation for both goods and people, telegraph messages sped to the far corners of the British Empire in minutes, education was compulsory, a man's religion (or lack of it) no longer barred him from sitting in Parliament, and women were not only wives and domestic servants but also physicians, dentists, elected school-board members, telephone operators, and university lecturers. Virtually every aspect of life had been transformed either by technology or by the massive political and legal reforms that reshaped Parliament, elections, universities, the army, education, sanitation, public health, marriage, working conditions, trade unions, and civil and criminal law.

The continuing popularity of Victoriana among decorators and collectors, the strong market for historical novels and for mysteries set in the age of Jack the Ripper and Sherlock Holmes, the new interest in books by George Eliot and Charles Dickens and Wilkie Collins whenever one is presented on television, and the desire of amateur genealogists and hobbyists to find out about the lives, as well as the names, of nineteenth-century British ancestors all reveal the need for accurate information about the period's social history and material culture. In the years since my book *Daily Life in Victorian England* was published in 1996 I have been contacted by many people who want more detailed information about some area covered in that overview. Each book in the Victorian Life and Times series will focus on a single topic, describe changes during the period, and consider the differences between country and city, between industrial life and rural life, and above all, the differences made by class, social position, religion, tradition, gender, and economics. Each book is an original work, illustrated with drawings and pictures taken from Victorian sources, enriched by boxed quotations from Victorian publications, based on current research and written by a qualified scholar. All the authors have doctoral degrees and many years' experience in teaching; they have been chosen not only for their academic qualifications but also for their ability to write clearly and to explain complex ideas to people without extensive background in the subject. Thus the books are authoritative and dependable but written in straightforward language; explanations are supplied whenever specialized terminology is used, and a bibliography lists resources for further information.

The Internet has made it possible for people who cannot visit archives and reference libraries to conduct serious family and historical research. Careful hobbyists and scholars have scanned large numbers of primary sources— nineteenth-century cookbooks, advice manuals, maps, city directories, magazines, sermons, church records, illustrated newspapers, guidebooks, political cartoons, photographs, paintings, published investigations of slum conditions and poor people's budgets, political essays, inventories of scientists' correspondence, and many other materials formerly accessible only to academic historians. Yet the World Wide Web also contains misleading documents and false information, even on educational sites created by students and enthusiasts who don't have the experience to put material in useful contexts. So far as possible, therefore, the bibliographies for books in the Victorian Life and Times series will also offer guidance on using publicly available electronic resources.

The Victorian family is often idealized as a model of parental authority, loving relationships, inner harmony, and secure values untroubled by pressures from the public world. England's queen was a married woman who bore nine children; pull-out portraits of the royal family at home were a regular feature of the illustrated magazines that had, by the middle of the period, grown cheap enough for almost everyone to afford. Claudia Nelson's *Family Ties in Victorian England* describes the sources from which Victorians themselves constructed a sentimental vision of family life and explains the alternate versions found in some autobiographies, novels, and sociological studies. By paying attention to economics, birth and death rates, class differences, and legal developments, Nelson reveals that Victorian families were in many ways as varied and as complicated as those of the present day and shows how examples from both literature and social investigations can uncover some of the fears and difficulties that lay beneath the surface of family life. She also demonstrates that for the Victorians as for ourselves, conceptions of the ideal family had an important influence on individual psychology and the internal workings of actual families as well as on public and political debates.

The author, Claudia Nelson, is Professor of English at Texas A&M University, where she also directs the Women's Studies Program. She has written or edited scholarly books on children's fiction, nineteenth-century girls, Victorian fatherhood, ideals of motherhood, adoption, and sex education. Her book *Little Strangers,* on portrayals of adoption, won the 2005 Children's Literature Association award for the best scholarly book in the field of children's studies. At Texas A&M she teaches graduate, undergraduate, and honors courses in Victorian literature, the English novel since 1870, children's literature, and representations of motherhood.

Sally Mitchell, Series Editor

ACKNOWLEDGMENTS

My primary thanks must go to Sally Mitchell for inviting me to contribute to this series on Victorian Life and Times. Without her, this book would not have been written—and without the models of informed and approachable scholarship that she has provided throughout her career, my work would be poorer. Thanks, too, to the Department of English at Texas A&M University for funding graduate research assistants Sunjoo Lee and Amy Montz. Amy's energy and unfailing cheer during the more fraught moments of finding and preparing illustrations for this volume are particularly appreciated. For permission to use images drawn from its collection, I am grateful to Texas A&M's Sterling C. Evans Library.

I have profited from reading any number of earlier works on the subjects discussed in the present study, from discussions with my colleagues Terry Hoagwood and Bob Boenig, and from participating in an assortment of collaborative projects while this book was in progress. Of these I should mention especially Trev Lynn Broughton and Helen Rogers's *Gender and Fatherhood in the 19th Century* (forthcoming from Palgrave) and Dennis Denisoff's *Nineteenth-Century Childhood and the Rise of Consumer Culture* (forthcoming from Ashgate), as well as the contributions to the Ashgate Studies in Childhood series. The field of nineteenth-century family and childhood studies is presently a rich and lively one, and I count myself fortunate to be working in it.

Finally, on the home front, I am grateful to my daughter, Mary Isabel Nelson, for sometimes letting me work on this book and sometimes reminding me that a game of chess or a swim might be a good idea, too.

INTRODUCTION

When the eighteen-year-old Victoria inherited the throne in 1837, England's economy was primarily agricultural. Of the approximately 15 million people whom the 1831 Census had counted in England and Wales, fewer than 5 million lived in cities. They traveled slowly, in horse-drawn vehicles or by sailing ship or on foot, and although the Industrial Revolution was already in its sixth decade, most work connected with daily life—dressmaking, cleaning, food production, hauling water for sanitation and consumption—was still done by hand. Religious tracts for the poor and didactic literature for children emphasized the need to accept one's place and respect authority, a message reflecting the early nineteenth-century fear that Britain, which experienced joblessness and high prices following the Napoleonic Wars, would undergo the same sort of revolution that had engulfed France in 1789. Over the sixty-three years of Victoria's reign, England did indeed undergo a revolution. But it involved not military force but rather technological, commercial, and social developments that fundamentally changed English life, replacing the world into which Victoria was born with one that looks much more familiar to the twenty-first-century eye. Simultaneously, these developments changed the English family.

Demography offers one way to measure the difference between the England of 1837 and that of 1901. By the dawn of the twentieth century, the population of England and Wales had grown to 32.5 million, roughly two-thirds of its present size. Eighty percent of these people, or about 26 million souls, lived in or near cities; the population of London alone had doubled, to 4 million, over the six decades after 1841. The explosive growth of urban centers led first to appalling conditions in slum quarters and subsequently to more effective sanitation. Turning points here were the cholera epidemic of 1853–1854, the London "Summer of the Great Stink" in 1858, and the Prince Consort's death in 1861 from typhoid fever, a disease caused by contaminated water; all sparked campaigns for better control of refuse and sewage. By the end of the century, life expectancies remained substantially lower than they are in most developed nations today. A baby born in 1880 had, on the average, only forty-one years of life ahead of it if it was a boy, forty-four if it was a girl. Nevertheless, public health had improved significantly. The birth rate, which peaked at 36 births per thousand individuals in 1870 (more than three times the 2004 figure), was outstripping the death rate—in 1880, 22.2 deaths per thousand men and 19.5 deaths per thousand women. All these factors affected the composition of families, as well as the degree of health and comfort to be found in daily life.

Technology had made greater advances still, resulting in dramatic changes to both commercial and domestic life. The pace at which news traveled was no longer limited to the speed at which a person could carry it, but had become more nearly instantaneous with the commercial telegraph system, developed in the 1850s and linking Britain and North America after 1866. The construction of a national rail network, which extended to most of the country by 1850, drastically increased pollution, but also brought jobs for railroad personnel, laborers, engineers and machinists, and miners of coal and iron; fresh food, which could now be speedily transported from country to city; and, increasingly, a national culture, as travel became easier and news and fashions more readily broadcast. By the 1890s, telephones were a common feature in business life, making communication still more rapid. An efficient penny post, introduced in 1840, and the intertwined growth of literacy and the penny press likewise contributed to an unprecedented boom in the public and private dissemination of information. People, too, were moving more swiftly, carried along by passenger trains and steamships (from the 1840s onward), the London Underground (opened in 1863), the inexpensive "safety bicycle" (invented in 1885), and (by the 1890s) automobiles.

In a social sense as well, mobility seemed to many Victorians both more common and more rapid than had once been the case. To be sure, Britain experienced economic downturns. Among these were the decade called the "Hungry Forties," which contained not only the potato blight that caused the death or emigration of more than one-fifth of the population of Ireland, but also high food prices and unemployment in England; the "cotton famine" caused by the Union states' blockade of the Confederacy during the American Civil War, which temporarily devastated the Lancashire textile industry in the early 1860s; and the agricultural depression of the 1870s. But the prevailing trend was against poverty. Paupers made up 4.2 percent of the population in the late 1850s, 3.7 percent in the early 1870s, and only 2.7 percent in the early 1880s. Although England's increasing urbanization was partly a product of labor woes in the countryside, the movement from an agricultural to a manufacturing economy and the development of new kinds of business endeavors provided opportunities for some workers to rise above their impoverished origins. If the

NO SMOKE.   NO SMELL.

Price,
as drawn,
£2 12s. 6d.

NO
TROUBLE.
NO DUST.

FRANK RIPPINGILLE'S _{PATENT} STOVES

UNIVERSALLY ADMITTED THE BEST IN THE WORLD.

Oven temperature in 12 minutes from time of lighting over 400 degrees. Will bake, roast, fry, stew, toast, warm plates, boil water; in fact, do all and even more than a Kitchen Range.

SOLD BY ALL THE LEADING STORES AND IRONMONGERS IN THE WORLD.

See the name **FRANK RIPPINGILLE** on every Stove and do not be put off with worthless imitations.

WILL COOK A DINNER FOR SIX PEOPLE AT THE COST OF ONE PENNY.

Prices from 5s.   Write for Catalogue, free.

MADE BY THE

FRANK RIPPINGILLE STOVE CO.

PLUME STREET, ASTON, BIRMINGHAM.

The technological boom that extended throughout the Victorian period changed not only England's public face but its domestic life as well. This advertisement for Frank Rippingille's Patent Stoves was incorporated into the 1890 edition of *Mrs. Beeton's Cookery Book and Household Guide*. [London: Ward Lock & Bowden; collection of the author.]

self-made man who went from mill hand to mill owner in a generation was a rare creature, he nonetheless became a prominent figure in Victorian mythology. On a larger if less dramatic scale, the increased availability of education for the poor, which the government began partially to fund in 1839 before passing a series of Education Acts to put ever more children in school, created a more literate workforce with a better chance for social advancement. The pre-Victorian tracts about humble shepherds praising God for making them contented with their lot gave way to secular works for those aspiring to improve their situation, most famously Samuel Smiles's best-selling *Self-Help* (1859). Such commentaries emphasized that home and family were crucial factors in the struggle to rise.

> Whatever may be the efficiency of schools, the examples set in our Homes must always be of vastly greater influence in forming the characters of our future men and women. The Home is the crystal of society—the nucleus of national character; and from that source, be it pure or tainted, issue the habits, principles and maxims which govern public as well as private life. The nation comes from the nursery.
>
> —Samuel Smiles, *Self-Help*, 1859

Social rise was desirable on any number of fronts, as life in the middle class was not merely more comfortable than life in poverty, but generally longer as well. If members of the working classes married earlier than members of the middle classes, they also died sooner, particularly in childhood. In England as a whole, infant mortality had diminished substantially since the eighteenth century, although it remained frighteningly high by today's standards. Dr. T. R. Edmonds noted in the medical journal *The Lancet* in 1836 that in the years between 1730 and 1749, nearly 75 percent of all children born had died before age five, a figure that had fallen to just over 50 percent by 1789.[1] By 1880 the rate was closer to 6 percent—but in the slums of big cities such as London and Liverpool, children were still dying at late-eighteenth-century rates at the very end of Victoria's reign. While the average citizen in the Victorian era was much more likely to live long enough to produce children than someone living a century or two earlier had been, the large families associated with the period were in part a recognition that many children would die before adulthood. Significantly, by the end of the period middle-class family sizes had shrunk to reflect the improved life expectancies of the well to do, while working-class families remained large.

As the power of the middle class grew, the moral authority of the aristocracy declined. The court of George IV, Victoria's uncle, who served as Regent for his mentally incapacitated father from 1810 to 1820 and then ruled in his own right until 1830, was known for its sexual permissiveness. A series of scandals in high life peaked with the remarkable spectacle of the newly crowned King suing his estranged wife for divorce when she attempted to claim her position as Queen. Although it was evident that neither spouse's behavior could stand much scrutiny, the country's sympathies were with Queen Caroline, and the prestige of both George and his cabinet (which had, at his direction, instituted the divorce proceedings) suffered a serious blow. Subsequently, the political agitation that extended from the 1820s through the 1840s pitted the working classes against the landed gentry; if the former came off as violent and excessive in their demands, the latter struck some observers as intransigent in their attempts to maintain their traditional privileges and income. Ultimately, perhaps, neither scandal nor agitation had as much influence over the shift in power toward the middle classes as did the changes that were taking place in the way England made its money, but the emotional climate of England was shifting as well, undergoing a reaction against self-indulgence. In this new atmosphere, the middle classes' more modest pleasures and more evident productivity seemed better suited to the age than the profligacy of many Regency nobles, and family life took moral precedence over public display.

George's younger brother William, who inherited the throne from him, proved sensitive to the change of national mood; after William's death in 1837 and that of his wife, Queen Adelaide, in 1849, both were eulogized as having been excellent models for middle-class family life. (William's ten illegitimate children were tactfully omitted from such tributes.) Profiting from this example, Victoria, too, soon established herself as a monarch middle-class in spirit if not in station. Her success in turning herself into a national icon was not immediate, however. After a brief honeymoon period at the time of her accession and coronation, her popularity among her subjects began to slip, injured particularly by the negative publicity surrounding her treatment of one of her ladies in waiting, Lady Flora Hastings. A friend of Sir John Conroy, whom Victoria particularly disliked because of his attempts to shift a modicum of royal authority to himself, the attractive Lady Flora had begun to complain of pain and swelling of the stomach. Victoria jumped to the conclusion that the unmarried young woman was carrying Conroy's child, a determination that widened the rift between Victoria and her mother, Conroy's longtime ally. Within a few months, Lady Flora was dead of liver cancer, and the periodical press trumpeted the people's anger at the Queen's behavior. Eager to enter upon a new phase of her life and reign and to end the irksome authority exercised over her by her mother and, indirectly, Conroy, Victoria began discussing with her prime minister the possibility of marrying her cousin Prince Albert of Saxe-Coburg-Gotha.

The marriage was solemnized in February 1840. By 1857, the Queen had borne nine children, and her devotion to her consort and to her home life had established her as a model bourgeois housewife—if one uniquely rich, famous, and active in national affairs. After Albert's sudden death in December 1861, Victoria embarked upon an ecstasy of mourning, secluding herself as much as possible from the public gaze for the next fifteen years and making it obvious that like the ideal woman of her age, her chief priorities were domestic. If her private letters were frank about her disappointment in her eldest son, her belief that marriage was often a disaster from the woman's standpoint, and her feelings of revulsion toward infants, symbolically Victoria's role as matriarch of a large family was crucial to her public image. The opinions that she voiced to trusted confidants such as her daughter Vicky sometimes coincided with those of nineteenth-century feminists, but the persona that she constructed for her subjects—and that they helped to construct for her—established her as a model for women who sought their fulfillment from family life.

> All marriage is such a lottery—the happiness is always an exchange—though it may be a very happy one—still the poor woman is bodily and morally the husband's slave. That always sticks in my throat. When I think of a merry, happy, free young girl—and look at the ailing, aching state a young wife generally is doomed to—which you can't deny is the penalty of marriage.
> —Letter from Queen Victoria to her eldest daughter, May 16, 1860

The Queen was not alone in seeing familial devotion as the answer to the woes of public life. Faced with a rapidly changing world, English society clung to the idea that family might provide stability and access to eternal values. But the pattern of family life was itself in flux. Once a site of economic productivity, the home was increasingly separate from the workplace, as the new availability and cheapness of mass transportation, and the rise of factories and corresponding decline of cottage industries, made commuting to work common. For wives who did not work outside the home, the domestic space could thus become a private fiefdom, to be managed with minimal interference from husbands who had to absent themselves in order to make a living. To be sure, women of the laboring classes frequently held down paying jobs; approximately one-third of the Victorian workforce was female, although mothers of young children tended to stay home unless the financial situation was unusually dire. But even though at least 85 percent of the population was working-class, it was middle-class ideology that was dominant in Victorian society, because it was the middle class that controlled the presses, writing and producing most of the books and periodicals that voiced and shaped public opinion. Thus it was the middle-class model, in which work was generally divorced from home, that gave rise to an idea crucial to the era's construction of family, namely the concept of separate spheres.

In a lecture entitled "Of Queens' Gardens," delivered in 1864 and published the following year as part of *Sesame and Lilies*, the Victorian sage John Ruskin famously articulated his view of the relationship proper between the sexes. Man, Ruskin explained, was to be the risk-taker, the protector, the partner toughened by contact with the world. His strength, and his willingness to be coarsened morally by his exposure to conflict and corruption, would provide a safe place for woman to carry out her own duties, including not only the maintaining of a pleasant and tranquil home but also the moral uplifting of its occupants. Home would therefore function both as a respite from the knockabout public sphere and as an antidote to it—even, perhaps, a means of transforming it, if the woman succeeded in expanding her domestic power to serve and improve the state, as Ruskin encouraged her to do. If man's protection of woman enabled home to exist, the woman would use the home she ruled to protect man in turn.

> By her office, and place, [the woman] is protected from all danger and temptation. The man, in his rough work in the open world, must encounter all peril and trial:—to him, therefore, must be the failure, the offence, the inevitable error: often he must be wounded, or subdued; often misled; and always hardened. But he guards the woman from all this; within his house, as ruled by her, unless she herself has sought it, need enter no danger, no temptation, no cause of error or offence. This is the true nature of home—it is the place of Peace; the shelter, not only from all injury, but from all terror, doubt, and division. In so far as it is not this, it is not home: so far as the anxieties of the outer life penetrate into it, and the inconsistently-minded, unknown, unloved, or hostile society of the outer world is allowed by either husband or wife to cross the threshold, it ceases to be home; it is then only a part of that outer world which you have roofed over, and lighted fire in.
> —John Ruskin, "Of Queens' Gardens," 1864

As constructed by Ruskin and countless other cultural commentators, home and family were potent forces, amounting, at least in the abstract, to a secular religion. But the ways in which Victorian society practiced this "religion" varied enormously. Feminists invoked "mother power" in order to urge the expansion of women's rights, while antifeminists invoked it to explain why women should not have the vote. Institutions from schools to churches to government used family as a metaphor to explain or justify their own social authority. And individuals sought to keep these institutions at a distance by pleading that family was a private matter. Moreover, the abstractions voiced by Ruskin and his ilk might bear little or no resemblance to particular cases. Ruskin's own marriage, for instance, failed publicly and spectacularly when his wife, Effie Gray, left him for the painter John Everett Millais, justifying her action by revealing that the union had never been consummated.

Such disjunctions between the ideal and the real contributed to the many stresses and anxieties surrounding the Victorian family. While the literature of sentiment presented family in a quasi-sacred light, the literature of sensation (and, sometimes, autobiography) suggested that family might rather be the incubator of twisted emotions and disreputable secrets. Sociologists sketched a lurid portrait of family life among the poor that suggested that domestic peace was not an instinct but a luxury. And sundry important pieces of legislation passed during this period and impinging on family life provided official recognition that wives might need financial protection from their husbands, that parents might not be very good at child rearing, and that a marriage might be a prison rather than a refuge.

The first of these new laws, the Custody of Infants Act of 1839, was passed partly in response to the vigorous lobbying of one estranged wife, Caroline Norton, whose 1836 separation from her abusive husband had left him—as was customary at the time—with near-complete power over her property and children. Divorce would have required the passage of a private Act of Parliament, and while if Norton had managed to secure a divorce she would have controlled any money she might earn or inherit in future, English law held that except in extraordinary circumstances, children belonged entirely to their fathers. The 1839 Act, first in a series of laws that gradually gave judges (not parents) more power to determine custody arrangements, established that women separated from their husbands could petition the Court of Chancery to give them custody of children under seven and visitation rights to children under sixteen. (Chancery, of course, was free to refuse such requests.) While this procedural change may seem less than adequate to some of us today, as indeed it did to many early Victorians, it nonetheless represented the first crack in English law's assumption that the family had only one face, namely the husband's.

A more dramatic change in the law occurred with the passage of another bill for which Norton had fought, the Divorce and Matrimonial Causes Act of 1857. Before the Divorce Act, legal dissolution of marriage was possible only for the wealthy and well connected; after its passage, divorce was within the reach of the middle classes as well. (The poor, cut off by financial and cultural reasons from the recourses available to their social superiors, evolved less formal ways of dealing with failed marriages.) The Act gave to women who had separated from their spouses the legal status of spinsters, who, unlike wives, could own property and control their own money. It also established a divorce court, making the termination of marriages substantially easier. The rules for divorce differed for men and women. A husband could divorce his wife simply by proving that she had been unfaithful to him. A wife, however, had to prove that her husband was not only adulterous but had also deserted her, committed incest or bigamy, or abused her in a way that went beyond his legal right to chastise her physically. This double standard reflected the widespread view that a wife's adultery was more serious than a husband's, not only because it might foist upon him children not biologically his, but also because woman's sexual drive was, or should be, different from man's in being focused on pregnancy rather than pleasure. A husband's straying was regrettable but natural; a woman who forgot her marriage vows betrayed both her family and all womankind.

But perhaps the most radical of all the assumptions underlying Victorian family legislation was the admission that even women who stayed with their husbands might need legal powers of their own. Nineteenth-century feminists fought long and hard for reforms that would change the principle, once fundamental to English law, that a wife had no legal identity separate from her husband's. Thus, for instance, suffrage leader Millicent Garrett Fawcett recalled with bitterness in her memoirs the experience of appearing in court to bear witness in a criminal case. When she heard the bailiff read out the charge that the accused had stolen "from the person of Millicent Fawcett a purse containing £1 18s. 6d., the property of Henry Fawcett," she felt that her own title to the money was as nonexistent as the thief's.[2] While the Married Women's Property Acts of 1870 and 1882 did not take the ultimate step of giving wives property rights and a legal status equal to those of their husbands, they decreed that husbands could no longer exercise complete control over their wives' earnings, savings, and inheritances. After 1882, the money in Millicent Fawcett's purse might be described as hers.

The 1882 Act, the more far-reaching of the two, defined as married women's "separate property" all that came into their possession after January 1, 1883, and gave them the right to dispose of it as they saw fit. Wives could enter into contracts in their own right and could sue or be sued to the limit of their separate finances. They also became liable for their own debts, which put an end to a tactic employed by some aggrieved wives, including Caroline Norton: when Norton's husband reduced her separation allowance in 1851, she responded by refusing to pay her bills, thus making him the target of lawsuits from creditors. To be sure, the Acts were carefully framed to distinguish women's right of "separate property" from men's right of "own property," which was intimately connected to the right to vote, something Englishwomen would not have on equal terms with men until 1928. Nevertheless, they consciously sought to protect the economic interests of women married to improvident, unscrupulous, or cruel husbands.

Parliament passed laws of the sort described above only reluctantly, and for each law enacted, many more radical and sweeping measures failed. But that these Acts made their way through Parliament at all, and that they excited considerable pamphleteering and editorializing pro and con, signaled two things. First, the Victorian family was not the stable repository of absolute virtue that the literature of sentiment claimed that it was, but was changing in response to a changing world. Second, the discrepancies between the ideal vision of the family and the family as it might exist in real life were giving rise to discussion so heated as to reveal deep cultural anxieties.

> [I am] old-fashioned enough to believe that by the law of Nature and the law of
> God the father [is] the person who ought to have the care of his child, and that
> to disestablish the father altogether of his rights and to say that the Judge should
> act solely with reference to his own view of the welfare of the infant would be to
> disregard rights held sacred from the beginning of our polity.
> —Speech of the Marquess of Salisbury in the House of Lords,
> reported in *Parliamentary Debates* for April 30, 1885

We may see the controversy surrounding other pieces of Victorian legislation as arising from similarly family-related concerns. While throughout the century Parliament refused to limit the number of hours men could work, laws such as the Mines Regulation Act of 1842 and the Factory Acts of 1850, 1874, and 1878 set caps on the length of the female workday in certain industries. Both proponents and opponents of such restrictions observed that the caps were motivated partly by the idea that women's place was in the home and that working women jeopardized both their families' comfort and the health of their present and future children. For every commentator who proclaimed that family life was at the root of England's strength, there was another who saw families as damaged or vulnerable.

This book examines that paradox. The chapters to follow will focus both on the historical facts influencing Victorian domestic life and on the conflicting and powerful images of family that Victorians produced in their fiction and nonfiction—which continue to influence and to help explain visions of family today. Our investigation will be organized around familial roles, with chapters on husbands and wives, fathers and mothers, sons and daughters, brothers and sisters, the extended family, and nontraditional families (blended families, adoptive families, and single-parent households). As is the case in our own culture, the Victorians did not always agree about how the family should operate and what the role of any given family member should ideally be. Moreover, assumptions about family dynamics and roles were influenced by social class, religious beliefs, opinions on woman's place, and many other social factors. It should be noted that these factors include geography; both the patterns of family life and, to some extent, beliefs about roles within the family varied according to whether the people in question were English, Welsh, Scottish, Irish, or expatriates living in one of Great Britain's possessions overseas. This book generally confines its investigation to England. It seeks to highlight ways in which disparate views of family life and domestic duties cooperated and conflicted, and to increase our understanding of how both positive and negative visions fulfilled the practical, emotional, and moral needs of the nation.

Chapter 1 examines Victorian views on marriage, specifically the roles of husband and wife. Victoria's reign witnessed the publication of popular advice manuals, magazine articles, didactic novels, and other middle-class texts

A wood engraving depicting afternoon tea shows the purchasers of the cheap shilling edition of *Mrs. Beeton's Cookery Book and Household Guide* what they might aspire to: spacious rooms with elegant furnishings and a leisured social environment in which women predominate but men participate as well. [London: Ward Lock & Bowden, 1890; collection of the author.]

treating marriage as a topic on which readers would need instruction; these writings' clear assumption is that many people, women and men alike, don't understand marriage's complexities and risks. Motivations for marriage included romantic love and the longing for companionship and children, but also the desire for productive work (wives), for financial security and social status (wives, but also many husbands), for an acceptable outlet for sexual urges (husbands, but also many wives), and for a dependable housekeeper (husbands). Remarriage after the death of one's original spouse was also common, especially when the earlier marriage had resulted in children, since the bereaved partner often hoped that a new husband or wife would bring the family back to economic and/or emotional stability. Once married, couples might or might not find that the expected results materialized, and thus Victorian texts commonly offer advice not only on reaching these goals but also on coming to terms with disappointment.

Chapter 2 discusses expectations for—and criticisms of—fathers and mothers. That nineteenth-century fathers increasingly worked outside the home lessened their domestic authority, so that many were seen as withdrawn, overbearing, or ineffectual or were viewed more in financial than emotional terms; in middle-class practice, mothers were often the dominant parents. Hence mothers might be presented as either making up for their mates' failings or complementing a more distant, but still powerful, male. Working-class parents were often judged according to the extent to which they appeared to have embraced middle-class mores. Thus fathers who devoted too much time to the leisure pursuits of the poor (which in the nineteenth century often took place outside the family context) or mothers who worked outside the home were condemned as socially dangerous. And even in the case of middle-class

maternity, which generally had a halo of sanctity, many Victorian texts con-
demn individual mothers, who are pilloried as weak and childlike, complacent
and hypocritical, or even physically and emotionally abusive. These negative
portrayals improve our grasp both of the ideal and of the depth of Victorian
fears that this ideal might prove elusive.

Chapter 3 deals with sons and daughters, and specifically with how their roles
diverged. Child rearing often differed radically for boys and girls; for example,
middle-class boys were much more likely than their sisters to attend boarding
school (typically from age seven on), and there was a general expectation that
sons were to be prepared for independence while daughters might well not
be. Similarly, the duties of sons—to follow their fathers in a particular line of
work, say—could also seem very different from the duties of daughters, who
might be required to serve as caregivers in their parents' old age or to take
over the child-care responsibilities of mothers who had died. Social workers
ministering to the working classes might see girls, far more than boys, as a
mechanism through which mothers might be taught middle-class standards of
domestic comfort. This approach, like some other Victorian commentary on
parent-child ties, suggests a belief that the mother–daughter relationship was
based on sameness to an extent that might not be true for mothers and sons,
fathers and daughters, or perhaps even fathers and sons.

Chapter 4 focuses on siblings, a significant issue in an era of large families.
Earlier scholars have noted that the brother–sister tie was unique in Victorian
society because it was presumed not to have a sexual component. As a result,
siblings of opposite genders could experience an intimacy and freedom otherwise impossible between male and female; thus artist Dante Gabriel Rossetti
could draw his sister in the nude not despite but because of their kinship. Yet
many Victorian depictions of family acknowledge also the inequality of sibling
relationships. A disproportionate share of the domestic burden might fall on
the eldest child in a working-class family, who often had to help support or
care for younger siblings; while some children took pride in their usefulness
and felt a quasi-parental solicitude toward their charges, others resented the
demands made on them. In addition, in a world that expected different things
of boys than of girls and that (at least in the landowning classes) observed
primogeniture, sibling relationships might be fraught with jealousy. Finally,
the possibility that the passionate bonds among siblings that Victorian culture
sought to promote might have a covertly or even overtly sexual dimension
was a source of tremendous anxiety to respectable middle- and upper-class
Victorian England, as the emotional debate over the Deceased Wife's Sister Bill
suggests. The tension between the Victorian ideal of a large, loving family and
the actuality, in which some siblings felt exploited or rejected or the love gave
rise to anxiety, fueled many literary explorations and personal experiences of
family in the nineteenth century.

The subject of Chapter 5 is the extended family, in particular the extension
of the household beyond what we now consider the standard pattern of mother,

father, and children. Not only did well-to-do Victorians employ live-in servants whose duties included child care (wet-nurses, nannies, and governesses, as well as other servants, some of them in their teens, who might provide companionship for their masters' offspring), but families at all income levels often took in miscellaneous relations. Marriage between first or second cousins was relatively common, reflecting—among other things—the close emotional ties that could exist among members of an extended family. Other factors shaped the configuration of households as well. Reductions in pension schemes after 1870 meant that grown children were increasingly responsible for supporting their parents, so that grandparents often resided in the home. Girls might join their married sisters to help with the children and, perhaps, improve their own chances of finding husbands; nieces and nephews whose parents were dead or resident in countries deemed unhealthy for children, such as India, might be folded into their cousins' nurseries. Portrayals of such households often betray anxiety about their emotional and moral climates, so that discussions of the extended family may help to reveal the areas in which Victorians were concerned about family as an institution.

Finally, Chapter 6 explores what we would now term nontraditional families—although blended families, in particular, were an ordinary feature of the Victorian domestic landscape. To be sure, the blended families now created by divorce were unusual, but nineteenth-century mortality patterns were such that partial families headed by a widow or widower and blended families containing stepmothers, stepfathers, and stepsiblings and half-siblings were common. England had no adoption law until 1926, but informal adoption, including adoption by single parents, existed among both the proletariat and the bourgeoisie. As in the case of the families examined in Chapter 5, nontraditional families often function in fiction and nonfiction texts to permit criticism of various family members. When the Brothers Grimm revised their 1812 collection of German fairy tales, they turned wicked biological mothers into stepmothers to soften the evil, feeling that the stories might otherwise unsettle their audiences and diminish the reverence in which motherhood should be held. Victorian novelists used a similar stratagem, in that stepparents sometimes display in exaggerated form failings elsewhere attributed more tentatively to biological parents. Conversely, adoptive parents may demonstrate a devotion that throws into relief the inadequacies of their children's blood kin, and households in which a single parent occupies the place of both father and mother encourage observers to ask how distinct these roles really are. Nontraditional families, then, appear in literature both because they existed so often in life and because they permitted writers to raise potentially controversial questions.

The book that follows this brief introduction might seem to have two focuses, Victorian families as they were and Victorian families as they were imagined. But I want to suggest that "history" and "imaginative literature" are not always the separate entities that we sometimes assume them to be. Just as domestic fiction (a genre at which the Victorians excelled) works partly by incorporating believable and often trustworthy details about daily life, sociological commentary, housekeeping manuals, diaries, interpretations of population statistics, and other documents that we might consider "factual" all have their own assumptions about what families should be. I would argue that in order to gain an understanding of how Victorian families worked in practice, it is important also to think about how they were supposed to work on the level of the ideal. For the Victorians, who wrote voluminously on any topic with which they were familiar, were particularly ready to write about an experience that almost all of them shared, that of being part of a family, and inevitably, they wrote by blending what they had observed with what they longed for. It is those writings—whether in census documents or novels, instructions to district visitors or autobiographies, magazine editorials or Parliamentary debates on female labor—that make up the historical record with which we must concern ourselves.

1

WIVES AND HUSBANDS

Women outnumbered men in Victorian England. In the 1850s, for instance, commentators on the condition of women frequently pointed out that there were 104 females for every 100 males, or half a million "superfluous" women. This population imbalance was only partly attributable to the advantage in life expectancy that women typically enjoy over men in industrialized countries, which amounted only to 1.9 years of extra life in 1840 and 3.27 years by 1880. It also reflected the disproportionate exodus of men to the colonies, whether as soldiers or as settlers; of every ten emigrants, seven were male. Although women sometimes accompanied their husbands to destinations such as India or Australia, and sometimes emigrated on their own in the hope of finding adventure, fortune, and/or a suitable marriage partner, Britain's imperial possessions contained more Englishmen than Englishwomen, the reverse of the situation at home. While approximately 90 percent of the population of Victorian England eventually married, marriage might come late in life, and was not inevitable for either men or women. The 1851 census, for example, listed more than 1.7 million spinsters and nearly 800,000 widows, over half of the adult female population of Britain.

Partly as a result of such demographic patterns, partly as a result of social changes in employment, the position of women, and many other factors, Victorians understood that marriage in their society was changing. Not only did they realize that a significant sliver of the population would never marry, they saw as well that the roles of husband and wife were not matters of unalterable instinct, but rather required instruction and adaptation. The middle-class marital ideal involved love, companionship, and mutual respect based upon the complementary strengths that the partners were expected to bring to the union. Simultaneously, however, both lived experience and the world of popular culture indicated that the ideal did not always reflect reality. Middle-class criticism of working-class unions was common, as social workers and journalists expressed anxiety about drunkenness, sexual immorality, domestic violence, and other antifamily behaviors that they associated particularly with the poor. Yet to some extent, such criticism often seems to be a displacement of an anxiety whose real focus was the affluent.

WIFELY ROLES

Victorian conceptions of the nature of the ideal wife varied. The qualities that a working-class man was expected to value, or did value, in a wife differed in a number of particulars from the qualities that a wealthier man might seek. For instance, a comfortably situated middle-class husband could, if he chose, afford a wife in delicate health, and—once she had produced an adequate number of children—he might even prize her all the more for her fragility. After all, the religion of the day suggested that physical suffering refined the character; in addition, by keeping her homebound, an organic weakness would help to keep a woman safe from the potential contamination of the public sphere. To be sure, marriage manuals sometimes advised that chronic invalids refrain from marrying, for fear that any children might inherit their mother's weakness. In theory and in sentimental fiction, however, an invalid wife might look especially well poised to become the moral center of the home, thereby performing the kind of wifely duty emphasized by commentators such as John Ruskin. But middle-class wives had the luxury of delegating more down-to-earth responsibilities. Their households contained at least one servant, and often three or more, to see to the house, kitchen, and children; if such wives were confined to sickbeds, the sickbeds were likely to be located in tidy homes in which meals would come to the table on schedule.

In contrast, the working-class wife was typically responsible for cooking, cleaning, washing and sometimes making the clothes, marketing, budgeting, and either providing or (if she went out to work) arranging child care. If she fell ill, the family's comfort would suffer. Workingmen were thus well advised to seek energy and competence in prospective mates. And since, as we shall see below, working-class wives were likely to be employed outside the home at least occasionally during the marriage, their ability to generate income was also important. As the eminent Victorian sociologist Charles Booth pointed out in *Life and Labour of the People in London* (1889–1893), a wife could be the major factor determining a workingman's precise social class.[1] A drunken wife, for instance, would substantially handicap her sober husband's efforts to rise; she would waste his money, exhaust him emotionally, and fail to make the kind of home that he needed. An industrious wife would provide not only moral encouragement but also considerable practical and financial help.

The disastrous consequences for poor men of choosing the wrong wife are highlighted in novels such as Charles Dickens's *Hard Times* (1854). Here the

This advertisement by Lilian Young for Brooke's Monkey Brand Soap suggests some of the many duties of the good working-class wife, among them cleaning, caring for children, and cooking. It is noteworthy that this image was bound into the September 1890 issue of the *Boy's Own Paper*, a periodical whose contents did not generally highlight domesticity. [Collection of the author.]

decent workingman Stephen Blackpool is tied to a worthless alcoholic, which prevents him from marrying the upstanding woman to whom he has given his heart. Because divorce, although technically possible for those in a position to arrange a private Act of Parliament, is considerably beyond his means and station, and because he is too respectable to offer his true love anything but legal marriage, Stephen is trapped for life. While Dickens's novels contain many failed marriages (a preoccupation that reflects the author's own marital unhappiness), Stephen's situation seems more dire than those of his middle- and upper-class counterparts.

For one thing, when well-to-do wives err in Victorian fiction, their crimes are almost always sexual—and a wife's adultery, unlike alcoholism or drug addiction, was grounds for divorce after 1857. Even in novels published before the passage of the Divorce Act, such as Dickens's *Dombey and Son* (1847–1848) or Anne Brontë's *The Tenant of Wildfell Hall* (1848), wealthy husbands whose wives have been unfaithful, or, like Edith Dombey, merely appear to have been unfaithful, can arrange formal separations. And novels that show well-bred men yoked to working-class women dependent on drink or opiates, including George Eliot's *Silas Marner* (1861) and Samuel Butler's *The Way of All Flesh* (completed 1885, published 1903), suggest that such a husband does not always have to live with the consequences of his marital mistake. Unlike his poorer brethren, he derives his class status more from his family background and educational level than from his current income—or his wife's earning capacity and thrift.

In real life, even cases as dramatic as that of author George Gissing, the son of the proprietor of a small pharmacy, might be retrieved. Gissing was expelled from Owens College in Manchester and sentenced to a month's hard labor for stealing money, books, and clothing in an attempt to support the girl he loved, Nell Harrison, so that she would not have to return to a life of prostitution. His fall made it difficult for him to find work and, especially in his own eyes, declassed him; moreover, his marriage to Nell, an alcoholic, quickly fell apart. Nevertheless, Gissing was able to separate from Nell (who died destitute six years later), to establish himself as a professional writer, and to make his way

> "I ha' read i' th' papers that great fok (fair faw 'em a'! I wishes 'em no hurt!) are not bonded together for better for worse so fast, but that they can be set free fro' *their* misfortnet marriages, an' marry ower agen. When they dunnot agree, for that their tempers is ill-sorted, they has rooms o' one kind an' another in their houses, above a bit, and they can live asunders. We fok ha' only one room, and we can't. When that won't do, they ha' gowd an' other cash, an' they can say, 'This for yo' an' that for me,' an' they can go their separate ways. We can't. Spite o' all that, they can be set free for smaller wrongs than mine. So, I mun be ridden o' this woman, and I want t' know how?"
> —Charles Dickens, *Hard Times* (1854), Book the First, Chapter 11

back into the middle classes, despite contracting another disastrous marriage to a mentally unstable working-class woman. Had Gissing, like Nell, lost his family early in life and received no meaningful education, the obstacles to his career would have been still greater than they were.

Dickens, Eliot, and Butler were all writing for an educated audience. Their discussions of working-class wives should thus not be taken as direct practical instruction to the middle-class reader—if you marry beneath you, be sure to marry a provident and sober woman—but rather as a warning that misplaced sexual desire can lead one badly astray. Wives, in other words, were supposed to bring out one's best side, not one's worst. For the working-class man, that best might be viewed largely in economic terms, as a capacity for hard work and careful saving could result in social transformation. For the middle-class man, it might be described rather in terms of moral character. While wives provided an acceptable outlet for male sexual desire, many Victorians believed that they also existed to tame and control such desire, turning it into the motivation to protect and provide for one's spouse and children rather than focusing it on sensual gratification.

An important part of the middle-class wifely ideal, accordingly, was sexual innocence. For some men, this criterion was so important that their symbol of romantic perfection became the girl rather than the woman. To be sure, the possibility that men (or adolescent boys) might take sexual advantage of girls—*working-class* girls, some legislators and reformers stressed, since other possibilities were usually too uncomfortable to contemplate—was a matter of some concern in the later part of the Victorian period. But until 1875, the legal age of consent in England, the point at which a girl was considered competent to decide to engage in sexual activity, was twelve, and legislation of 1875 raised that number by only one year. Not until 1885 did the Criminal Law Amendment Act set the barrier as high as age sixteen. (That there was no corresponding law protecting boys reflects the assumption that male sexuality was active rather than passive; boys, it was assumed, would be seducers, not victims, and in any case many adults considered their innocence less valuable than girls'.) After all, the Victorians had inherited from their forebears of the late eighteenth century a readiness to celebrate the "girl-wife," young, sweet, and clinging.

In this context, it makes sense that the Victorian "cult of the little girl" embraced more than the close, but apparently not overtly sexual friendships with children on which some men, most famously Charles Lutwidge Dodgson (better known as Lewis Carroll), based the major part of their emotional lives. It included as well a substantial number of engagements, and often marriages, contracted between adult men and teenagers, sometimes teenagers who had first attracted their future husbands in childhood. Among the many prominent individuals whose romances (in many cases unsuccessful) took this latter path were Ruskin; William Clarke Hall, chief barrister for the National Society for the Prevention of Cruelty to Children; artists George Frederic Watts, Frederic Shields, Edward Ward, Frederick Sandys, and Philip Wilson Steer; poet Ernest Dowson;

adventure novelist Mayne Reid; and clergymen Stephen Gladstone, son of the prime minister, and Edward White Benson, later archbishop of Canterbury. As much as the Criminal Law Amendment Act, these socially sanctioned relationships remind us of the premium that Victorian society placed upon female virginity, and, correspondingly, of the anxiety with which many Victorians viewed sexuality. In Victorian terms, middle-class marriage sometimes looked like an arrangement that exchanged one valuable commodity, a woman's sexual inexperience, for another, a man's agreement to confine his sexual urges to a single partner to whom he was legally bound. And while selecting a wife for her immaturity and naiveté could lead to ill-assorted unions, as in Emily Eden's novel *The Semi-Attached Couple* (published 1860, though written in the early 1830s), in which the eighteen-year-old bride prefers her family of origin to the inexplicable passions of the wealthy aristocrat whom she has obediently married, the girl-wife's presumptive innocence might nonetheless be viewed as a guarantee of her worth.

DISTRACTED FROM DOMESTICITY: WIVES AND WORK

But while it was not uncommon for middle-class Victorian men to be attracted to girlhood, with its connotations of freshness, purity, and dependence, and while Victorian society objected to marriages between adult men and teenagers less vigorously than we do today, not all brides were straight from the schoolroom. In fact, the average Victorian bride first married around age twenty-five; her bridegroom, who was expected to have demonstrated before the wedding his ability to support a family, was typically two or three years older. (The age gap was wider among the wealthy than among the poor, and might be wider still when one of the parties had been married before.) And if many marriages involved women younger than twenty, many others involved women in their middle years.

For instance, author Anne Thackeray married Richmond Ritchie when she was forty and he twenty-three; educator and feminist Elizabeth Wolstenholme was forty when she married Ben Elmy; author Dinah Maria Mulock married George Craik (eleven years her junior) at thirty-nine; journalist Eliza Lynn married William Linton at thirty-six; physician Elizabeth Garrett married J.G.S. Anderson at thirty-five; children's writer Beatrix Potter married William Healis at forty-seven. There are many other examples of late unions. And as the cases of these individuals suggest, middle-class women sometimes found it possible to embark upon careers before—or instead of—marrying, and might even continue these careers after marriage. When the socialist political economist Beatrice Potter married Sidney Webb in 1892, both were in their thirties and had begun to make their marks as reformers and social commentators; they agreed not to produce children so that both could go on devoting their energy to public questions.

As we may see from the careers of Beatrice Potter Webb and Elizabeth Garrett Anderson, the kinds of jobs that a gentlewoman might hold expanded considerably as the century progressed. Entities as diverse as the feminist Society for Promoting the Employment of Women, founded in 1859, and the Religious Tract Society's popular magazine *The Girl's Own Paper*, founded in 1880, addressed the question of middle-class women's employment in a variety of fields, from office work to civil service to the professions. The three Brontë sisters, born between 1816 and 1820, had few alternatives to finding work as governesses. In contrast, the heroine of George Bernard Shaw's 1898 play *Mrs. Warren's Profession* sets up as an actuary in partnership with a woman barrister, after considering and rejecting a number of other possible career paths—marriage among them. And while in the 1830s it was (marginally) acceptable for young middle-class women such as the Brontës to work outside the home only if there was real financial need, by the 1890s popular novels and magazines stressed the pleasures and benefits of independent earnings for affluent girls as well.

Somewhat less constrained than their wealthier sisters by Victorian ideals of feminine propriety and fragility, working-class women were yet more likely to earn their own way. Whether exercising traditionally feminine skills as domestic servants, schoolteachers, dairy workers, nursery-maids, or seamstresses; laboring in factories or mines or offices; or selling anything from shop goods to fish to sex, women were a prominent part of the economic landscape. According to the 1851 Census, half of the six million adult women in England, Wales, and Scotland worked for pay, and two million were self-supporting. Among unmarried women more than fourteen years old, three-quarters were wage earners. Few of these women could afford to abandon their jobs altogether after marriage, and some not until their children began to contribute to the family economy. For financial reasons, those who did "retire" in early married life frequently found themselves returning to the workforce upon their husbands' deaths. And although over the latter half of the nineteenth century women were increasingly edged out of the higher-paying jobs in manufacturing and industry, and beginning in the 1870s census figures showed a decline in the proportion of women employed in any trade, many women continued to work. In short, what middle-class Victorians (like their twenty-first-century heirs) saw as the traditional concept of marriage, in which the husband is the breadwinner and the wife devotes herself to homemaking without ever having entered the public sphere, was by no means the only pattern to be found in English society. Feminists' long attempt to push a Married Women's Property Bill through Parliament, and Parliament's eventual accepting of this piece of legislation (see Introduction), reflected the fact that a large proportion of married women had funds of their own and wanted to control them.

Inevitably, the degree to which Victorian women were employed influenced both sexes' views of marriage. Among other things, as political economist Harriet Martineau pointed out in 1859, being employable caused some women to see marriage more as an option than as a necessity.[2] For instance, she suggested, women brought up in rural poverty who entered domestic service in the homes of the wealthy—these live-in jobs were often reserved for single women—might legitimately hesitate before they left their luxurious surroundings to return to a hardscrabble cottage existence as wives. Although Martineau's argument would not have applied to all members of the servant class, whose work was often backbreaking in its difficulty, her point that being self-supporting gave women additional choices is undeniable. Moreover, her implication that marriage might well prove the inferior choice reminds us that many Victorians refused to take a romantic view of family life. The rise in the late 1840s of organized feminism, which saw many of women's problems as family related, was one symptom of this skepticism about the extent to which ideals of domesticity overlapped with reality.

> From that time (the uprising of a middle class) to this, the need and the supply of female industry have gone on increasing, and latterly at an unparalleled rate, while our ideas, our language, and our arrangements have not altered in any corresponding degree.... We are (probably to a man) unaware of the amount of the business of life in England done by women; and if we do not attend to the fact in time, the knowledge will be forced upon us in some disadvantageous or disagreeable way. A social organisation framed for a community of which half stayed at home, while the other half went out to work, cannot answer the purposes of a society, of which a quarter remains at home while three-quarters go out to work.
>
> —Harriet Martineau, "Female Industry" (1859)

Anne Brontë's *The Tenant of Wildfell Hall* stands as a useful indication that Martineau's insights applied to the middle classes as well as to the poor. Brontë's heroine, Helen Huntingdon, has contracted as a teenager a disastrous marriage to a man who turns out to be an abusive alcoholic. It is Helen's artistic talent, by which she expects to earn a living, that emboldens her to leave the marriage and take her young son beyond the sphere of his father's corrupting influence. Setting up housekeeping in a corner of a decaying mansion owned by her half-brother, Helen establishes herself as a professional artist who need not depend on a man to provide for her. When she remarries after her first husband's death, Helen enters upon a union in which the power dynamics will be very different from those of the earlier relationship, not only because her second husband is her social inferior but also because she has demonstrated her independence. Like her sister Charlotte, whose 1849 novel *Shirley* (in particular) also pleads for meaningful employment and equality for women, Anne Brontë argues that domesticity can be as stifling as it can be satisfying, and that marriage does not inevitably bring permanent happiness. In *The Tenant of Wildfell Hall* as in many other Victorian feminist texts, paid work offers women both an alternative and a corrective to the causes of marital unhappiness.

The careers taken up by fictional Victorian women are frequently glamorous, as Helen Huntingdon's work as artist suggests. But in fact, in 1851, about one in every ten Englishwomen, and a higher proportion of English girls in their upper teens, worked as a domestic servant. The numbers rose toward the 1880s and then began to fall again by the end of the century as new kinds of employment beckoned and new household appliances reduced the need for human labor, but despite these fluctuations, historian John Gillis has estimated that at least one in every three working-class Victorian women was, had been, or would be employed as a servant during her lifetime.[3] What being a servant might entail varied widely. As her title implied, a maid of all work in a lower-middle-class household would be expected to participate in all the indoor chores, from cooking to cleaning to laundry, usually alongside her mistress. In contrast, the duties of individual staff members in an aristocratic household were highly specialized and hierarchical, the housekeeper, lady's-maid, and cook ranking above the housemaids, laundry maids, kitchen maid, nursemaid, and scullery maid, and each performing a separate range of duties. But because being "in service" at any level clearly demanded familiarity with at least some household tasks, the work was done in a domestic setting, and servants were expected to submit to their employers' authority, Victorian commentators usually saw this profession as an appropriate one for women.

Work that could be accomplished in one's own home, such as sewing or writing or, as *The Tenant of Wildfell Hall* notes, painting, was also acceptable. So was work that involved caring for or educating children or—after nursing sisterhoods and Florence Nightingale turned nursing into a profession between the late 1840s and the mid-1850s—tending the sick. As technological progress offered new types of employment, jobs such as typewriting and operating a telephone switchboard appeared and were quickly defined as "women's work" because they involved fine motor skills rather than strength and because they seemed to call more for subservience than for assertiveness. While there were certainly Victorians of both sexes who held that women should focus all their attention on their families and not be distracted by even the most "feminine" ways of earning money, the larger society regarded with equanimity career paths that seemed to have a domestic side.

But many commentators were much more anxious about women engaged in tasks that could not be said to hone innately feminine skills. Concerned observers noted repeatedly that female factory workers, for example, had neither the time nor the expertise needed to keep their houses clean, their families properly fed and clothed, and their husbands soothed and amused. (One should note here that because factory work was more lucrative than most jobs open to women on this social level, many male workers objected to the competition and supported legal limits to factory owners' ability to hire women for these positions, less on ideological than on practical grounds.) Female street vendors

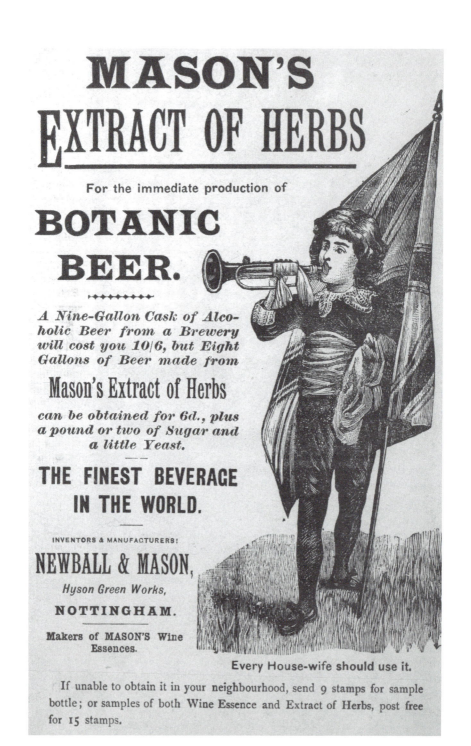

MASON'S EXTRACT OF HERBS

For the immediate production of

BOTANIC BEER.

A Nine-Gallon Cask of Alcoholic Beer from a Brewery will cost you 10/6, but Eight Gallons of Beer made from

Mason's Extract of Herbs

can be obtained for 6d., plus a pound or two of Sugar and a little Yeast.

THE FINEST BEVERAGE IN THE WORLD.

INVENTORS & MANUFACTURERS:

NEWBALL & MASON,

Hyson Green Works,

NOTTINGHAM.

Makers of MASON'S Wine Essences.

Every House-wife should use it.

If unable to obtain it in your neighbourhood, send 9 stamps for sample bottle; or samples of both Wine Essence and Extract of Herbs, post free for 15 stamps.

Wives in modest circumstances who did not work outside the home were expected to make the family money go as far as possible. This advertisement included in the shilling edition of *Mrs. Beeton's Cookery Book and Household Guide* suggests that making one's beverages rather than purchasing them is the housewife's duty—a thrift that the illustration associates with patriotism. [London: Ward Lock & Bowden, 1890; collection of the author.]

such as flower girls and watercress sellers were also perceived as potential social threats, on the theory that they might combine these jobs with part-time prostitution. And both Parliamentary commissions and the Victorian reading public were warned that the practice of hiring women and permitting them to work long hours endangered the future of the nation by sapping strength needed for childbearing. As will be developed further in Chapter 2, the work of women in all social classes, particularly in the early and mid-Victorian years, was often thought to jeopardize their function as wives and mothers.

ADVICE TO WIVES

Such criticisms reflect a sense on the part of many Victorians that if women failed to fulfill their wifely responsibilities, their husbands' and children's health and behavior would suffer accordingly. The wife's primary function was to make home pleasant. As journalist Thomas Wright warned, a working man who came home to a messy house, a slatternly wife, and no prospect of an appetizing dinner had two choices: to do the household tasks himself or to flee to the nearest pub.[4] In the absence of indoor plumbing and a safe municipal water supply, drunkenness was in any case rife among the urban poor, but according to Wright, the alcoholism of countless working-class Victorian men might be laid at their wives' doors.

The man who goes home from his work on a Saturday only to find his house in disorder, with every article of furniture out of its place, the floor unwashed or sloppy from uncompleted washing, his wife slovenly, his children untidy, his dinner not yet ready or spoilt in the cooking, is much more likely to go "on the spree" than the man who finds his house in order, the furniture glistening from the recent polishing, the burnished steel fire-irons looking doubly resplendent from the bright glow of the cheerful fire, his well-cooked dinner ready laid on a snowy cloth, and his wife and children tidy and cheerful.... Drunkenness is in many cases, doubtless, the result of innate depravity, and a confirmed drunkard is rarely to be reclaimed by home comforts, which to his degraded mind offer no charm; but at the same time there can be no doubt in the mind of any person who is acquainted with the manners and habits of the working classes, that thousands of working men are driven by lazy, slovenly, mismanaging wives, to courses which ultimately result in their becoming drunkards amid disreputable members of society.
—Thomas Wright, *Some Habits and Customs of the Working Classes* (1867), Part III

Wright is typical of the many Victorian commentators who believed that married life was deteriorating and that this deterioration reflected poorly on the wives of England. But the problem was not thought to lie solely in the working classes; middle-class wives, too, were seen as potentially incompetent, ignorant, or distracted. Dickens's wildly successful novels, complex panoramas of all levels of Victorian society, contain a number of critical portraits of failed middle-class wives, usually intended as examples of particular types within the culture. They range from *David Copperfield*'s Dora in 1850, a girl-wife who is too young and inexperienced to run a home successfully, to *Bleak House*'s Mrs. Jellyby in 1853, a middle-aged woman who devotes all her energies to philanthropy and ignores the needs of her large family. Many other writers of fiction and nonfiction shared Dickens's view that wives did not always do their job properly.

Accordingly, the Victorian era witnessed a boom in advice manuals, and particularly in advice manuals aimed at women. So common were such books in the early years of Victoria's reign that the humor magazine *Punch* could parody them by 1844, offering "Hints to Make Home Happy" that instructed first husbands and then wives in infallible methods of irritating their partners.[5] Guidance of a more serious sort, such as Isabella Beeton's *The Book of Household Management* (1861) or Sarah Stickney Ellis's series, begun in 1839, on female domestic roles (*The Women of England, The Wives of England, The Mothers of England, The Daughters of England*), could readily achieve the status of best seller. Indeed, while Beeton died of puerperal fever in 1865, such was her success that books on household hints and food preparation continued to be issued under her name throughout the remainder of the century (and afterward), updated to take account of the new popularity of developments such as vegetarianism and "colonial cookery."

Such works provided a number of desirable things to their readers, including the recognition that wifehood did not always come naturally and that the job of the middle-class Victorian wife was neither uncomplicated nor easy. Beeton's lengthy compendium of household instruction, Alexis Soyer's cookery tips and suggested menus, Eliza Acton's *Modern Cookery for Private Families* (1845), and other successful manuals gave clear and detailed directions of a practical sort. They often contained not only recipes but also advice on meal presentation, laundry (a complex and time-consuming task in the days before washing machines and temperature-regulated irons), the managing of the kitchen staff, household economy, and the like; Beeton, indeed, touches upon subjects from drainage and ventilation to domestic law. Such volumes offer evidence of the everyday tasks expected of many Victorian women in comfortable circumstances. Middle-class wives' jobs typically included keeping the account books, overseeing home decoration, planning menus in consultation with the cook, ordering groceries and household supplies, sewing or purchasing clothing for all members of the household, hiring and firing employees to care for house and children, teaching the youngest children, maintaining the family's network of acquaintances by making and receiving morning visits, and acting as hostess at social occasions from children's parties to formal dinners.

The wealthier the wife, the more likely it was that she would be supervising the housekeeping rather than engaging in it directly, and by the mid-Victorian years the household tasks of some aristocratic women had dwindled into the purely symbolic, such as flower arranging and recreational embroidery. For instance, in the novels of Emily Eden, sister of the governor-general of India, wealthy wives exist primarily to bear children and to attend social functions; other tasks are delegated to women of less exalted social standing, so that in *The Semi-Detached House* (1859), the sea captain's wife Mrs. Hopkinson is called upon to go over the household inventory for one titled neighbor and to see another through childbirth. As this reassignment of tasks suggests, among the bourgeoisie, housewives were expected to be competent.

> As with the commander of an army, or the leader of any enterprise, so is it with the mistress of a house. Her spirit will be seen through the whole establishment; and just in proportion as she performs her duties intelligently and thoroughly, so will her domestics follow in her path. Of all those acquirements, which more particularly belong to the feminine character, there are none which take a higher rank, in our estimation, than such as enter into a knowledge of household duties; for on these are perpetually dependent the happiness, comfort, and well-being of a family.
> —Isabella Beeton, *The Book of Household Management* (1861), Chapter 1

In addition to her practical duties, the wife was instructed that she was responsible for the "moral tone" that turned an establishment from a house into a home and kept married men mindful of their own domestic duties. To some extent this tone was seen as a function of good housekeeping. Tidy, clean, and pleasantly decorated rooms, carefully chosen and well-cooked meals, serene rather than frazzled wives, would encourage husbands to hurry home from their work instead of spending their evenings in dissipation. It was also a matter of behavior and training; for instance, middle-class girls were typically given music lessons so that in later life they could entertain their husbands by singing to their own accompaniment on the pianoforte or harp, and reading aloud well was another valued accomplishment. But moral tone was first and foremost an outgrowth of a particular cast of mind. As noted toward the beginning of this chapter, middle-class wives were expected to exert a positive influence over their husbands by exuding virtues such as purity, devotion, and selflessness.

This expectation helps to explain the emphasis, relatively new at the start of the Victorian era, on romantic love as an important factor in marriage. To be sure, in the nineteenth century as today, couples frequently married without being passionately in love on their wedding day. Many were motivated rather by a desire for children (or for a stepparent for existing children), for sexual release, for financial support, for higher social status, or for companionship, or simply by a feeling that the surrounding culture expected adults to pair off. Nevertheless, there was a cultural insistence, often rather desperate in tone, that especially among the middle classes, marriage should mean a loving lifetime commitment. Fiction might question this presumption, as may be seen in feminist works from *The Tenant of Wildfell Hall* forward, social satire of the Dickens or William Makepeace Thackeray type, and sensation novels about the dark underside of domesticity, but such fiction derived its force precisely from bucking the dominant trend. For love was thought to make moral influence easy. Wives who adored their husbands, commentators chorused, would eagerly seek out ways to add to their happiness and would show the kind of interest in their lives and experiences that would keep men attached to their homes. Conversely, husbands who adored their wives would be ready to leave their business woes at the office and revel in the domestic delights of the home, which was supposed to remain separate from the public sphere, uncontaminated by commercialism or competition.

HUSBANDS AND MONEY

While housekeeping manuals aimed at wives were common, and while husbands retained responsibility for a few areas within the home—the stable and carriage-house, the wine cellar, and the library among them—advice books offering practical hints to middle-class men typically focused on personal matters rather than on domestic tasks. Titles such as *Etiquette for Gentlemen, with Hints on the Art of Conversation* (2nd ed. 1838), *The Gentleman's Manual of Modern Etiquette* (1864), and *The Gentleman's Art of Dressing with Economy* (1876) suggest the proliferation of works on manners and grooming for the newly or would-be successful. Meanwhile, texts such as Samuel Smiles's *Self-Help* provided instruction in the character traits, such as industry, punctuality, and attention to detail, that might enable social rise in the first place. Yet as much as wives, husbands lived under certain codes and expectations. On the masculine side of the partnership, too, these expectations varied somewhat from class to class.

Among the upper classes, the husband's primary task was to be a gentleman. In this context, "gentlemanliness" referred not only to an internalized code of conduct (as in the belief that, for instance, "no gentleman would cheat at cards") but also to a way of life. While a gentleman might occupy himself by taking up a position in government, serving as an officer in the army, or—if he were a younger son and thus unlikely to inherit the family estate—becoming a clergyman, he was not expected to devote himself primarily to earning money. At least theoretically, the money was already present, usually generated by rents received from the farmers who lived as tenants on the family land. And if a noble family had fallen on hard times, it was often possible for its sons to contract marriages with women who had money but lacked social position.

For example, the daughters of self-made mill owners or, toward the end of Victoria's reign, American heiresses of plebeian ancestry and six-figure dowries might enter the aristocratic marriage market, exchanging a welcome infusion of ready cash for a title.

Freed from the necessity of earning a living, the upper-class husband might potentially spend considerably more time in the home than his middle- or working-class counterpart. Yet in the early years of the nineteenth century, the lifestyle of such men was expected to focus more on entertainment than on domestic bliss. Hunting, gambling, drinking, and wenching were all accepted behaviors for wealthy men in Regency England, and all were best engaged in without a wife's scrutiny. As the middle class grew, however, and with it the authority of evangelical religion, moral earnestness became the hallmark of Victorian England, so that both the poor and the wealthy increasingly aspired to bourgeois respectability. The Prince Consort led the fashion for domesticated aristocratic husbands, setting a standard of marital fidelity and husbandly attentiveness, sharing parenting responsibilities, and generally showing a high degree of consideration for his wife's feelings. If after Albert's death the Prince of Wales established a rather different pattern, the creep back toward sexual laxity in high life was associated with the end of the century rather than the middle.

The middle-class husband's life was different from that of his social superior, not merely because it was less luxurious but also because it was considerably less leisured. A key distinction between the middle and upper classes was that the former were not independently wealthy. Members of the aristocracy and gentry would sign deeds of settlement upon their marriages, agreements that established a trust for the wife. Settlements, which might be hotly negotiated, consisted of a stipulated amount of money, often a combination of a portion of the wife's dowry, a contribution from the husband or his parents, and a paid-up insurance policy on the husband's life. The sums in question might consist of principal sufficient to generate interest (which the wife would control) equivalent to the allowances paid to the wife's brothers once they reached age twenty-one. In any case, they were expected to be substantial, commonly in the five figures. They could be higher; historian Pat Jalland reports that when Mary Leiter married George Curzon in 1895, her parents settled £140,000 on her, with an additional £25,000 coming from the Curzon family and the whole generating a hefty £7300 in interest annually.[6] Settlements, which could be willed to the children of the marriage and thus might be recycled in due course to form the basis of a daughter's marriage portion, enjoyed legal protection from a husband's creditors and from the husband himself, should he turn out to be a spendthrift or a scoundrel. Well-to-do wives, then, did not need to worry about their husbands' earning capacities in case of bankruptcy, since their financial futures were already secured.

But settlements were less common among the bourgeoisie; only about 10 percent of all Victorian wives had them. In the middle classes, therefore, a husband's

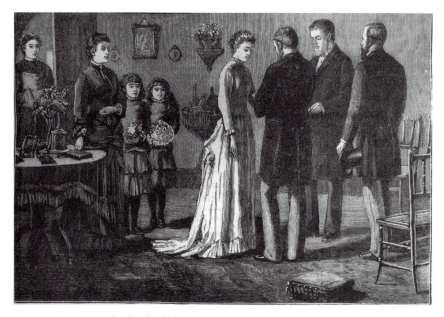

Marriage was very much a family affair. In Nellie Hellis's "Donald and I," concluded in *The Girl's Own Paper* on November 29, 1884, the heroine is alone in the world; her family is symbolically supplied by the household of the clergyman who performs the ceremony, as his daughters act as flower girls, his wife takes the place of the bride's mother, and his servant witnesses the event from the doorway. [Detail; collection of the author.]

ability to provide economic support for his wife and future children became correspondingly more important, although courtship patterns might bear some resemblance to those prevalent among the wealthy. Like his class superior, a middle-class man who developed a wish to marry a woman living in her father's house was not supposed to approach her directly (although, human nature being what it is, this rule was sometimes broken). Rather, he was to ask her father for her hand, at which the responsible father would respond with searching questions about his character, his background, and his prospects as regarded money and career. And as in the upper classes, the religion, politics, and social standing of bride and groom were usually expected to match; when they did not, families and friends were likely to express disapproval, even if the marriage went forward. Indeed, in the absence of the right kind of financial and family information, sterling virtue might well prove inadequate to secure agreement to the marriage.

In many cases, once the wedding had taken place, the middle-class husband might spend relatively little time at home. One way in which the Victorian era differed from those preceding it was in the increasing likelihood that adults, and particularly men, would commute to their work. As the nation became more and more urban and industrial, a smaller segment of the population lived by farming. Living "above the shop," with one's wife helping to serve customers and keeping the accounts, also became somewhat less common, in part because it was perceived as lower middle class. And the establishment of a network of railways and the London Underground meant that large numbers of people could efficiently be moved, and distinctions between residential suburbs and districts devoted to offices and factories became newly marked. While a wife who earned money might do so at home, then, a husband might well catch an early train to a job in the city and not return until evening.

Thus while pre-Victorian texts such as Mary Martha Sherwood's *The Fairchild Family* (first volume, 1818) show middle-class men playing an active domestic part, particularly in parenting, later in the century the typical middle-class husband's principal function was to provide economic support for the family. He was expected to use his salary to pay rent, taxes, and other expenses having to do with the public sphere, and to turn over to his wife either whatever was left or a housekeeping allowance sufficient to cover food, clothing, home decor, household supplies, servants' wages, and sometimes children's school fees. In exchange for this contribution, it was assumed that he would be predominantly a consumer rather than a creator of the home. Within the dominant rhetoric of the conventional Victorian world, each evening that the middle-class husband spent in the domestic environment was to be a tiny but essential vacation from the cares of public life.

Man is strong, but his heart is not adamant. He delights in enterprise and action; but to sustain him he needs a tranquil mind and a whole heart. He expends his whole moral force in the conflicts of the world. To recover his equanimity and composure, home must be to him a place of repose, of peace, of cheerfulness, of comfort, and his soul renews its strength again, and goes forth with fresh vigour to encounter the labour and troubles of the world. But if at home he finds no rest, and is there met with bad temper, sullenness, or gloom, or is assailed by discontent, or complaint, or reproaches, the heart breaks, the spirits are crushed, home vanishes, and the man sinks in despair.

—"The Good Wife," *Family Friend* 8.87 (1852)

HUSBANDS AT HOME

Generally, married men who were comfortably situated financially were not expected to take a role in day-to-day housekeeping decisions or activities, the care of young children, or in controlling the household budget. Marriage thus potentially offered them considerably greater comfort than might be found in bachelor lodgings, since, ideally, wives would be organizing the household around the husband's convenience. In an antisocialist tract of 1840, for example, the Reverend C. B. Tayler praises marriage as a civilizing force that offers men the stability and free time to develop new intellectual avocations.[7] This was not the language used of wives, whose hours at home were not supposed to be particularly leisured. Moreover, Tayler's stance signals the extent to which husbands' domestic lives might be carried on separately from those of their wives. He is not suggesting that marriage partners might explore new hobbies together as a way of cementing their companionship, but rather that the wife's efforts on the home front will create a realm in which the husband has peace and quiet to pursue his own interests.

To be sure, some men played an active part in the workings of the home, shopping for little household luxuries, wallpapering or painting rooms, or (especially in the artisan class) making furniture. This involvement frequently encompassed the emotional side of domesticity as well as the practical side. By his daughter Beatrice's account, Richard Potter, chairman of the board of the Great Western Railway, was considerably readier than was his wife to put the happiness of spouse and children before his own, even though this ethic of unselfishness was normally assigned to the female partner.[8] And Victorian fiction, which might be seeking either to reflect real-life practice or to provide a model calculated to influence readers' habits for the better, contains any number of portraits of domestically active men.

Then too, matters on the domestic front might run more smoothly if the husband did *not* take, or believe that he needed to take, control over them himself. Charles Dickens offers a case in point. By temperament, Dickens was unusually energetic, not only producing many thousands of pages of fiction before his death at age fifty-eight, but also editing magazines, going on speaking tours, and interesting himself in various philanthropic endeavors. His wife, Catherine, was slower and less charismatic, especially after the births of her ten children, and Dickens, always one to relish being in charge, evidently decided that he was not only her intellectual superior but also better equipped than she to make the home. As a consequence, Catherine Dickens became something of a cipher even within the domestic realm. Her failure, which was not entirely her fault, to live up to what mid-Victorian society saw as the wife's responsibility to exert domestic control clearly contributed to the collapse of the marriage. Although the most obvious signal of the union's demise was Dickens's public infatuation with a young actress named Ellen Ternan (who was not the first woman to have caught his eye during his marriage), Dickens's doubts about Catherine's ability to embody Victorian culture's ideal of the wife posed a significant problem. The contrast between the husband envisioned by Tayler and the examples provided by Potter and Dickens reminds us that husbands' domestic involvement might vary considerably from one house to the next.

Notwithstanding his constant and arduous work, [Dickens] was never too busy to be unmindful of the comfort and welfare of those about him, and there was not a corner in any of his homes, from kitchen to garret, which was not constantly inspected by him, and which did not boast of some of his neat and orderly contrivances. . . . [His orderliness] enabled [him] to make time—notwithstanding any amount of work—to give to the minutest household details. Before a dinner-party the *menu* was always submitted to him for approval, and he always made . . . a list of 'who was to take in who' to dinner. . . . [In a sickroom he was] always quiet, always cheerful, always useful and skilful, always doing the right thing, so that his very presence seemed to bring comfort and help.

—Mary Dickens, "Charles Dickens at Home,"
Cornhill Magazine n.s. 4.19 (1885)

Working-class husbands, too, might play an assortment of roles on the domestic front. Among this group as well, marital patterns were changing. Whereas between 1750 and 1850 common-law marriage, spousal desertion, and illegitimacy rates were relatively high, by the middle of the nineteenth century, except among the lowest orders of society or under unusual personal circumstances, conventional marriage was increasingly the only game in town. As middle-class observers defined them, the "deserving poor" were not only those with steady jobs but also those who aspired, on a smaller scale, to emulate the bourgeois pattern of man as breadwinner, woman as homemaker. Family magazines for readers in modest circumstances, such as the *Family Friend* in the 1840s and 1850s, promised skilled workingmen that if they chose their wives carefully, found steady employment, saved up enough money to marry on, and laid out that nest-egg wisely, they could enjoy comfortable homes and afford to educate their children. The key, according to the *Family Friend* and similar voices, was for the husband to make home, not entertainment, his first priority. Money squandered in popular working-class haunts such as theaters, music halls, dancing academies, or saloons would vanish without a trace, or, worse still, would establish a permanent taste for dissipation. In contrast, money put into the home, whether expended on rent or on beautification projects, could be considered a sound investment.

Like commentary on the middle classes, discussions of working-class life often hint that husbands' inclinations, and perhaps their standing, might preclude much active—as opposed to financial—participation in homemaking. In a section of *Some Habits and Customs of the Working Classes* entitled "Working Men's Saturdays," for instance, journalist Wright describes how a workingman in reasonably comfortable circumstances might spend his Saturday-afternoon leisure in the late 1860s: reading the newspaper, joining other men in army drill or rowing clubs, improving himself by studying mathematics or mechanical drawing, doing carpentry. But when Wright mentions the possibility that such a man might do the grocery shopping for, or even with, his wife, an edge of disapproval enters his tone. He suggests that this excessively helpful husband "is probably regarded by his own wife as a bore, and by his shopmates as a mollicot."[9] Indeed, among the working classes as among their social betters, a husband's friends would frequently all be male, a wife's all female, so that except during courtship, leisure activities tended to be gender-segregated. As long as both partners functioned in a way not deleterious to the home, then, observing the distinctions between husband's and wife's roles was one mark of respectability.

At the same time, in addition to supporting the family financially (or helping to support it, if the wife also worked for pay), the good working-class husband was supposed to behave in a fashion suited to the domestic sphere. Another early Victorian magazine aimed at the modestly situated, the *Family Economist*, endeavored in 1850 to spell out the code of conduct expected of the small householder. In particular, he was to behave toward his womenfolk with gentleness and consideration. Even when given every provocation to lose his temper, he was to express himself temperately, and at all times he should guard his speech so as not to give vent to coarse language. In other words, whatever his income, the respectable husband was to comport himself as a gentleman.[10]

Such advice reflects a complex social situation. On the one hand, it helps to illustrate the degree to which middle-class mores, propelled by both evangelical religion and worldly ambition, were extending into the upper tier of the working class. On the other, it suggests the existence of middle-class fears about those less well off than themselves. Without instruction, perhaps, superior workingmen of the artisan class could not be trusted not to swear at their wives. Indeed, since this magazine's readership would have embraced the lower middle class as well, it was evidently recognized that politeness might not come naturally to the artisan's immediate social superior, either. And as middle-class observers looked further down the social ladder, the domestic excesses that they reported (whether accurately or not) got worse and worse, encompassing intemperance not merely linguistic, but physical and sexual as well. Commentators were ready enough to speak of incest and wife beating among the poor. But in most contexts, such matters were distinctly *not* to be discussed with regard to more affluent families, although newspapers' titillating practice, after 1857, of publishing detailed accounts of divorce proceedings made painfully clear that even among gentlefolk, husbands' gentlemanly instincts and wives' purity of heart might be lacking.

HUSBANDS AND SEXUALITY

The common middle-class Victorian conception that life among the poor was rife with brutality, infidelity, drunkenness, and squalor was compounded of both realism and fantasy. It is undeniable that many hundreds of thousands of English citizens lived in appalling conditions, enduring overcrowded and ramshackle housing, poor food, and inadequate sanitation, and that these circumstances were conducive not only to disease of all kinds but also to violence and crime, frequently domestic in nature. The impoverished inhabitants of urban slums were indeed dirty and ragged; in the absence of indoor plumbing, changes of clothing, and space to hang out the wash, cleanliness was hard to manage. It is also true that the poor often married younger and had more children than the well to do (in part, a reflection of higher infant mortality rates), as well as being—at least at the beginning of the period—significantly more tolerant of illegitimacy. Middle-class observers tended to interpret these facts as indicative of a lack of self-control, a virtue that the middle class particularly prized. While social workers and others who had direct contact with the home lives of the poor often wrote about them with considerable sympathy, stressing in particular the strength of their feelings for their families, to those at a greater distance the poor, and particularly poor *men*, frequently seemed terrifying.

For while the very poor looked different from the middle class—shabbier, dirtier, smaller (owing to poor nutrition), less healthy—and spoke with a different accent, their chief failing in middle-class eyes was their presumed lack of restraint. They could not be trusted to repress, as their social superiors purportedly could, their antisocial rage and desire. Implicit in this conception was the acknowledgment that the middle-class male, controlled though he might be, nonetheless had to contend with these same impulses. The stereotypical poor man on a spree, reeling home from the corner pub to blacken his wife's eye before making up with her in bed, might merely be acting in a fashion of which all men were secretly capable. The revelation, after Charles Darwin began to publish his evolutionary theory in *On the Origin of Species* in 1859, that humanity was part of the animal kingdom rather than a separate creation from it, confirmed suspicions that had already bedeviled any number of Victorians. The Puritan belief in humankind's innate depravity still had many adherents.

Particularly toward the end of the century, then, a common Victorian tendency was to see human nature as dual, compounded of both animal and spiritual elements. Marriage was frequently taken as a case in point. A union founded primarily upon physical attraction could drag the partners down by emphasizing their lower natures. Conversely, one founded upon feelings of mutual responsibility and self-sacrifice would raise husband and wife alike to a higher level, although romantic love was often a requirement as well. Romance by itself was not enough, however. While many commentators noted that feeling sexual desire toward one's spouse was a good thing, they stressed that this desire needed to exist within a framework of virtue. If marriage should work on the animal plane, it should work on the spiritual plane as well.

From the perspective of the privileged classes, working-class sexuality was particularly dangerous because cramped living conditions made it a public matter. Middle- and upper-class women who breastfed would have been unlikely to do so outdoors, like this mother in Dorothy Tennant's drawing "The Infant Ragamuffin" (*English Illustrated Magazine* 1885). [Courtesy Evans Library, Texas A&M University.]

In the later years of Victoria's reign, a domestically oriented feminism asserted wives' moral value, biological science saw the female principle as innately energy-conserving (and thus, perhaps, passive) and the male principle as innately active and energy-expending, and an influential social purity movement urged the containment of desire. In this cultural context, wives were frequently represented as the more spiritual partners, husbands as embodying the animal side of the equation. Writing in the high-minded periodical *The Nineteenth Century* in February 1892, for instance, Lady Mary Montgomerie Singleton contended that women typically view romantic love in a semi-sacred light, as it is linked to home, motherhood, and other experiences that they associate with virtue. She continued by noting that their prospective husbands are likely to be more selfish, and thus to find the prospect of settling down to domesticity less appealing. In other words, women enter into sexual unions because they long for the responsibility and purification that running a home and starting a family were expected to entail for Victorians of a certain class; men enter these unions because they long for physical release.[11]

Singleton's outlook, reflecting as it does a perceptible distrust of husbands' motivations and characters, was a common one at this time. Indeed, theories advanced by prominent male writers were compatible with it. Take Herbert Spencer, author of the magisterial *Principles of Sociology* (1876–1896), which examines human social evolution along a continuum stretching from primitive societies into a more ideal future world. Among less developed peoples, suggests William Schooling in an 1891 article based on Spencer's work, husbandly responsibility is unknown; women are essentially slaves, and in the absence of marriage, infant mortality is high and society violent and brutish. Once monogamous marriage becomes a culture's norm, men start cooperating with rather than domineering over women, and this cooperation, in turn, changes men for the better, making them less coercive and more altruistic. The closer a man is to his wife and family emotionally, the better he and the surrounding culture will be. But left in his natural state and separated from the improving influence of domesticity, man can be little more than a savage.[12]

Feminist texts, in particular, made use of such theories to critique not only working-class men but also their middle-class brothers. In a representative polemic entitled *The Awakening of Women* (1899), suffragist and activist Frances Swiney pointed to the writings of Dr. Ludwig Büchner, Havelock Ellis, and other male authorities to demonstrate that women, with their proportionately greater brain size, hairless bodies, and less simian pelvises, represent a higher stage of evolution than men.[13] In the pages of feminist periodicals of the 1890s, such as Swiney's *Awakener* and Margaret Shurmer Sibthorp's *Shafts*, men's supposed moral inferiority to women was evidenced especially by what many contributors saw as their unbridled sexual appetite, which was blamed for a host of social problems. These included prostitution, illegitimacy, adultery, unwanted or medically dangerous pregnancy, the sexual crossing of barriers of race or class, and venereal disease.

In an era in which syphilis was largely untreatable and thus a significant cause of disfigurement, infant mortality (between 60 and 90 percent of children infected with congenital syphilis died in their first year of life), insanity, blindness, and premature adult death, the latter issue was particularly explosive. Under the pen name Sarah Grand, novelist and feminist Frances Clarke McFall became a best seller with the appearance of *The Heavenly Twins* (1893), which deals, among other formerly taboo topics, with a well-born wife who contracts syphilis from her husband and passes it along to their unborn child. Nor was this concern exclusively feminist. Adherents of the social-purity movement, an attempt to establish high moral standards in private life that also embraced temperance, included not only feminists but also evangelical Christians and proponents of eugenics, the scientifically oriented belief that the fit should be encouraged to marry and the unfit discouraged. As all these voices pointed out, infection rates were dangerously high; indeed, purity reformer Josephine Butler charged that nearly all men would suffer from syphilis at some point in their lives.

The battle against syphilis extended to Parliament, which passed the Contagious Diseases Acts in 1864, 1866, and 1869 but repealed them as failures in 1886, since not only did infection rates remain unabated, but the Acts also appeared to many to abrogate the civil rights of the wrong party. Opponents held that legislation permitting the imprisonment in a "lock hospital" of any woman even suspected of prostitution, but making no provision for dealing with her clients, could not effectively protect society, since for many Victorians the real problem was male sexuality rather than the women who accommodated it. Popular culture, too, raised the syphilis issue. Newspaper advertisements hawked dubious nostrums promising relief; a Blackpool wax museum incorporated figures showing the ravages of the disease in an effort to persuade patrons into habits of decency. By 1894, the twenty-third edition of Dr. Henry Allbutt's popular marriage manual *The Wife's Handbook* (originally published in 1886) advised prospective brides to ask for a medical report before accepting a proposal, as uncleanness, Allbutt cautioned, was rampant even among men of the respectable classes. The brutishness imputed to the poor was clearly not confined to them.

> Before giving her consent to marry . . . she should also be sure that he is free from any contagious disease which can be communicated through sexual relations. . . . A young woman may be ruined in health for life, and have her innocent offspring diseased, if she is allied to a man who has disease lurking in his system. I refer to what is called syphilis. I should like to see it the custom for women or their parents to demand a recent certificate of freedom from syphilis from all man proposing marriage. In this matter false delicacy should be dropped.
>
> —Dr. Henry A. Allbutt, *The Wife's Handbook*, 23rd edition (1894)

MARRIAGE AND EMOTION

Inevitably, rhetoric presenting men as diseased and sinful had repercussions for some middle-class marriages. In Victorian England, many boys left home for all-male boarding schools at age seven; earned degrees from universities that usually did not officially admit women (although a handful of female students began attending lectures at Oxford and Cambridge in the 1870s); and entered professions that in most cases were open only to men. It was entirely possible in the upper middle classes for boys and girls alike to grow up associating with no one of the opposite sex who was not closely related to them by blood, and therefore to regard one another as members of an alien species. Even after marriage, as historian Amy Milne-Smith points out, many upper- and middle-class men used their all-male clubs as an alternative domestic space in which they could enjoy the benefits normally associated with the ideal home, such as peace and quiet, good food, and pleasant company, without the perceived drawback of women's presence.[14] In this context, the very audible discourse of social purity, the agitation for women's rights—frequently cast as necessary above all to protect women from male aggression or injustice—and the omnipresent warnings about the dangers of choosing a spouse ignorantly would have made marriage a frightening prospect for many.

The gender segregation imposed upon working-class children was considerably lighter than it was for their more prosperous peers. For one thing, at least in cities, the poor lived cheek by jowl with their neighbors; indeed, among the very poor, multiple families might occupy a single room. For another, working-class children were much more likely to attend a coeducational school, although their time in it might be brief. And while boys and girls might earn money in different ways—girls perhaps selling fruit and vegetables, tending a working neighbor's baby, or joining their mothers in taking in piecework to sew, boys working as messengers or (once they reached age ten, the legal minimum after 1842) in coal mines—many jobs were performed by both sexes, among them street sweeping, factory labor, and various types of handwork. Under these circumstances, members of the opposite sex would have seemed more familiar. Nevertheless, ignorance and fear about sexuality appear to have shaped any number of working-class marriages, a situation that, as historian of sexuality Lesley Hall has chronicled, lingered on well into the twentieth century.[15] It was not only middle-class commentators who saw working-class men as sexually threatening; many working-class women did too.

But, of course, anxiety and guilt are far from the whole picture here. Private diaries and letters produced by many Victorians of all classes (especially the middle and upper strata of society, where literacy was not only common but also comfortable) sometimes reveal extremely happy, successful marriages, in many of which sexual desire was clearly open and welcome. Unions such as that of clergyman and novelist Charles Kingsley and his wife, the former Fanny Grenfell, had a strong physical as well as emotional component, apparent even before the wedding.

I have been thinking over your terror at seeing me undressed, and I feel that I should have the same feeling in a minor degree to you, till I had learnt to bear the blaze of your naked beauty. You do not know how often a man is struck powerless in body and mind on his wedding night.

—Letter from the Rev. Charles Kingsley to his future wife (1843)

My hands are perfumed with [your] delicious limbs, and I cannot wash off the scent, and every moment the thought comes across me of those mysterious recesses of beauty where my hands have been wandering, and my heart sinks with a sweet faintness and my blood tingles through every limb for a moment and then all is still again in calm joy and thankfulness to our loving God. Tomorrow I fast. ... to acquire self-control and to keep under the happy body, to which God has permitted of late such exceeding liberty and bliss.

—the same to the same (1843)

Nor would it be accurate to divide marriages into only two camps, the failed and the fulfilling. What marriage meant in any given case might vary substantially from individual to individual. For some couples, it was a partnership of equals in which the wife enjoyed a full measure of power and respect. The nineteenth century's leading male feminist, John Stuart Mill, credited his wife and occasional collaborator, Harriet Taylor Mill, with shaping his philosophy and understanding of his world. Novelist George MacDonald taught his sons that their mother and sisters were their natural moral superiors. During their courtship, Sidney Webb happily accepted from Beatrice Potter advice calculated to raise his class status (for instance, coaching to turn his lower-middle-class accent into something more genteel) and reciprocated with constructive comments about her writing; after their marriage, they embarked on a number of weighty projects together, including the founding of the London School of Economics.[16]

Other men might insist on being dominant in the relationship. Potter's first suitor, Liberal politician Joseph Chamberlain, physically attracted her in a way that Webb initially did not. This advantage notwithstanding, the relationship foundered on the discrepancy between their understandings of a husband's role. She could not assent to his precept that a wife must subordinate her views to those of her spouse and was dismayed by his announcement that he would tolerate no open divergence of opinion in his home. He, in turn, was dismayed by her unconventionality and independence, which he considered likely to impede domestic happiness. Dickens's novel *Dombey and Son* explores a somewhat similar emotional situation. Edith Dombey eventually deserts her autocratic husband, who has tried his utmost to break her will and compel her subservience to him. In fiction and fact alike, male dominance was by no means assured.

SECOND MARRIAGES AND UNCONVENTIONAL UNIONS

It is also worth bearing in mind that the dynamics of a marriage might be significantly affected by one or both of the partners having been married (and subsequently widowed) before. The blended families that often resulted from remarriage will be discussed at greater length in Chapter 6, but one might recall at this juncture that the wish to provide a substitute parent for a child whose mother or father had died was a common motivation for marriage. Chamberlain, for instance, lost his first wife two years into their marriage, an event that left him the single parent of a newborn and a toddler. Five years later, he married again, only to be widowed a second time; his family now contained six children under the age of fourteen. Perhaps prudently, he waited until all the children were grown before marrying yet again, choosing a young American wife of good family (her father was in the Cabinet) who could help his daughters adapt to the social demands placed upon them by their father's increasing political stature. That marriage to a spouse who already had children meant marriage to a family, still more than to an individual, was signaled by the possibility that the youngsters might accompany the newlyweds on the honeymoon.

The idea of gaining stepchildren made some, though not all, prospective spouses anxious. Particularly among the middle classes, where children would neither be earning money nor be members of families whose wealth was fully secured, husbands might perceive their wives' children primarily as a drain on their finances; in all classes, wives might see their husbands' children as a drain on their energies. Jalland has chronicled the experiences of Lady Fanny Elliott and Margot Tennant, courted by, respectively, the political leaders Lord John Russell and Herbert Asquith. Both women were doubtful not only about the substantial age gaps between them and their future partners and about the initial absence of romantic passion (at least on their own part) but also about the stepchildren to be acquired: two Russells under age three, five little Asquiths.[17] In contrast, John Stuart Mill enjoyed a warm relationship with his stepdaughter Helen Taylor, in particular; after her mother's death, Helen, a young woman at the time of the wedding, stepped into the role of chief emotional support to her bereaved stepfather. Somewhat similarly, Robert Louis Stevenson was delighted to gain a son and imaginative playmate in Lloyd Osbourne. And Charlotte Yonge based her 1861 novel *The Young Step-Mother* on the premise that the prospect of gaining stepchildren, perhaps especially stepchildren still traumatized by the loss of their mother, would make a marriage more attractive to a bride eager for emotional occupation. The complex and diverse responses to marrying spouses who already had children defy generalization, but nonetheless remind us that many Victorian marriages were affected, for good or ill, by this factor.

Finally, discussions of Victorian marriage ought also to acknowledge that despite the increase over the second half of the century in the percentage of the population entering into legal matrimony, not all unions could boast a marriage license. Cohabitation arrangements were tolerated more readily among the poor at the beginning of the period than would be the case later on, but even at the end of the period they were by no means unknown. The privileged classes, too, might reject marriage, whether out of principle (one such case is anatomized in Grant Allen's scandalously successful novel of 1895, *The Woman Who Did*) or for reasons of personal expediency. In other words, although the dominant culture prized respectability, many individuals did not—or, like George Eliot (in private life Marian Evans), they constructed a definition of respectability compatible with living on terms of intimacy with someone who was not their legal spouse.

 Eliot could not marry her partner George Henry Lewes, even though his legal wife, the former Agnes Jervis, had engaged in a long-running affair with Lewes's colleague Thornton Hunt and thus would normally have been vulnerable to divorce. The obstacle was that Lewes, who supported free love, had condoned the adultery by registering the first of Agnes and Hunt's four children as his own, and hence, under English law, he could not subsequently decide to dissolve the marriage. Breaking with her family, Eliot took up residence in Lewes's household, which by that time no longer contained Agnes. She adopted the name Mrs. Lewes; acted as stepmother to his sons, to whom she offered nursing care and financial assistance as necessary; and behaved to the fullest extent possible like a legally wedded wife, devoted and responsible. Her modern biographer Kathryn Hughes notes that the decision to live together was nonetheless agonizing for both Eliot and Lewes, despite their intellectual espousal of ideals that were often at variance with tradition.[18]

 Eliot's importance as a novelist was widely acknowledged during her lifetime, and she attracted any number of admiring disciples, who saw her as a supremely moral voice. Although her brother refused to reconcile with her until after Lewes's death and his sister's marriage to the much younger John Walter Cross (honorary "nephew" to both Leweses), people outside the family often proved more tolerant. Lewes was presented to the Queen of Holland and to King Leopold of Belgium, who had both hoped to meet Eliot as well; Queen Victoria secured Eliot's and Lewes's autographs; and Princess Louise of England arranged that a dinner party that she was to attend would include Eliot as well. Her fan letters might, like one from fellow novelist Elizabeth Gaskell (whose husband was a clergyman), mingle praise with regret that Eliot was *not* "Mrs. Lewes," but in general, even England's most respectable citizens gradually came to accept Eliot's unconventional domestic arrangements.

 Clearly not only Eliot's undoubted greatness as a novelist but also the high-mindedness of her work were factors here. Her colleague Mary Elizabeth Braddon, who could not marry John Maxwell until their union was fourteen years old and had produced five children (they had to wait for the death of his wife, who had long been confined to an insane asylum), had a somewhat different experience. Although extremely popular in her chosen genre of the sensation novel, Braddon met with a much more equivocal response from reviewers, who were given to dropping snide hints about her personal life under the guise of commenting on her handling of the theme of illicit sexuality. But Braddon had begun her career as an actress, a scandalous profession for a middle-class woman in the 1850s, and her fiction is stuffed with wives in love with men not their husbands. Unlike Eliot, she did not impress her public as a woman who prized respectable matrimony.

Other middle-class Victorian domestic arrangements might appear to outsiders more conventional than they in fact were. Children's writer Edith Nesbit, for instance, was seven months pregnant at the time of her 1880 wedding to Hubert Bland, who was simultaneously engaged to another woman, Maggie Doran, on whom he had fathered a son; the liaison continued after he made Nesbit his wife. When in 1886 Nesbit, by then the mother of three, learned that her friend Alice Hoatson was pregnant out of wedlock, she invited Hoatson to join the household, have the baby, and give it to Nesbit, who would pass it off as hers. The invitation was accepted, the baby born—and it was then revealed that Nesbit's husband was the biological as well as the adoptive father of his new daughter. Hoatson, who bore Bland another child in 1899, remained an inmate of the Nesbit-Bland establishment (and honorary "Auntie" to all five of the children of the house) until Bland's death in 1914.

Romantic arrangements that crossed class boundaries also tended toward the unconventional, particularly because Victorian society was sometimes readier to overlook illicit relationships between men and their social inferiors than marriages between the same parties. In his memoir about Victorian family life in rural Lincolnshire, Geoffrey Robinson tells of a mid-nineteenth-century clergyman who, unable to reconcile his longing for sexual fulfillment with his understanding of married respectability, remained a bachelor for most of his life but conducted affairs with a series of his servants. Aware that marrying their employer was not an option, his inamoratas also cultivated suitors of their own class. When pregnancy ensued, the rector would provide them with dowries ample to permit them to marry his competition, and while the village was in no doubt about the goings-on at the rectory, his local popularity remained high. Only when the rector was seventy-five did he vary the pattern by marrying his twenty-year-old cook, who promptly bore him a legitimate son to inherit his substantial estate.[19]

It took barrister Arthur Munby less time to make up his mind to marry maid of all work Hannah Cullwick, whose remarkable diaries, edited by modern scholar Liz Stanley, were finally published in 1984. At Munby's instigation, Cullwick began keeping a journal of her experiences at work in 1854, at age twenty-one; she ended the practice in 1873, shortly after she and Munby married. But despite the longevity of their connection (which lasted until her death in 1909) and Munby's ongoing fascination with working-class women, whom he memorialized in his own journals and in an immense archive of photographs, the marriage lasted only four years. Evidently it was rendered impossible not by a want of affection between husband and wife but by the conflicting pressures imposed by secrecy on the one hand—only a very few people were aware of the true nature of their union—and by Victorian social expectations on the other. For Munby seems to have wanted his wife to share his own class status, as convention dictated, while Cullwick preferred to retain her identity as a member of the servant class.

I *like* the life I lead—working here & just going to M. when I can of a Sunday, & a chance time to clean [for him] of a weekday when I can get leave now & then, oftener of course if I could—better even I think than a married life. For I never feel as if I could make my mind up to that—it's too much like being a *woman*.
              —From *The Diaries of Hannah Cullwick, Victorian Maidservant*

Author Wilkie Collins, in contrast, maintained two concurrent quasi-marital relationships with working-class women. Caroline Graves (née Elizabeth Compton), whose father was a carpenter, was the widow of a stonemason's son turned shorthand writer. She and Collins set up housekeeping together in 1858, an arrangement that was interrupted in 1868, when Graves contracted an ill-fated marriage to a man of her own class after learning that Collins had formed a rival domestic establishment with a shepherd's daughter and erstwhile hotel chambermaid, Martha Rudd. Graves showed none of Hannah Cullwick's reluctance to become middle class; she claimed to be both the daughter and the widow of gentlemen, adopted elegant dress, and served as his hostess. Nevertheless, he clearly felt that a marriage between them was impossible, and officially she was known as his "housekeeper." Meanwhile, although he acknowledged his three children by Rudd, made her a generous allowance, and when in her company passed as "Mr. Dawson" to her "Mrs. Dawson," she too never became his legal wife.

Frances Braham was more successful. The daughter of a Jewish singer, she began life at a social disadvantage, but while still a teenager she embarked upon a series of matrimonial adventures, each highly successful in worldly terms. Her first husband was the illegitimate older brother of Lord Waldegrave, whose parents (who likewise came from different classes) had married in time for the birth of their second son but not their first. Despite the erratic behavior of both brothers, the three lived happily together until John Waldegrave's death in an epileptic fit, whereupon she married his titled sibling; the ceremony took place in Scotland, as it contravened English law for a man to marry his deceased brother's wife. After a brief stint in prison for assault, where his wife joined him in a comfortable apartment, the Earl also died young. Thus while still in her twenties Lady Waldegrave had inherited two husbands' estates, leaving her with extensive land holdings and an income in the neighborhood of £20,000 a year. In 1847, at age twenty-six, she married a sixty-year-old Member of

Parliament, Granville Harcourt, and became a political hostess, held in great esteem by her husband's party and by assorted members of the royal family. Widowed yet again at forty-two, in 1863 she married another M.P., Chichester Fortescue, who, due in no small part to her influence, became Chief Secretary for Ireland and was later raised to the peerage as Lord Carlingford.

Fascinating in themselves, relationships such as those sketched above also stand as important demonstrations that marriage—or its equivalent—meant many things to the Victorians. An individual's social class, religious convictions, ambitions, age, employment status, previous experience, worldly wisdom, and character and personality were only some of the factors affecting the form that his or her marriage, or failure to marry, might take. Moreover, society's attitude toward the union might prove similarly variable. The unconventional career of a Lady Waldegrave, the unlicensed marriage of a George Eliot, would not necessarily prevent one from gaining influence and favor, although in many cases they assuredly did. While the writers of advice manuals might imply that marriages would succeed only when the partners gave their earnest attention to playing their assigned roles as conventionally and respectably as possible, in fact such texts can present only a partial picture of Victorian matrimonial life. Neither for wives nor for husbands was marriage either uniform or static.

2

MOTHERS AND FATHERS

The Victorian cult of domesticity was above all a cult of maternity. The moral superiority that nineteenth-century convention attributed to women was firmly tied to women's ability to mother. Pregnancy and childbirth were often seen as evidence of an innate female predisposition to sacrifice for others, so that even bearing an illegitimate child might be represented as a hallowing experience. In addition, that the responsibilities of child rearing enforced an association between women and young children, who were presumed by those who accepted sentimental and Romantic tradition to be at once innocent and spiritually wise, was considered to extend this sanctifying process. Accordingly, middle-class women who embraced the maternal role that Victorian society defined as their natural destiny were celebrated in forums from art to journalism to popular science—even though in practice some might have found motherhood less fulfilling than advertised. In addition, the idea that the capacity to bear children brought with it special virtues permitted some women to take on new roles in the public sphere, as long as these roles seemed connected in some way with nurturing. As John Ruskin noted in "Of Queens' Gardens," the ideal woman could leave the home, because wherever she might go, "this home is always round her."[1]

Paternal roles were not so vividly imagined. In contrast to the physical hardships that bringing forth children entailed for women, the act of procreation seemed to require no sacrifice for men, who, moreover, were effectively excluded from the lengthy mother–child bonding process that many Victorians believed pregnancy to be. If mother and unborn baby were one flesh, the father enacted, at best, the part of concerned onlooker. Even after the baby's birth, fathers, unable to breast-feed and, at least in households affluent enough to afford a nursemaid, unlikely to change diapers or button clothing, often had little intimate contact with infant offspring. In the middle classes, their major domestic responsibility was played out in the public rather than the private sphere: they were to earn the money that sustained the family. With this model as the ideal, men whose temperaments so inclined them could remain emotionally distant from their children while still being regarded as satisfactory fathers. At the same time, fiction and nonfiction held out the possibility that paternity might be a major and positive force for change in a man's life—while noting as well that father and mother alike might fail miserably at their task.

PREGNANCY AND CHILDBIRTH

The mystique surrounding motherhood was partly based on an awareness of the discomfort and danger that accompanied producing a baby. Although childbirth was not the principal cause of death among Victorian women of childbearing age (that dubious honor belonged to tuberculosis), it was nonetheless perceived as involving more physical peril than any other part of the average woman's life. First, the chances of women dying in labor were considerably higher than they are today; for every thousand living infants born, approximately five mothers died. Miscarriages—which for nineteenth-century women were not only more risky than live births but also, according to the late-Victorian physician A. L. Galabin, accounted for perhaps 20 percent of all pregnancies[2]—raised maternal mortality still further. Women who employed obstetricians ran a significant risk of contracting puerperal fever, a potentially fatal infection spread by physicians' habit of attending multiple patients in a day without sterilizing their hands or clothing as they moved from one to the next. The official (and conservatively reported) death toll from this cause peaked at 2.6 per thousand newborns between 1885 and 1896, some years *after* the medical establishment's 1879 acceptance of Joseph Lister's call to embrace higher standards of antisepsis. In addition, women who bore more than five children were likely to find subsequent births more difficult, and some doctors joined birth-control advocates in warning that undergoing labor too many times could be fatal.

Even when it did not result in death, childbirth was frequently also associated with debilitating complications such as prolapsed uterus and abscesses, and, of course, with pain. Early in the period, a verse from Genesis, "in sorrow thou shalt bring forth children," was sometimes invoked to show that suffering in childbirth was part of God's punishment of the daughters of Eve. Queen Victoria's use of chloroform for the births of her final two children, Leopold in 1853 and Beatrice in 1857, within a decade of the anesthetic's 1847 introduction, made the alleviation of pain under such circumstances more or less acceptable, although debate over chloroform's safety continued for some time. Nevertheless, this apparent advance had its negative side. Under the mid-Victorian licensing acts, chloroform, like many other drugs, could legally be administered only by a qualified physician. This circumstance, together with charges by the medical establishment that midwives were usually ignorant and incompetent, helped to make obstetricians more popular than midwives. Because midwives typically attended only one patient at a time and thus had hygienic advantages over their more professionalized rivals, the shift away from their services led to a rise in the incidence of puerperal fever.

While many women took pregnancy and parturition in stride, popular fiction reflected the trepidation with which others surrounded childbirth. Victorian novels return again and again to the image of the mother dying as she brings forth new life. Familiar examples include Charles Dickens's *Dombey and Son* (1846–1848) and Emily Brontë's *Wuthering Heights* (1848), but many other works employ the device, usually in a manner designed to wring the reader's heartstrings on behalf of the dying mother, the bereaved husband, the orphaned baby, or all three. The commonness of this literary trope is connected to the frequency with which mothers were invested by the larger culture with Christlike qualities of self-sacrifice and altruism. Toward the end of the period, indeed, some parenting manuals recommended to women that they describe to their young children the travail that a mother must undergo to give birth. According to the writers of these works, the child's resulting guilt and gratitude would give the mother additional influence over him or her. While children were also to be reminded of what their *fathers* had given up on their behalf, the latter acts of self-denial had to do with men's toil in the workplace to provide for their families, an everyday drudgery that was invested with considerably less melodrama than surrounded childbirth.

I think, dearest Uncle, you cannot *really* wish me to be the "Mamma d'une nombreuse famille," for I think you will see with me the great inconvenience a *large* family would be to us all, and particularly to the country, independent of the hardship and inconvenience to myself; men never think, at least seldom think, what a hard task it is for us women to go through this *very often*. God's will be done, and if He decrees that we are to have a great number of children, why we must try to bring them up as useful and exemplary members of society.
                    —Letter from Queen Victoria to Leopold, King of the Belgians
                                                               (January 5, 1841)

Pregnancy, and even the years before pregnancy, also posed anxieties. Before giving birth, women might be warned to avoid stimulation and to live for their offspring, not for themselves. They were not to overuse systems that might compete with the reproductive organs—or that might enable them to compete with men. The disturbingly assertive "New Women" of the final years of the century, for instance, were told that too much exercise could develop the woman's strength at the expense of her children's, while too much education could divert blood to the brain and impede menstruation, thus sapping fertility.

Pregnant women were not to become excited and were expected to use discretion about appearing in public. Manuals such as Dr. Pye Henry Chevasse's *Advice to Wives on the Management of Themselves during the Periods of Pregnancy, Labour and Suckling* (1843), which sold 390,000 copies, instructed women that they could ensure their unborn children's vitality by following guidelines for health laid down by the male medical establishment. Conversely, Chevasse and his fellows warned, women who did not follow their doctors' advice to the letter risked their offspring's very lives.

For many commentators, however, the concept of the fragility of the mother, which heightened the sacrifice that childbirth entailed, was linked to social class. To a significant extent, poor women existed outside the sphere of the caution preached by male physicians and other advice givers. For one thing, the poor were unlikely to invest in prenatal medical care. And even for the birth itself, unless they went to a hospital charity ward (of which many were justifiably suspicious), any professional assistance that they might have would come from a midwife rather than from an obstetrician, since midwives generally came cheaper. Moreover, the less affluent the woman, the more durable she was often considered; women who could not afford to be treated as invalids might be deemed not to stand in need of consideration or care. Stories of female factory workers giving birth on the job and instantly returning to their machines were used as ammunition in legislative efforts to curtail women's employment. In fact, working mothers of small children were in the minority. Census data reveal that during the third quarter of the century, most fathers did in fact fulfill their role as financial provider, as only 20–25 percent of mothers of children under five worked for pay if they had husbands present in the home. Anecdotes that conflate labor in the workforce with obstetrical labor may thus have served a function that was more symbolic than practical. They illustrate not only male anxieties about the possibility that economic forces might distract women from their nurturing function, but also the tendency among some members of the privileged classes to see working-class women as tough and unfeminine. That Victorian fiction affords relatively few examples of women of the lower orders dying in childbirth goes hand in hand with the culture's inclination to idealize motherhood primarily above the poverty line.

PRACTICAL PARENTING

Once the child was born, practical parental duties, like spousal duties, also varied with social level. Despite the Victorian image of the perfect mother as essentially middle-class, working-class mothers and fathers alike might well do more hands-on parenting than their wealthier counterparts, a situation necessitated by the fact that working-class families occupied much smaller living quarters than the affluent and did not employ live-in nannies. To be sure, life in the workforce complicated matters. Women who worked outside the home commonly contracted out the care of their infants and toddlers, often to the youngsters' siblings or to neighbors too young or too old to engage in more strenuous labor. Women who earned money at home, for instance as seamstresses or lace makers, could see to their children themselves, and indeed frequently drafted them into the business, partly to keep them out of trouble and partly because the money thus generated was sorely needed; most home industries paid poorly. Nevertheless, stay-at-home working mothers were sources of concern for Victorian reformers, who published numerous exposés of the effects on family life and childhood of combining workplace and domesticity.

She kept herself and her child, a stunted, half-starved girl of nine, making, as it appeared from her wage book, an average of 7s. 6d. a week, working all day. [. . .] The child went to and fro with the work, wrangled with the costermongers of every description who supply the scanty needs of the street, did such intermittent cleaning as seemed good in her eyes, prepared the poor food hastily snatched in the intervals of work, and evaded the School Board officer with all the ingenuity of the true slum child. The mother had not left the house for weeks. When the day's work was over, she threw herself on the bed, too tired even to get "a bit of victuals." [. . .]

Everywhere these "homes" in which leisure is unknown, or if it comes as the rarest of visitors, it comes as a curse. In them, these mothers with no time to rejoice in their motherhood, to give or receive love and sympathy and care from those for whom they are responsible; and children, who, from the time they are first launched into their troubled sea of life, must be a law unto themselves, who are born and nurtured in life's darkest places, "like plants in mines that never see the sun."

—Edith F. Hogg, "The Fur-Pullers of South London,"
The Nineteenth Century (November 1897)

Jobs might run in families in the male line as well, although reformers were less likely to see this situation as a problem—in part because associating work with masculinity seemed more natural than associating it with femininity. A major responsibility for the good working-class father was to ensure that his sons were given the means of supporting themselves. Thus a coal miner, say, might arrange for his sons to follow him into the pit once they reached the legal age for such employment. If it was not provided by the father, vocational training could strain the family's resources, as apprenticeships cost money and some entry-level berths in the business world (such as office boy, for instance) might pay no salary. In many families, the effect of such practices was to encourage sons to enter the same line of work as their fathers.

That the preceding discussion focuses on mothers working alongside young children and fathers working alongside rather older ones is no accident. While individual cases might deviate from the pattern, Victorian parenting conventions assigned the major responsibility for girls and all young children to the mother; fathers were expected to concern themselves more with the up-bringing of older children, primarily boys. To put matters another way, mothers nurtured, fathers disciplined. As a result, mothers sometimes felt themselves to be superfluous to the lives of their grown sons, a phenomenon explored in female-authored novels such as Elizabeth Gaskell's *North and South* (1854–1855) and George Eliot's *Felix Holt* (1866). Conversely, we have noted in Chapter 1 that the first reform made to Victorian marriage law was the 1839 Custody of Infants Act, which made it possible for wives estranged from their husbands to gain custody of children less than seven years old. The movement away from the principle that the father's rights to his offspring were paramount reflected not only an increasing disinclination to define children as chattel but also the growing belief that whatever might happen when the children grew up, the bond between a mother and her small children was sacrosanct.

But, again, middle-class mothers might have relatively little to do with the physical care of the young, and fathers still less. In a household with three ser-vants (a number betokening middle-class respectability but no unusual degree of wealth), the third, after the cook and housemaid, was typically a nursery-maid, responsible for the hygiene of both nursery and child. The nursery itself was the children's territory, and they were commonly expected to remain in it except when invited into adult spaces such as the parlor or dining room, a ritual that might occupy only an hour or two a day. Young children of the middle and upper classes did not typically eat with their parents, nor did they eat on the same schedule; children's main meal was usually taken at midday, while adult dinner occurred in the evening. Well-to-do mothers who found themselves unable to breast-feed might even contract out the task to wet nurses, although this practice drew criticism from commentators. For all classes, bottle-feeding was also a possibility, particularly in the final two decades of the century when infants' hygienic and dietary needs were becoming better understood.

But if many affluent mothers did not bathe, dress, diaper, or feed their own infants, they nonetheless were considered to fulfill important functions in their children's daily lives. It was part of such mothers' duties to interview prospec-tive nurserymaids and, in the upper classes, governesses. Often, mothers themselves served as their children's first teachers, drilling them on the alpha-bet, guiding their first efforts at forming their letters, providing elementary religious instruction, and perhaps continuing with the rudiments of French, history, and geography. If, under Victorian stereotypes, middle-class fathers waited downstairs for the "children's hour," mothers were expected to penetrate the nursery occasionally. In the last two decades or so of the century, with the rise of the social purity movement, it was also increasingly the mother's duty to provide sex education for her young daughters and perhaps also her sons. The idea was that having learned the facts of life in so holy an environment, children would approach sexuality with a reverence that would preclude error in later life.

MELLIN'S FOOD
For INFANTS AND INVALIDS.

"*The Brewery House,*
"*Addlestone, Surrey.*

"*I send photo of one of the children I have brought up on your food (I am now bringing up the third on it). The photo was taken 2 years since, when the child was 12 months old, and she has been fed on your Food and Milk from one month.*

C. H. Clarke

MISS CLARKE,
AGED 12 MONTHS.

"*February 26th,* 1889."

SAMPLES, PAMPHLET, AND PROSPECTUS POST FREE ON APPLICATION TO

G. MELLIN, Marlboro' Works, PECKHAM, S.E.

The development of infant formula as a potential substitute for breast milk occurred during the Victorian era. This testimonial for Mellin's Food appeared in the advertising pages prefacing the *Boy's Own Paper* in September 1890. [Collection of the author.]

Still more than active participation, however, mothers' supervisory role in their youngsters' upbringing was considered important. For instance, if they did not make their children's food or clothing, they nonetheless chose it; it was assumed that they would vet at least their daughters' reading; and responsible mothers exercised absolute authority over their children's social circles, forbidding contact with prospective playmates who came from the wrong kind of family. Just so, in later life, would they chaperone their marriageable daughters, keeping a watchful eye out at parties and maneuvering the girls out of the orbits of ineligible bachelors. While wealthy fathers had complementary duties—negotiating their daughters' marriage settlements, say—mothers' were typically more time-consuming.

WORKING-CLASS PARENTS THROUGH MIDDLE-CLASS EYES

Although complacency has been identified (sometimes by the Victorians themselves) as the besetting sin of middle-class Victorian life, social commentators from the affluent classes did not invariably consider their own form of domesticity ideal. Sociologist Charles Booth noted in the first volume of *Life and*

Religious training was an important part of the ideal mother's role among all classes. Here, a fashion drawing by H. Baude from an 1878 issue of the *Englishwoman's Domestic Magazine* illustrates suitable confirmation apparel for boys and girls—and the need for the mother's presence at this sacrament. The father is not in evidence. [Microfilmed illustration reproduced by permission of National Archive Publishing Company, Ann Arbor, Michigan.]

Labour of the People in London (1889) that while children just above the poverty line are less likely to live to adulthood than their wealthier peers, "I certainly think their lives are happier, free from the paraphernalia of servants, nurses, and governesses, always provided they have decent parents." Not only do they have more to occupy their time, he explained, with school, household chores, and friends who live in close proximity, they also get more attention from their parents.[3] Benjamin Waugh, who edited the journal known as *The Child's Guardian* that the National Society for the Prevention of Cruelty to Children established in 1887, included among the accounts of abuse a number of cases involving middle-class parents. "The Story of the Shrewsbury Case" (February 1887), for instance, details the brutality of both mother and father in the corporal punishment of their three-year-old daughter. This behavior is witnessed and eventually reported to the authorities by the family's five servants—a number that identifies the parents as comfortably situated. And one may point to any number of novels, from Charlotte Brontë's *Jane Eyre* to Samuel Butler's *The Way of All Flesh*, that address the shortcomings of what pass for respect-worthy families among the professional classes.

Nevertheless, working-class fathers and mothers might well find it difficult to live up to the standards set by the ideal mother from the affluent classes. Working parents could not readily supervise their children, so that during business hours, mothers who held jobs in factories or shops or offices or even homes, like fathers (even affluent fathers) who commuted to posts in the public sphere, were distanced from their children not only physically but also emotionally. Or, at any rate, so claimed many commentators. Influential Parliamentary commissions of 1840 and 1844, charged with investigating conditions in the cities, reported that neglectful and incompetent slum parents were undermining the moral training provided to their children in Sunday schools run by those of a somewhat higher caste. For the remainder of the century, these and related findings helped to shape attitudes about poverty. So powerful was the disapproval of the home life of the poor that members of the artisan and lower middle classes frequently sought to distance themselves from working-class behaviors. One illustration of this tendency is that child labor in the lower middle class dropped by almost two-thirds between 1851 and 1881, a sign of the increasing dismay with which the phenomenon, which remained common at a lower social level, was regarded. Similarly, middle- and upper-class sociologists and journalists were often ready to believe the worst of the domestic practices of their social inferiors.

For example, the ways in which the different classes spent leisure time were perceived as indicative of the relative strength of their family ties. Middle-class leisure often involved the private sphere; the good bourgeois housewife was expected to be able to coordinate domestic entertainment ranging from music to croquet to the parlor games in which respectable Victorian society delighted. Such pastimes could readily incorporate children beyond a certain age, as audience if not as participants, and even the very young might absorb the implicit message that home was to be viewed as a major site of pleasure. Among the working classes, in contrast, entertainment was primarily to be found in public, and often in sex-segregated environments. Music halls, pubs, workingmen's institutes, athletic teams, and the open street were appealing alternatives to the cramped and airless dwellings vouchsafed to the Victorian masses (historian George Behlmer notes that even in 1911, one- or two-room establishments accommodated three-quarters of the English population[4]), but they were conducive neither to parent-child bonding nor to good domestic press.

Working-class parents thus experienced something of a public-relations paradox. On the one hand, as Booth points out, they might spend more hours than the wealthy in direct interaction with their offspring. On the other, middle-class commentators often defined the families of even the working poor as facing a crisis. Among other factors here was that the working classes were most visible to their social superiors in the streets—and the streets were full of parents and children who were clearly not traveling together or engaged in the same activities. As approximately 35 percent of the population of England and Wales in the third quarter of the nineteenth century was under fifteen years of age, children were much in evidence in the Victorian landscape. The large number of children working as vendors, crossing sweepers, bootblacks, and the like, with no parents in evidence, inspired considerable anxiety in the hearts of well-to-do observers and contributed to a belief, sometimes well founded, that mothers and especially fathers among the very poor neglected and abused their young.

> There were swarms of children. . . . Nothing could be more dismal than these livid little bodies, the pale stringy hair, the cheeks of flabby flesh encrusted with old filth. They kept running up, pointing out the "gentleman" to each other with curious and avid gestures. Their mothers watched from doorways with dull uninterested eyes. The interiors were visible, exiguous, sometimes a single room in which the family lives, breathing the foetid air. The houses are generally of a single storey, low, dilapidated, kennels to sleep and die in. What can it be like in winter when, during weeks of continuous rain and fog, the windows remain closed? And in order that each numerous brood shall not die of hunger, it is essential that the father abstain from drink, be never out of work and never ill.
> —Hippolyte Taine, *Notes sur l'Angleterre* (1864, translated 1872)

Reform-minded writers thus stressed ways in which the families of the poor did not appear to resemble those of the privileged. Even texts sympathetic to the plight of the slum dweller tended to present their subjects as alien beings whose behavior and outlook required interpretation. The author of "Travels in the East," for instance, a series of articles published in *All the Year Round* in 1884, notes that mothers in London's East End exhibit no feeling while discussing their children's deaths, but that concealing emotion is typical of their class; secretly, this writer assures us, these mothers do care.[5] Somewhat similarly, waif fiction, a widely read genre that combined pathos with an earnest desire to improve society, depends rhetorically on the existence of a nearly unbridgeable gulf between the poor and their social superiors, a gap that such texts claim to want to span.

Yet waif fiction does not dwell on the traits that rich and poor may share nearly so much as it does on the damage that drink, illness, and godlessness pose to domestic life among the marginal classes. Popular tracts such as *Jessica's First Prayer* (1867), by "Hesba Stretton" (Sarah Smith); *Froggy's Little Brother* (1875), by "Brenda" (Mrs. G. Castle Smith); *Bravely Borne* (1882), by Louisa C. Silke; and many others feature brutal, drunken, or dying adults whose conditions make productive parenting impossible. Works of this type dramatize the observation, also made by more highbrow social commentators such as the French philosopher and historian Hippolyte Taine after an 1858 visit to the London dockyards, that the only hope of the very poor lies in the male breadwinner's ability to remain healthy, sober, connected to his family, and employed—four states that in combination might well prove impossible. Often written by middle-class authors but read by consumers at a wide range of economic levels, waif tracts suggested that the poor could parent effectively only if they had God's help, and that getting it might require a small miracle.

One way in which the respectable classes sought to encourage God to alleviate the domestic problems of urban slum dwellers was by continuing a late eighteenth-century practice known as district visiting. A predominantly middle-class device invented by Methodists and quickly adopted by other Protestant denominations as well as by Catholics, Jews, and secular reform organizations, district visiting involved making house calls to save souls. The visitor, who was often a wife and mother, might go from door to door in the territory assigned to her, attempting to enlighten poor women about how best to run their households. From the standpoint of the middle-class woman, this activity represented an acceptable way to parlay one's maternal capacities into a valuable role in the public sphere. For as the *English Woman's Journal* indicated in 1859, reforming the way in which slum women approached maternity was particularly necessary for the long-term good of society. Working-class mothers were instructed in how important it was for their children to be properly nourished and to receive schooling, both secular and sacred. They were also informed that it was necessary to teach their children quiet ways and obedience to adult authority, behavior that would assist women in establishing the peaceful domestic atmosphere idealized in middle-class writings. Beginning in the early 1850s, district visiting was complemented by mothers' meetings; usually run by middle-class women for their poorer sisters, these get-togethers promoted religious observance and good housekeeping. This emphasis on missionizing the home and encouraging the domestic ties for which women were thought to be the primary vector still ran strong at the end of the period, as the remarks of social reformer Octavia Hill in the 1890s illustrate.

It is for woman, in her functions of mother, housewife, and teacher, to effect those urgently needed changes in infant management, domestic economy, education, and the general habits of her own sex, without which humanity could never attain to its destined state of bodily perfection, though all injurious external circumstances were changed.

—*English Woman's Journal* (June 1, 1859)

This I will say, that the deep honour for home-life is essential to the best kind of work for the poor now. Thrift?—yes, if you like; education?—yes, if it be good; preparing girls for service, sanitary improvement, skilled nursing, country holidays, amusements, drill, open spaces, and fifty more things, all are valuable; but one spark of honour for and love of home, if it were granted to you to fan it into life, would be a better gift, one more far-reaching in its influence, and bearing better fruit, *without* which all the other gifts are very poor—*with* which they will bring much good.

—Octavia Hill, "Trained Workers for the Poor,"
The Nineteenth Century (January 1893)

For many visitors, coordinators of mothers' meetings, and tract authors, fathers were the chief obstacles to tranquility in the homes of the poor. The community feeling and clubby atmosphere of the mothers' meeting, for instance, was not infrequently cemented by lectures (and conversations among the constituents) implying that a major purpose of the organization was to overcome the coarseness and violence of the members' husbands. Middle-class women, after all, were idealized as the great purifiers of mankind, and working-class women who attended mothers' meetings were demonstrating their willingness to follow in the paths of the middle class. Certainly many among the bourgeoisie acknowledged that working-class women might be slatterns and shrews; Parliament's urban investigations of 1840 and 1844 had noted that inadequate housekeeping and incompetent parenting by slum women might discourage their men from staying home. But it was surely the man's own innate flaws that caused him to spend his temporary exile getting drunk and to beat his family on his return, as many assumed would be the case.

Similarly, some tracts—*Froggy's Little Brother* and *Bravely Borne* are examples—depict the protagonists' mothers as tender parents of instinctive refinement, essentially middle-class women with working-class accents, while fathers are presented as considerably harder to civilize. Froggy's father is initially sullen, inconsiderate, and given to spending too much time at the pub; not until his wife dies does he mend his ways, only to be killed in a street accident shortly thereafter. Archie's father in *Bravely Borne* is still more culpable. Not content with having crippled his son in infancy, he kills Archie's beloved dog, repeatedly beats and abuses the boy himself, and generally acts in a way calculated to arouse the hatred of both Archie and the reader. While this father too is eventually redeemed, the tendency of these and many other tracts is to paint a picture of family life among the poor in which, in sharp contrast to mothers, fathers are failures not only economically but also emotionally. Although there are certainly exceptions to this pattern—in *Jessica's First Prayer*, for instance, Jessica's mother is a drunken actress who displays no interest in her daughter— texts such as *Froggy* and *Bravely Borne* translate into slum settings the cult of maternity established among the middle classes.

FEARS OF FATHERHOOD

But fatherhood was not only suspect among the working classes. Fiction and nonfiction often expressed concern about how men of the privileged classes, too, approached their paternal role. Anne Brontë's *The Tenant of Wildfell Hall*, for one, has its aristocratic heroine's rebellion against her husband (discussed in Chapter 1 of the present book) depend upon his readiness to corrupt their son by teaching him to drink and to withhold respect from his mother. Dickens's *Dombey and Son* focuses on a father whose pride in his success in business renders success in familial terms impossible; only after his financial collapse can he learn to prize his daughter as she deserves. Florence Montgomery's sentimental best seller *Misunderstood* (1869) examines a wealthy Member of Parliament who entirely lacks insight into the character of his elder son, a blindness that has tragic results. *The Way of All Flesh* pillories its protagonist's clergyman father as a self-satisfied and hypocritical mediocrity incapable of providing either love or meaningful guidance to his children. The protagonist of *A Superfluous Woman* (1894), by Emma Brooke, dies in bearing the last of three infants whose mental retardation has been caused by their syphilitic father's debauchery. And even the idealized hero of Dinah Mulock's *John Halifax, Gentleman* (1856) is less successful as a father, at least of grown sons, than he is as husband, friend, businessman, and public figure, although he is represented as a better father than any of the other men in the novel.

Part of the problem that the Victorians faced here was that fathers' roles were considerably vaguer than mothers'. The ideology of separate spheres held that the public world was dominated by masculine values of competition and achievement, the private world by feminine ones of nurturance. Women who intruded into the public sphere in the capacity of wage earners (and as we have seen, many did) could be spoken of disapprovingly as unwomanly and as shirking their domestic responsibilities. But what of men's relationship to the home? Was it to be seen as a corresponding intrusion into women's turf, as a welcome

Among the prominent men whose style of fatherhood was a subject for public discussion was Charles Dickens, whose daughters seem to have found his parenting style more successful than did his sons. This 1865 photograph by Robert Hindry Mason for Mason & Co. shows the famous author with his daughters Mary Dickens and Kate Macready Dickens; the positioning of the figures conveys to the viewer that the assertive father is in charge and the daughters respectfully attentive to him. [© National Portrait Gallery, London.]

worshipping at Victorian society's secular shrine, or as yet another area in which natural masculine authority should assert itself?

Because of the shift in nineteenth-century understandings of family, all three answers were possible. We have seen in Chapter 1 that men were often expected to be consumers of domesticity rather than its creators. This expectation gave them a clearly delineated set of behaviors vis-à-vis their wives; for example, it was the wife's part to plan the dinner and perhaps to cook it, the husband's to join her at the table to eat it. It was much less clear what consuming domesticity meant where fatherhood was concerned. Historian John Tosh has noted that fatherhood came in for less public discussion than any other aspect of the masculine role, from husbandhood to work.[6] Among other symptoms of this condition: advice books that offered instruction and encouragement to mothers were plentiful, but although until the eighteenth century parenting manuals usually addressed men rather than women, the nineteenth century furnishes no masculine counterpart to Sarah Stickney Ellis's highly successful 1843 volume, *The Mothers of England: Their Influence and Responsibility*. For many (non-)commentators, this silence reflected uncertainty rather than disinterest or reticence.

Commentators who did speak of fatherhood, like individual fathers in practice, saw paternity in a wide range of lights. Memoirs and letters from the period often record the existence of fathers who were tender, involved, adoring, and fun. Queen Victoria's husband, Prince Albert, was one of many men who participated in the fashion of being present in the room for the delivery of one or more of their children. A number of beloved children's classics by writers from George MacDonald to Rudyard Kipling started life as tales told orally to these Victorian fathers' own offspring, a circumstance that suggests that warmth and involvement as well as creativity characterized these relationships. As the wife of socialist poet, printer, artist, and designer William Morris became increasingly wrapped up in her love for his associate Dante Gabriel Rossetti, Morris became the primary parent to their two daughters, who became strongly identified with him. When the older girl developed epilepsy in her teens, he wrote her daily letters in an effort to counter the disorientation that followed upon her attacks, and the younger daughter, May, not only embraced his socialist principles and edited his literary works after his death but also entered the family business by heading the embroidery department in the household furnishings company that he had founded.

Yet one may also find many traces of fathers who were distant, fathers who were domineering, fathers who were abusive, fathers who were irresponsible. While still a motherless teenager, for instance, the future novelist Dinah Mulock was left the sole support of her two younger brothers when her mentally unstable father abandoned the family. Patrick Brontë appears to have expended little affection on his brilliant daughters in their youth and to have displayed rage at the prospective marriage of Charlotte, his last surviving child.

This idealized image of country life, published in *The British Workwoman* in 1874, shows the father as the center of a happy group. In the background, the mother waits at the cottage door to welcome her family home. [Reprinted in *Children: A Pictorial Archive from Nineteenth-Century Sources*, selected by Carol Belanger Grafton, Dover Publications, Inc.; used by permission.]

Conversely, John Ruskin condemned his father for having been overly indulgent and permitting John to grow up in an atmosphere of excessive comfort instead of toughening him up. Although the father's domestic authority was officially beyond challenge, in practice many Victorians found much to complain about in their fathers' approaches.

The many legal challenges to paternal rights over the course of the period reflect the extent to which Victorians worried that such rights might be abused. The growing tendency to allow judges the power to award custody of children to mothers was only one manifestation of this trend. Whereas English fathers had once enjoyed absolute legal authority over the persons and disposition of their children, this authority was gradually curtailed by Parliament. Work offers a prime example of this point. Child-labor legislation, which began in the 1830s by making it a crime to employ young children in mines and factories, moved on to regulate chimney sweeping, farming, brick-making, and various other trades. While such legislation originally governed children's relationship with an employer who was not their parent or legal guardian, by the late 1870s it also embraced some forms of labor instigated directly by the parent. The father's traditional right to demand such labor from his child as he saw fit, whether in the home or through apprenticeship, was eroding.

And the state was making other decisions once vested in the father. Some had to do with education, some with discipline, some with the well-being of both child and public. Compulsory infant vaccination against smallpox was the law from 1853 to 1898, when an amendment was passed permitting parents to opt out if they had conscientious objections to the practice. A series of Education Acts from 1870 onward not only made state-sponsored schools available throughout England but also mandated that all children be in school for a stipulated length of time, instead of giving fathers their traditional right to control the activities of their offspring. (By today's standards, to be sure, this right was not much interfered with; in 1880, the minimum legal age for leaving school was ten.) Another series of Industrial Schools Acts, passed between 1857 and 1880, empowered the courts to commit children to a residential "barrack school" if they were destitute, beggars, vagrants, incorrigibles, or frequenters of bad company. Fathers, clearly, could not be depended upon to control their children, and indeed fathers whose children were placed in barrack schools had demonstrably failed in their duty, financially or morally or both. Another piece of legislation that encroached upon the disciplinary function primarily associated with the father was the 1889 Prevention of Cruelty to and Protection of Children Act, which gave magistrates the authority to remove children from abusive domestic situations. Although corporal punishment was still taken for granted and might be vigorously applied, the 1889 Act imposed limits. No longer could fathers assert that they had absolute power to correct and rear their offspring as they saw fit.

Such legislation reflects the suspicion and anxiety with which the dominant classes viewed the family lives of the poor. It was not wealthy children, after

all, who were remanded to barrack schools or whose education had to be safe-
guarded by the state. The middle classes did not send their children to sweep
chimneys or labor in factories. (The horror felt in the mid-1820s by one twelve-
year-old member of the petit bourgeoisie, the young Charles Dickens, at being
put to work in a blacking warehouse when his father was imprisoned for debt
illustrates the degree to which the boy perceived his plight as wrenchingly ab-
normal. His shock and dismay reverberate throughout his fiction, which teems
with examples of injustices done to the young by their parents or guardians.)
And while affluent children are not immune from parental abuse, the investigations of the Society for the Prevention of Cruelty to Children were far more
likely to involve tenements than mansions.

Nevertheless, as Chapter 1 has already suggested, the fascination—and in
many cases the disgust—with which well-off Victorians frequently regarded
the home life of the marginalized classes was surely fueled to some extent by
a repressed sense of recognition. That working-class fathers, still more than
working-class mothers, were so often represented as violent, drunken, cruel,
irresponsible, and indeed downright bestial, exaggerates criticisms leveled in a
more tentative way against many fathers on higher rungs of the social ladder.
Tosh has argued that there were four basic modes of middle-class fatherhood in
Victorian England, namely physical absence, emotional distance, tyranny, and
intimacy.[7] That the first three of these patterns suggest negative or potentially
damaging approaches to the paternal role is no accident. We have merely to
examine Victorian divorce-court records (which, because of divorce's costliness,
reflect the failed marriages only of the financially secure) to see that at least
for the minority of citizens who sought to dissolve their marriages, wealthy
fathers' mishandling of their children was often an issue.

FATHERHOOD'S REDEMPTIVE POSSIBILITIES

At the same time, Victorian literature and lived experience often depict fatherhood as a potential emotional watershed. If, as nineteenth-century ideology
asserted, mothers' association with young children could help to preserve the
women's innocence and secure their moral influence, the same process could
work for fathers as well. Edward White Benson, an eventual Archbishop of
Canterbury, is a case in point. Until their first child, Martin, was born in 1860,
Benson's marriage to Mary Sidgwick seems to have fallen short of the Victorian ideal. Mary, who had been conscious since she was twelve that Edward
wanted to marry her, was nineteen upon her marriage. She was slightly over
a decade younger than her husband, whose superior intellectual attainments
evidently overawed her, and the age difference doubtless contributed to the
strain that initially characterized communication between the pair. Historian
David Newsome quotes a letter written by Edward to Mary's aunt during their
engagement, asking whether something might be done to make Mary express
herself to him in a more open and fond fashion. Yet Martin's birth, as Newsome

notes, entirely altered the climate of the marriage.[8] In the role of mother of his children, Mary became her husband's emotional equal, even his emotional guide, alleviating his fits of depression and providing the kind of haven that was the particular task of the Victorian wife.

Meanwhile, Edward, who as headmaster of Wellington was known as a stern disciplinarian swift to cane erring pupils, became a doting and attentive father. He actively sought his children's society, enjoyed playing with them, took pride in their achievements, and was shattered by Martin's death from meningitis at seventeen. The guilt that he felt at the thought that Martin's illness might have been brought on by intellectual overwork caused him to revise the parenting strategies that he used on his younger children, holding them to less exacting standards and giving more weight to the value of pleasure in their lives. In short, Edward White Benson approached fatherhood with a mixture of conscientiousness and delight, making companions of his children and investing the bond with all the longing for intimacy that his wife had initially found it difficult to respond to. Already a professional success by the time of Martin's birth, he found in the baby's arrival the commencement of a new domestic success as well.

Victorian fiction sometimes represented fatherhood in a similarly redemptive light. As we shall see in Chapter 6, the second half of the century saw something of a vogue in novels and short stories showing how adopting a baby or young child, usually female, might transform the least sympathetic old bachelor into a loving and noble person. The same phenomenon might be seen where fathers and their biological children were concerned. W. M. Thackeray's *Vanity Fair* (1847–1848) details the disastrous marriage between the conniving Becky Sharp and her initially laughable husband, Rawdon Crawley. Although Rawdon's love for Becky is sincere enough until their marriage begins to disintegrate, it can do little for him emotionally because she is incapable of sincerity herself. His clumsy but heartfelt love for their son (whom Becky regards as a tiresome nuisance) is thus the only successful emotional intimacy of his life, the narrative's signal that Rawdon deserves the reader's sympathy and perhaps even admiration. As a military man Rawdon is negligible, as a husband he is a dupe, but as a father he comes into his own. Somewhat similarly, Thackeray's *The Newcomes* (1853–1855) also displays love between father and son as potentially more successful than romantic love—a conclusion that may have been encouraged by Thackeray's own experience, since his wife had become incurably insane after the birth of their third child.

There are other examples of Victorian novels that employ an essentially sentimental approach in stressing the moral benefit that men may derive from learning to love their offspring. Dickens's *Dombey and Son* is an especially pertinent example, as a paternal melodrama that begins with many hundreds of pages illustrating the elder Paul Dombey's inability to love his daughter and consequent inadequacy as a human being, but ends by taking the opposite tack. Mr. Dombey's failure in business precipitates a realization that only fatherhood can save him; he reconciles with his daughter, pours out his love on his grandchildren, and provides both a happy ending and an object lesson for the reader. Although his approach to fatherhood is considerably more convoluted than Rawdon Crawley's, the two men end up in somewhat similar emotional circumstances, and each situation is presented with a degree of pathos within these novels.

But sentiment is not the only mode within Victorian fiction to accommodate messages about the improving power of the father–child bond. The popularity of this theme is illustrated by the fact that it may be found even in humorous works such as *Vice Versa* (1882), by Thomas Anstey Guthrie, who wrote under the pen name "F. Anstey." This novel, the ancestor of popular twentieth-century American works such as *Freaky Friday* and *Big*, takes fatherhood's transformative possibilities literally by describing how a father and son magically trade places. Predictably, many disasters ensue for both, the father in particular finding life as a student in a second-rate boys' boarding school made uncomfortable by bad food, corporal punishment, and the social embarrassments that arise from his inability to imitate boyish deportment in a convincing way. Yet the humor overlays a message that is far from farcical: fathers owe it to their sons and to themselves to establish true sympathy and understanding between the generations. By occupying his son's place for a time, Paul Bultitude gains willy-nilly an insight that improves his own character and the dynamics of his family life ever afterward. The persistence of such claims about fatherhood's potential illustrates both Victorian anxieties (since clearly not all fathers were getting the point) and Victorian hopes.

THE SINS OF THE MOTHERS

Although Victorian fiction and nonfiction often represents mothers as making up for the delinquencies of fathers, we may also point to any number of expressions of concern about motherhood. Because the culture's vision of the qualities of the good mother—purity, selflessness, tenderness—was so powerful, women who deviated from this ideal inspired dismay, even disgust. The more pronounced the deviation from the stereotype, the more horrified the public reaction might be.

Thus Hannah Lynch's *Autobiography of a Child* (1898), which details at length the physical and emotional abuse that Lynch's mother meted out to all her children, would have been deeply shocking to many Victorian readers, the more because the family in question was not working-class. Lynch describes her mother as cold and unloving instead of nurturing, notes that her stepfather was by far the kinder parent, and recounts anecdote after anecdote revealing her mother's intolerance of the young. Nevertheless, for all Lynch's stated antipathy toward her mother, she adds at several points in her memoir her conviction that in some ways these painful childhood experiences were beneficial to her character, as well as asserting her belief in the existence of maternal love as a strong force for good. To deny the benevolence and moral power of mothers in general is a heresy greater than Lynch's memoir can encompass, even though the book seems designed to debunk precisely this cultural belief.

[It] transpired, as we approached a railway station, that we were going to visit Shakespeare's grave. "Who is Shakespeare?" I flippantly asked, looking at my sister, who sat beside my mother.

Pif-paf! a blow on the ear sent sparks flying before my eyes, and rolled my hat to the ground. Two years inhabiting a sacred county and not to have heard of the poet's name! a child of hers, the most learned of women, so ignorant and so unlettered! Thus was I made acquainted with the name of Shakespeare, and with stinging cheek and humiliated and stiffened little heart, is it surprising that I remember nothing else of that visit to his tomb? [. . .]

My mother had not seen me for two years. This was the measure of maternal tenderness she had treasured up for me in that interval, and so royally meted out to me. Other children are kissed and cried over after a week's absence. I am stunned by an unmerited blow when I rashly open my lips after a two years' separation. And yet I preserve my belief in maternal love as a blessing that exists for others, born under a more fortunate star, though the bounty of nature did not reserve a stray beam to brighten the way for that miserable little waif I was those long, long years ago.

—Hannah Lynch, *Autobiography of a Child* (1898), Chapter 20

While texts that, like Lynch's, explore maternal violence among the middle classes are rare, Victorian fiction is readier to identify less egregious forms of maternal error. Christina Pontifex in *The Way of All Flesh* is posturing and hypocritical, so wrapped up in projecting the image of a good wife and mother that she cannot feel the emotions that should support this persona. Hyacinth Gibson in *Wives and Daughters* (1864–1866), by Elizabeth Gaskell, is shallow and self-absorbed, satisfying her own social desires rather than spending time with her daughter, Cynthia Kirkpatrick, and defining maternal duty entirely in terms of marrying Cynthia off. David Copperfield's mother, Clara, is too weak to protect his interests; needing someone to lean on in her widowhood, she makes a disastrous choice of second husband and then dies, leaving David at his stepfather's mercy. The worldly Flora May in Charlotte Yonge's *The Daisy Chain* (1856), wrapped up in securing the political advancement of her dimwitted husband, neglects her baby, who consequently dies after being dosed with an opium-laced cordial by an ignorant nursemaid.

All the accounts mentioned in the preceding paragraph fault mothers who are not sufficiently absorbed in their children, even when the children's rival for attention is the mother's husband. This sense that mothers might be distracted from their duty to nurture was an ongoing fear in Victorian society. We may trace it not only in the many expressions of concern about working mothers among the poor, but also in the outpouring of texts attacking the phenomenon of the "New Woman" toward the end of the century. New Women were often described in terms of their likeness to men. Predominantly middle class, they aspired to higher education, to the vote, and to careers; they might ride bicycles, smoke cigarettes, or embrace dress reform, and they uniformly displayed an uncomfortable readiness to shock the sensibilities of traditionalists. Their opponents, most famously the pioneering woman journalist Eliza Lynn Linton, found their views and behavior antithetical to the principles of good motherhood and thus to the stability of the nation. According to Linton and her followers, women who aped male prerogatives were both challenging their husbands' authority, to the detriment of domestic peace, and unfitting themselves for motherhood, emotionally, morally, and physically. Directing their energies in inappropriate channels, New Women might bear feeble children and teach them wrong values.

Anxiety about mothers using their influence over their children in misguided ways was redoubled when the question of sexual purity was at issue. The Custody of Infants Act of 1839, which remained in force until 1873, barred mothers who had committed adultery from gaining custody of their young children. The presumption was that unchaste women were unnatural women, and that unnatural women could not bring up children to be morally upright adults, although adulterous fathers could retain their common-law rights over their offspring. After this law was superseded by the Custody of Infants Act of 1873, the question of whether a woman's extramarital affair made her an unfit mother was left to the individual judge to decide. But especially after the passage of the Guardianship of Infants Act of 1886, which stipulated that a father's adultery should be considered as culpable as a mother's, the custom in divorce cases (since adultery was a prerequisite in any divorce) was for custody to go to the innocent parent. Although a few exceptions existed toward the end of the century, in general women who had been found unfaithful to their husbands had little chance of retaining their children. The stereotype of the sexual purity of the good mother was so powerful that mothers who failed to live up to it appeared not to be mothers at all.

A case in point is that of Annie Besant, the central figure in one of the most widely publicized custody cases of the Victorian era. When barely out of her teens, she had married an Anglican vicar, Frank Besant, a union that soon produced a son and a daughter. As historian Nancy Fix Anderson has detailed, however, the marriage quickly fell apart.[9] Among the pressures contributing to its demise were the naive young wife's shock at the sexual side of marriage, her husband's violent conduct toward her, and her loss of religious faith, expressed, much to the clergyman's chagrin, in anonymous pamphlets doubting Christ's divinity. The couple obtained a legal separation in 1873, only six years after the wedding, and agreed that for eleven months out of every year, Frank would take charge of four-year-old Digby, Annie of three-year-old Mabel.

Mother and daughter then relocated to London, where Annie found friends whose views meshed with her own. She joined the National Secularist Society, headed by Charles Bradlaugh, and with Bradlaugh began coediting a journal that reflected their rejection of standard Christian doctrine. In 1878, she and Bradlaugh were tried on obscenity charges for another joint publishing venture, an edition of an American birth-control manual entitled *The Fruits of Philosophy*, whose new illustrations had already been judged an offense against decency. Although the court's verdict went against them, the conviction was overturned, and Annie went on to publish another, similar volume, this one of her own writing.

Appalled at his wife's behavior and seeing a chance to punish her disobedience, Frank sued to regain custody of their daughter. What made the Besant custody trial of 1878 so unusual, though, was that the estranged husband was not alleging that his wife had committed adultery (in which case he could have divorced her). Rather, Frank's case depended on the claim that Annie's unconventional views, and particularly her readiness to make her frank thoughts about sexuality a matter of public record, disqualified her from raising a daughter. In the care of such a mother, Mabel could not expect to form the social ties that would enable her to marry well, much less the moral standards that she would need in order to fulfill her own maternal function appropriately. Although the jury convicting Annie of obscenity had found that her motives in publishing *The Fruits of Philosophy* had been high-minded, and although Annie pointed out that Frank's physical abuse of his wife made him a questionable parent, Frank won both the original case and the 1879 appeal.

The Besant case illustrates that where mothers were concerned, purity encompassed more than sexual fidelity. Although not an accused adulteress, Annie Besant was so vociferous in her refusal to abide by conventional standards of respectability as to be just as disturbing to Victorian propriety as an unfaithful wife would have been. Her crime was not only that she was an atheist, an advocate—just a little too early—of sex education for the young, and a publisher of material that was then deemed more acceptable in medical texts than in writings for lay readers. Still more problematic was that she was *publicly* all these things. Both the judges involved and most of the journalists and letter writers whose reactions saw print appear to have believed that Annie was so wholly a creature of the public sphere that she could not hope to create a suitable domestic environment for an eight-year-old daughter. Although it was evident that she was a concerned and affectionate mother (both Mabel and her brother, Digby, left their father to rejoin her once they had come of age), these qualities counted for little against her notoriety.

FALLEN MOTHERS

If some mothers might fall from grace by becoming distracted from motherhood, whether by getting swept up in a cause like Annie Besant or by indulging personal vanity or ambition like the fictional women cited at the beginning of the preceding section, others might fall by becoming mothers in the first place. As the outlook of the middle classes became more and more dominant over the course of the period, illegitimacy became less acceptable. The reporting of births outside wedlock declined. In 1845, the first year for which statistics exist, 7 percent of all newborns were acknowledged to be illegitimate, although this figure excludes unregistered births and births deliberately misreported by the mother. By 1880, fewer than 5 percent were. In addition, as time went on, fewer parents made open provision for illegitimate children in their wills, a fact that may reflect a genuine dearth of illegitimacy among the will-making classes but that may also reflect the increasing stigma attached to the condition.

This stigma was applied unevenly. Parents who married after the birth of a child might be accepted more readily than parents who never married at all. Illegitimacy among the poor was both more common and more acceptable than it was among the well to do, so that the illegitimacy rate in industrial cities such as Manchester was higher than that for the country as a whole. A single woman who worked in a factory might bear a child without losing her job, whereas a single woman who worked as a domestic servant probably could not. And while unwed fathers might be tolerated by genteel society, unwed mothers (and indeed the children themselves) were much less likely to meet with such a response. All these phenomena were to some degree reflections of the double standard that governed both gender and class in Victorian England. The more closely a given situation affected middle-class women, the more important ideals of purity and selflessness tended to be. Thus a pregnant scullery maid might be dismissed while a pregnant mill worker might be retained, not because the scullery maid's class differed substantially from that of the mill worker but because the former worked within the genteel home, a space that was not to be polluted.

Under the provisions of the New Poor Law of 1834, the financial responsibility for an illegitimate child rested entirely with its mother. The mother also had the legal rights over such a child—deciding its apprenticeship or education, granting permission for marriage during its minority, and so on—that would normally have been vested in the father. Inevitably, some women found the prospect of assuming this double mantle of fatherhood and motherhood too burdensome, especially in combination with society's disapproval. As many Victorian commentators pointed out, this situation potentially led to any of a number of dismaying results: abandonment, "baby farming" (the placing of unwanted children with paid foster mothers, who in effect ran unlicensed orphanages that might prove fatal for the inmates), infanticide. A number of reformers and public figures, including authors Dickens and Gaskell, Prime Minister W. E. Gladstone, and other luminaries, consequently interested themselves in rescue work designed to teach Christian virtue and/or household skills to fallen women, whether the latter were repentant prostitutes or victims of seduction. Once retrained, these "Magdalens" might be given the means to emigrate, accompanied by their babies, to Australia or another colony in need of a larger population.

But some women opted to retain both their illegitimate children and their homeland. If the father of the baby remained in the picture, at least to the extent of providing financial assistance, or if the mother had another matrimonial prospect, emigrating or relinquishing the child became less necessary. Women who could support themselves likewise had more options. The actress Ellen Terry had two children by her lover Edward Godwin after separating from her first husband at the age of nineteen. When they were aged four and two, and the household was experiencing severe financial difficulties, Terry returned to the stage. Although the relationship with Godwin ended shortly thereafter, Terry was soon on her way to becoming a major Victorian star, a success that gave her the luxury of arranging her private life to suit herself. And at least one novel, Elizabeth Eiloart's *Woman's Wrong* (1872), observes that having legal rights to one's children might seem more desirable to some mothers than respectability. Eiloart's widowed heroine, on finding that her husband's will has left the guardianship of their children to a third party, falsely claims that they were never married so that she can retain custody of her son. Conversely, a woman who lived outside marriage with her children's father might be forced into lawful matrimony if the family were poor enough; home visitors sometimes arranged for local government to place illegitimate children in care, with their return contingent upon the securing of a marriage certificate.

Victorian reactions to illegitimate mothers were thus inflected to a considerable degree by context. Bearing a child out of wedlock might be viewed in a matter-of-fact way by the very poor and with horror by the bourgeoisie. It might be accepted, however reluctantly, in an Ellen Terry, famed for her beauty and charm and a success in a profession notoriously tolerant of deviations from respectability, but condemned in a woman who had no special talent to offer. Hence representations of "fallen mothers" in Victorian fiction also vary widely. When farmer's niece Hetty Sorrel produces an illegitimate baby in George Eliot's *Adam Bede* (1859), her reaction is one of desperation; not knowing what else to do, she abandons the newborn and is subsequently tried for infanticide. The protagonist of Gaskell's *Ruth* (1853), however, is an entirely different type. Seduced, like Hetty, by a man considerably her social superior, Ruth finds herself in similarly dire circumstances but is then offered help by kindly strangers. Over the years that follow, Ruth is hallowed by the experience of raising her child, and despite her original error develops into a noble woman. Her eventual heroic end (she dies of a fever contracted while saving the life of her erstwhile seducer) identifies her as a selfless woman who has thoroughly imbibed the ideals of middle-class motherhood. Still another variety of illegitimate mother is Herminia Barton, heroine of Grant Allen's *The Woman Who Did* (1895), who, as a committed feminist, has conscientious objections to marriage. When her daughter, Dolly, reaches adulthood and takes a more conventional stance, Herminia kills herself in order to clear the way for Dolly's own marriage. Again, demonstrating selflessness and idealism reveals the "fallen" mother not to be fallen at all.

The many discussions of erring mothers in Victorian fiction and nonfiction serve multiple functions. For one thing, they help to define the maternal ideal. Usually, the erring mother provides an example of what not to do, an example that is given more force by being associated with unpalatable consequences—the death of a child, say, or sensationalized social ills such as baby farming, or simply the failure to inspire love in one's offspring. Conversely, that fallen mothers may, like Gaskell's Ruth, be redeemed by maternity is intended as a demonstration of the power of motherhood, which is shown to outweigh both social convention and the woman's own human frailties. But simultaneously, Victorian narratives about mothers frequently indicate concern about women's ability to live up to the standards associated with ideal maternity. Even as popular science asserted that maternal instinct was biologically programmed into all but a few unnatural women, assuring nineteenth-century society that most women could not help loving and nurturing their young, voice after voice arose to offer counterexamples. Perhaps, it was suggested, women couldn't be mothers in the truest sense of the word if they were too poor, or if they worked for a living, or if they attended universities, or if they had extramarital affairs, or—the list, it seemed, lengthened with each new publication. While Victorian culture as a whole unquestionably celebrated and revered motherhood in the abstract, many Victorians openly discussed individual exceptions to the mother's "natural" angelic qualities. As for fathers, their status seemed more doubtful still.

Parenthood, in short, was invested with a great deal of emotion, not all of it consistent, in Victorian culture. Nineteenth-century observers saw a direct correlation between parenting methods and the nation's strength. Individuals who lived up to what middle-class society defined as their responsibilities vis-à-vis their children—most basically, financial support from fathers, moral guidance from mothers, and a positive home environment from both partners jointly—were considered to be making an important contribution to England. Individuals who betrayed their trust by rejecting their assigned roles, starting families outside the confines of legal marriage, or failing to establish a harmonious domestic atmosphere were often perceived as a significant social threat. The amount of discussion devoted to ways in which fathers, mothers, or both might fall short of the ideal reflects the degree of anxiety with which parenting was invested in Victorian England.

3

SONS AND DAUGHTERS

Victorian society—and, frequently, Victorian parents—did not have the same expectations for sons as for daughters; children who grew up in the same family might have radically different experiences, depending on gender and birth order. Although the lives of young children might not be much inflected by gender, as boys and girls grew older their lives increasingly diverged. This was especially true among the affluent. Yet across the economic spectrum, both sons and daughters had certain complementary responsibilities; while what we might term the job description of an aristocratic or a middle-class daughter diverged in obvious ways from that of her working-class counterpart, the former, too, had well-defined functions within their families. This chapter will examine how sonship and daughterhood worked, both in practice and in theory and imagination, in a variety of class contexts.

GENTLEMEN'S SONS

In many ways, the upbringing typically given to the sons of the well to do was designed to impress upon them something that sons in all but the poorest classes were also expected to learn, namely the importance of maintaining—or better still, improving—the family's social and economic position. Historians examining the factors influencing the decline in family size toward the end of the period have suggested that as education became more expensive, smaller families became more desirable precisely because of the perceived need for sons, especially, to be given every advantage so that the family might prosper. The traditional practice among upper-class families was to keep the property intact rather than to divide it equally among the children, a strategy that similarly reflects an emphasis on the economic value of the head of the family. Standard inheritance practice among aristocratic English families was based on primogeniture, the principle that the oldest son (or in some sonless families, the closest legitimate male relative in the male line) would inherit not only the family title but also the estate and the income that it produced.

Frequently, this system was enforced by deeds of entail, drawn up in an earlier generation to protect the family lands should an irresponsible person inherit them. Compulsive gamblers or spendthrifts, say, could raise money on the property by renting it to a stranger. They could mine it, cut down its trees and market them as timber, or dispose of art collections or other valuable household contents not mentioned in the entail. But they would not have the power to contract a mortgage, sell their houses, or reduce the size of their land holdings to pay their debts unless they broke the entail, a legal proceeding that required the acquiescence of their adult heirs. The hope was that although a man with expensive tastes and inadequate business skills might burden his successors by neglecting essential improvements to the property, stripping its assets, and squandering whatever ready cash came to hand, his son or grandson might put the family back on a sound financial footing. When he did so, the property would still be there, so that the family's return to solvency would not require the establishment of a completely new social position.

But entails did not cover all the wealth at a family's disposal. The elaborate system of marriage settlements that prevailed among the aristocracy and the gentry, and the fact that the income generated by an estate might be disposed of as its owner saw fit, produced additional income streams. The money that entered a family via a shrewd marriage or a profitable investment, or that a provident estate owner saved from his rent-roll, could be used to establish those children who would not be inheriting the house and lands, as well as to provide pensions for faithful employees. An aristocrat who bought himself an additional piece of property outside the entail could sell it again if times got lean, or could will it to someone other than his principal heir. Eldest sons thus operated within a world that potentially offered considerable financial freedom—if their fathers and grandfathers had demonstrated fiscal responsibility. The awareness of this principle put a fair amount of pressure on the new owner to live up to this standard in his turn. For the principal family duty of the well-born young man was not, like his unmarried sister's, to provide love and companionship to his aging parents, but rather to secure the smooth transition of the family property to the next generation, both by providing a son and by providing *for* that son.

The heirs-apparent of aristocratic families, then, knew from earliest childhood what their adult lives were likely to involve. While they could employ bailiffs and estate managers to assist in the business of overseeing the property, they would probably also live on the estates themselves, at least for some portion of the year. To be sure, some absences from home were anticipated, even expected. The possession of a title also brought with it a seat in the House of

Lords, which for conscientious noblemen meant spending May through July of every year in London; these months were also known as "the Season," during which the fashionable parties took place and many people left their country homes in order to enjoy city life. But with the exception of these parliamentary duties, men were generally not expected to engage in other professions after inheriting. A young aristocrat might join the Army during his father's lifetime, for example, but upon his father's death it was considered appropriate for him to resign his officer's commission and return home. If he had not done so already, he would be expected to contract a suitable marriage and to produce legitimate offspring (ideally including at least one boy) so that the cycle could continue in the next generation.

Because estate holdings were given such weight within this system, and because a substantial minority of landed aristocrats and gentry lacked a town house in London,[1] the upbringing given to the sons of the upper classes tended to emphasize pursuits calculated to engender a love of country life. Custom held that young men of this social stratum would be good at riding and shooting and other outdoor activities; they were also typically expected to develop a workable relationship with those social inferiors who were likely to rent property from them later on. Although novelists writing about the land-owning classes, from Anne Brontë to Charlotte Yonge to Elizabeth Gaskell to George Eliot to W. M. Thackeray, note the presence of snobbery and aristocratic irresponsibility of one kind or another, they often also note the necessity of communication across socioeconomic boundaries. In describing his title character's childhood in *Tom Brown's Schooldays* (1857), for instance, Thomas Hughes stresses young Tom's athletic endeavors, the experiences that bind him to his home county, and the friendships that he forms with village youngsters. All are presented as appropriate training for someone who will eventually succeed his father as Squire Brown. And when Tom's father sends him to a preparatory school, to Rugby, and later to Oxford, the point is not to turn the boy into an intellectual (which might cause him to look down upon his parents and unfit him for the life he is to lead as an adult), but rather to finish his training as a gentleman and a Christian. As Hughes and Tom's father see the matter, both roles are essential to the responsibilities of a country landowner, who will need to do the right thing by his tenants as well as by his family.

Younger sons had responsibilities as well. Unless the family controlled enough money and property to enable each of its sons to be independently wealthy in adulthood, or the sons married well enough to secure estates of their own, a younger son could expect to take up a respectable line of work. In the eyes of the conventional, where the nobility and gentry were concerned these employments were limited in number. Junior members of aristocratic families might enter government service by joining the diplomatic corps or standing for election to Parliament's House of Commons. Like the sons of the middle classes, they might become Army officers or Church of England clergymen; in the latter case, family connections might secure for well-born

> The few neighbours of the Squire's own rank every now and then would shrug their shoulders as they drove or rode by a party of boys with Tom in the middle, carrying along bulrushes or whispering reeds, or great bundles of cowslip and meadowsweet, or young starlings or magpies, or other spoil of wood, brook, or meadow: and Lawyer Red-tape might mutter to Squire Straightback at the Board, that no good would come of the young Browns, if they were let run wild with all the dirty village boys, whom the best farmers' sons even would not play with. And the Squire might reply with a shake of his head, that *his* sons only mixed with their equals, and never went into the village without a governess or a footman. But luckily Squire Brown was full as stiff-backed as his neighbours, and so went on his own way: and Tom and his younger brothers, as they grew up, went on playing with the village boys without the idea of equality or inequality (except in wrestling, running, and climbing) ever entering their heads, as it doesn't till it's put there by Jack Nastys or fine ladies' maids.
> —Thomas Hughes, *Tom Brown's Schooldays* (1857), Chapter 3

youths parishes with comfortable parsonages and good salaries attached, with perhaps a bishopric on the horizon. If funds permitted, they might become public figures in some dashing but probably unprofitable endeavor—exploring, say, or devoting themselves to amateur scientific investigation or the arts, or even owning a string of racehorses. But especially at the beginning of the period, most titled families would have expressed displeasure at their sons' embarking upon careers in business or in medicine, as these occupations then lacked the social cachet demanded in the occupations of the well connected.

Some class mixing was nonetheless possible for the sons of the nobility and gentry, and was seen principally in two areas, matrimony and education. The practice of primogeniture and the existence of the entail system meant that younger sons were not automatically well provided for upon their parents' deaths. Consequently, it became an accepted practice for parents to seek out, encourage, or at least agree to marriages for their children in which one partner brought the pedigree and the other brought a bankroll. Charlotte Brontë's *Jane Eyre* (1847) turns upon the revelation that the hero, Edward Rochester, the second son of a landed gentleman, has in his youth been coerced by his father into marrying a mentally unstable young woman from Jamaica because her money would provide much-needed funding for Rochester and his prospective offspring. This plot detail serves a number of purposes within the narrative, but it also reflects a common enough social practice—and the strength of the early-Victorian belief (which Brontë criticizes) that sons should unquestioningly accept their fathers' decisions about their lives. Self-made industrialists or, by the 1870s, New World millionaires might also marry their daughters to the sons of English noblemen, providing a useful infusion of cash in exchange for an unassailable social position. For instance, through this procedure an

American-born heiress, Lady Paget (the former Minnie Stevens), replicated her own Atlantic transplantation by arranging a match between Consuelo Vanderbilt and the Duke of Marlborough in 1895. Although both parties were in love with other people and the union ended in divorce, the bride came to the marriage with railroad stock worth $2.5 million, while the groom brought with him Blenheim Palace, one of the greatest properties in England.

Universities, too, could provide a forum for class mixing. Cecil Botting, in later life the father of novelist Antonia White, was the son of an alcoholic shopkeeper and clerk but won a scholarship to study classics at Cambridge in 1889. There he quickly formed an intimate friendship with an Irish aristocrat, Nevinson de Courcy, who taught him how to dress, eat, drink, and read after the fashion of the upper-class dandy set. The standards learned at Cambridge seem to have been a crucial influence upon Botting's subsequent life, particularly where his aspirations for his own family were concerned. He married Christine White, the descendant of a family that prided itself on its lineage although no family money remained, and took a teaching post at St. Paul's School, with Eton and Harrow one of the nine institutions for privileged boys that the mid-Victorians regarded as particularly important feeders for Oxford and Cambridge. At considerable financial sacrifice, for some years he sent his daughter, then known as Eirene Botting, to a convent school that catered primarily to the daughters of the Catholic aristocracy of Britain, Ireland, and the Continent. He also rescued his father from his unsuccessful business career and staked him to a version of the leisured existence appropriate to the fathers of gentlemen. Although it had to be conducted by post after their departure from Cambridge, his friendship with de Courcy, who served as Eirene's godfather, continued until the other man's death in 1919, and in the judgment of his granddaughter Lyndall Hopkinson was the high point of Botting's life.[2] Presumably de Courcy, too, derived emotional satisfaction from their comradeship, from Botting's undisguised admiration, and from the feeling that he was exercising such a formative influence over another man's life. Nor was their friendship unique; one can find fictional parallels in college novels such as Hughes's *Tom Brown at Oxford* (1861).

Perhaps even more important than the universities to facilitating the transferring of standards and ideals from one group to another were the public schools, in American terms elite private schools (usually boarding schools) for boys. In the early years of the Victorian era, the public schools were undergoing substantial reformation. Following the inspiration of Dr. Thomas Arnold, legendary headmaster of Rugby, these reforms were largely designed to attract pupils from the professional classes—the new center of economic power in England; the sons of the aristocracy and gentry often already attended such schools as a matter of family tradition. Increasingly, then, the offspring of noblemen and squires had opportunities to form close ties to the sons of their immediate class inferiors, friendships that might, like de Courcy's with Botting, continue into adulthood and that could in some cases result in intermarriage.

At the least, the mingling of the upper classes and the prosperous middle classes in the public schools provided a mutual set of formative experiences, a common background upon which both groups could draw in later life. These educational institutions were designed not merely to instill knowledge—indeed, the latter was often a relatively low priority—but also, and primarily, to forge character in a way that families presumably could not. In their different ways, all the great public schools saw themselves as producing leaders of men. Boys undergoing this process might perceive it as inspiring or as deeply traumatic; in either case, it was structured to be sufficiently emotionally intense as to rival or surpass one's early family life as an influence upon the personality. Whether emanating from the gentry or from the professional classes, boys frequently left home at age seven or eight to begin their formal education at an institution designed to prepare them for entrance to one of the major public schools at around age twelve. The products of this system were thus asked from an early age to understand that citizenship mattered more than domesticity, public involvement more than private ties. In contrast, the aristocratic "daughters of England" were less likely than their brothers to attend boarding school, and those who did were more likely to be told that their schools were preparing them to be good mothers to England's future rulers than that they would be shaping England themselves.

GENTLEMEN'S DAUGHTERS

The daughters of the upper classes usually led more circumscribed lives than did their brothers. To be sure, all the children in a wealthy family might start out in the same schoolroom, learning the identical lessons from the same nursery governess. The curriculum would often split when children reached the age of seven, however. At their preparatory schools, and subsequently at their public schools and universities, boys would pursue a course of study that emphasized Latin and Greek, since a background in these languages was a defining sign of gentility in men. (Curricular options expanded somewhat in the 1880s, so that some boys could opt for formal instruction in science, history, and a modern European language; classics nonetheless remained the more prestigious track.) Sons' enforced absence from the daily life of the family might engender homesickness, but would simultaneously promote a sense of emotional as well as physical distance from home. To a schoolboy, domesticity might be something to scorn, because of its associations with babyhood, rather than something to long for.

Girls' schooling, and thus girls' lives, worked rather differently. Although the eighteenth century saw the rise and fall of numerous small "female academies," the boom in the founding of girls' boarding schools would not occur until the mid-nineteenth century. Even then, many families who sent their sons away to school as a matter of course expected to keep their daughters at home. Thus girls would often remain in their fathers' houses, which for some represented

The ability to play the piano was often considered important for middle- and upper-class girls; not only did music provide an occupation for leisure hours, it could also be used to attract the interest of prospective suitors. The above illustration to a serial entitled *The Mountain Path* appeared in the *Girl's Own Paper* on December 27, 1884. [Collection of the author.]

security and continuity and for other, more rebellious spirits could seem like prison. Normally, their studies would not progress to Latin and Greek, although some ambitious girls, conscious of being shut out from opportunities vouchsafed to their brothers, pursued these subjects nonetheless. Rather, the genteel female curriculum emphasized French and German or Italian, music, history, watercolor sketching, and the kind of basic cultural knowledge that would fit young women to listen intelligently to their future husbands.

For, according to dominant opinion in the Victorian era, the primary goal of the upper-class girl should be a suitable marriage—that is, a marriage that would permit her to maintain her social standing. Accordingly, she was to be trained in the skills that would permit her to show to good advantage during the social season, such as dancing, etiquette, and conversation. If her mother was dead, she might also act as her father's hostess and oversee the running of his house and the management of his younger children before moving on to a household of her own. Thus, for instance, the young Sydney Bowles, future mother of the talented and unconventional Mitford brood, spent the years between ages eight and fourteen accompanying her widowed father and three siblings on an assortment of prolonged yachting trips. Still in her early teens, she then took over the household finances and the considerable task of directing the servants in her father's large London establishment before making her debut in society. From among the ranks of her aspiring suitors, she eventually married David Freeman Mitford, the second son of a close friend of her father, who would become Lord Redesdale on the death of his elder brother.

A similar but yet more exotic trajectory was that of Victoria Sackville-West, whose daughter, known as Vita, would go down in literary history as the inspiration for Virginia Woolf's fantasy *Orlando*. One of seven illegitimate children of a Spanish dancer and the diplomat Lionel Sackville-West (born the younger son of a titled family), Victoria became her father's hostess at age nineteen, when he was named Britain's ambassador to the United States, some ten years after her mother's death. Such an arrangement would not have been out of the ordinary had her parents been married, but the circumstances of Victoria's birth meant that her position in Washington had to be approved by both the Queen and President Garfield's wife. Despite the potential disapproval of society and an early upbringing that had in no way prepared her for her new role, however, Victoria's grandson Nigel Nicolson recounts that she performed brilliantly, not only supervising domestic matters superlatively well but also taking on an influential part in the highest circles of American society.[3] Lionel's brother's death in 1888 made him Lord Sackville, and he returned to England; over some opposition from her future husband's parents, Victoria then married her cousin, also named Lionel, who in due course succeeded to the family title.

The careers of Victoria Sackville-West and Sydney Bowles illustrate that the life of a well-connected girl before marriage might be neither devoid of challenges nor predictable, even if she chose her eventual spouse from her own extended family. Being a successful society hostess, a duty that fell to both these young women in adolescence, required a high degree of organizational skill and attention to detail. Guest lists might contain literally hundreds of names, and evening parties were likely to involve dancing (with attendant dance cards, musicians, and decorations), dozens of different foodstuffs, and a thorough knowledge of protocol. Yet Victoria and Sydney were exceptions to the general rule, not only in their unusual competence but also in their opportunities. For countless other aristocratic girls, being a daughter entailed considerably less autonomy because the social decision making fell to the lot of a living mother or stepmother. Making one's debut, being presented at Court, attending a whirl of fashionable parties, might all be accomplished under the authoritative guidance of an older woman, so that many young women of this class had relatively few chances before marriage to exercise their independent judgment.

Of course, not all members of the upper classes married, and the lives of spinsters of good family further illustrate the extent to which independence of mind often seemed undesirable in daughters. Historian Pat Jalland cites the case of Evelyn Murray, youngest daughter of the Duke of Atholl.[4] Bright and rebellious, Evelyn preferred studying Gaelic to attending social functions, refused to dress as her mother wished, and generally rejected authority both parental and medical. Fluctuating between illness and disobedience, she was believed by her physicians and her family to suffer from mental problems that included what her grandmother referred to as "persecution mania." If she harbored suspicions that those close to her were plotting against her, however, these would appear to have been well founded. When she was twenty-four, her parents forced her to move to Belgium. There, a new identity as an orphan was constructed for her to minimize the potential family shame, and her allowance was capped at £300 a year, a sum adequate for a middle-class existence but paltry by the usual standards of a duke's daughter. She never returned to Britain, in effect serving a life sentence for the crime of failing to live up to the requirements of the role of genteel daughter.

If a daughter is a source of discomfort at home (instead of happiness and delight as *you might be*) a Father can send her away and she must live wherever he provides a home for her. It cannot be expected that you can be placed in a home as comfortable or congenial as the one from which you have by your own conduct exiled yourself. . . . It is not for your own pleasure that you are living abroad. Your eventual return home will I believe depend on your own frame of mind. Should you come to see how undutiful, and unkind and cruel you have been to your mother—you should then write straight to her.
    —Letter from the Dowager Duchess of Atholl to Evelyn Murray (1892)

Yet if Evelyn Murray's chief problem was her failure to conform to her parents' expectations, unmarried aristocratic women who displayed a willingness to devote themselves to family might find little more happiness in life. Jalland also cites the case of Alice Balfour, in adulthood the chatelaine of the family estate inherited by her oldest brother, Arthur, who would become Prime Minister (succeeding his uncle, Lord Salisbury) in 1902.[5] The mansion housed not only herself and the bachelor Arthur, but frequently also two of their brothers and the brothers' wives and eight children. Relations between Alice and her sister-in-law and housemate Lady Frances Balfour were exceedingly strained, with the two competing for Arthur's attention, the love of Lady Frances's five children, and the right to attempt to curb the alcoholic excesses of Lady Frances's husband, Alice's brother Eustace. Running the household was a sore trial to Alice. She found little satisfaction in the task despite her organizational gifts, perhaps because entertaining and managing ate up time that she might have preferred to use in further developing her talent for painting. Yet as a single woman with a bachelor brother, by the unwritten laws of Victorian society Alice was required to subordinate her interests and needs to his. Removing her money from the family kitty and setting herself up in an artist's studio in London or Paris would not have been an option.

Even among the most privileged classes, in short, the role of daughter had its drawbacks. If aristocrats' sons were limited as to career choices, their daughters were still more so. Those who had an inclination toward the social whirl generally had the opportunity to indulge this taste, and those who did not might well find themselves entering society nonetheless. Girls passed from the authority of their fathers to that of their husbands. If they did not marry, reaching adult years sometimes made little difference in the degree of autonomy possible to them. The filial duty of a daughter in her teens to provide companionship and some degree of domestic help to her parents could extend for decades unless, through matrimony, that daughter entered another household. Moreover, the latter option might never be open to her, as some parents of large families expected that one daughter would forgo marriage so as to be in a position to devote herself to her mother and father in their old age. As some nineteenth-century women sardonically observed, if a woman wanted control over her destiny, the role most likely to provide it was neither daughter nor wife, but widow.

THE MIDDLE-CLASS DAUGHTER

Because of the ideological dominance of the middle classes in the Victorian era, the expectations for virtuous girls in all walks of society were strongly influenced by the mores of the bourgeoisie. Thus the similarities between the role of daughter in the land-owning classes and the same role in the professional and mercantile classes are attributable not only to the desire of the upwardly mobile to imitate their social betters but also to the reverse. Since in very real ways, the bourgeoisie occupied the moral high ground in Victorian England, it was they who took the lead in establishing the "correct" pattern for family life. Within this pattern, daughters might play a crucial part.

Middle-class daughters did not have the same kind of social experiences that were commonplace for their aristocratic counterparts—the balls for hundreds of guests, the ritual presentation to the Queen, and so on. Nevertheless, they too might have associations with luxury. As writers and social commentators from Dinah Mulock Craik to Florence Nightingale pointed out, middle-class girls often functioned as status symbols for their menfolk, prohibited from seeking paid employment by their fathers' need to demonstrate the ability to support "nonworking" members of the family. Such girls were expected to consume rather than to produce. They were to dress attractively and appropriately— nineteenth-century magazines proliferated to explore the intricacies of the world of women's fashions. They were to develop accomplishments that were valued without being readily marketable, such as "fancy work" or embroidery (as opposed to "plain sewing," which had potential commercial applications) and accompanying themselves on the piano or harp, instruments that Victorian culture regarded as well suited to female performers because one could look graceful while playing them. And they were to connect themselves primarily with the home, which dominant middle-class ideology saw as the antithesis of the marketplace.

The family uses people, *not* for what they are, not for what they are intended to be, but for what it wants them for—for its own uses. It thinks of them not as what God has made them, but as the something which *it* has arranged that they shall be. If it wants some one to sit in the drawing-room, *that* some one is to be supplied by the family, though that member may be destined for science, or for education, or for active superintendence by God, *i.e.*, by the gifts within.

This system dooms some minds to incurable infancy, others to silent misery.

And family boasts that it has performed its mission well, in as far as it has enabled the individual to say, "I have *no* peculiar work, nothing but what the moment brings me, nothing that I cannot throw up at once at anybody's claim"; in as far, that is, as it has *destroyed* the individual life. And the individual thinks that a great victory has been accomplished, when, at last, she is able to say that she has "no personal desires or plans." What is this but throwing the gifts of God aside as worthless, and substituting for them those of the world?

Marriage is the only chance (and it is but a chance) offered to women for escape from this death; and how eagerly and how ignorantly it is embraced!

—Florence Nightingale, "Cassandra"
(composed 1852, privately printed 1860)

Many middle-class girls were keenly aware of the constrictions of these expectations, which could be conducive to a dull and featureless existence. Thus a recurring question in Victorian fiction and nonfiction is that of how time may legitimately be used if one is a "home daughter" in a moderately well-to-do family. In a large household, elder daughters might assist their mothers in teaching the younger children, mending torn garments, arranging flowers, dusting the father's study (as a token of love or because he preferred not to entrust his sanctum to the housemaid), and the like. Girls were also viewed, at least potentially, as likely to provide help to their fathers, especially

Archery, which permitted attractive poses and had associations with the chaste goddess of the hunt, Artemis, became a fashionable pursuit for middle-class girls in the 1870s. Queen Victoria was among the sport's aficionados. The image above, an illustration by H. Winthrop Peirce to *Daniel Deronda*, shows Gwendolyn with her future husband at an archery tournament. [Boston: Dana Estes and Company, 1900; courtesy Evans Library, Texas A&M University.]

but not exclusively in cases where the mother was dead and the house in need of a mistress. Community service was another possibility, one that might be seen as an extension of family responsibilities. Daughters of clergymen, in particular, frequently helped out in the parish by teaching Sunday school or organizing community activities such as charity bazaars. They might also engage in district visiting, in which middle-class women communicated to the lower orders "appropriate" standards of domestic hygiene, dietary habits, table manners, and child rearing. Charles Dickens's *Bleak House* (1852–1853), for one, implies that girls might be more welcome in the homes of their social inferiors than middle-aged matrons, as the diffident and inexperienced young might approach charity in a less overbearing manner than their seniors.

Leisure activities suitable for respectable young women also proliferated, and sometimes served practical considerations beyond the temporary occupying of a girl's time. In George Eliot's *Daniel Deronda* (1876), the heroine, Gwendolyn Harleth, belongs to a family that has recently suffered major financial reverses after the failure of a business in which they are heavily invested. While her mother notes that Gwendolyn's assistance in the schoolroom will save the price of a governess, the senior members of the family also encourage the girl to join a local archery club and engage in her favorite sport of horseback riding. As her uncle observes once Gwendolyn is out of earshot, these pastimes take place in the public view and may enable her to marry well. Parlor games and musical performance likewise had potential usefulness in attracting a husband; for instance, the Victorians were fond of duets, a form of musical expression that facilitates courtship. Naturally, a talent for music would also have been a way for girls to gratify their parents and siblings by augmenting the pleasure available within the home. The roles of entertainer-in-chief and unpaid companion might continue as long as an unmarried daughter's parents remained to her.

After completing their quota of daily household duties and any community involvement, other girls used the time remaining to them in other ways. A group of fans and young friends of popular domestic novelist Charlotte Yonge began their own manuscript magazine, the *Barnacle*, which flourished between 1859 and 1871 and contained articles, illustrations, poems, and serial fiction promulgated under Yonge's supervision and heavily indebted to Yonge's own published works. As critic Julia Courtney has observed, the *Barnacle* provides valuable insight into the beliefs, concerns, activities, and abilities of a coterie of middle- and upper-middle-class girls in their teens and twenties.[6] Educated predominantly at home and emanating, in many cases, from households headed by clergymen or schoolmasters, the magazine's contributors produced work reflecting complex relationships to family. Some serials focus on their protagonists' difficulty in adjusting to a parent's remarriage, others on the inner lives—not altogether happy, notes at least one aspiring novelist—of girls who are morally and practically the most essential occupants of their homes. Meanwhile, articles focusing on travel, music, art, history, botany, translation, and literature suggest ways in which the "home daughters" of this class occupied themselves as young adults. Within this high-minded group, *productive* occupation was a major value, as it was for their mentor Yonge. Not all girls of this class would have been so focused on self-improvement, as is reflected in at least one serial, *A Tale of Four Months*, which expresses concern about the potential purposelessness of the existence of a "home daughter."

> I sleep away the mornings till past eight o'clock, I come down and fritter away an hour or two over breakfast and little nonsensical things, talk and letters and so on. Then if I feel inclined I practice a little, or loiter about in the garden, and do a little worsted work till luncheon. And then I spend the afternoon in riding or paying visits, and after dinner employ myself with bagatelle or a novel . . . I suppose if I were to marry or die you would miss me a little.
> —From *A Tale of Four Months*, a pseudonymous serial in *The Barnacle* (1867)

A daughter's idleness would have been disturbing to many Victorians for two reasons. From the viewpoint of many female commentators and of the conscientious girls who modeled themselves on Yonge, a girl who failed to find meaningful occupation faced tedium and lack of self-respect in an era that prized earnestness and saw work, whether or not it was remunerated, as a psychological necessity. From the viewpoint of the larger society, however, the major problem with the unproductive daughter was not the misery she might cause herself but the misery from which she would not be saving others. Victorian society expected middle-class daughters, like their aristocratic counterparts, to function as domestic centers of morality, in a way that even their mothers could not. Married women were hallowed by motherhood, to be sure, but they were also sexually knowledgeable, touched by experiences of a sort that the culture often found disturbing. In contrast, comfortably situated young women living in their parents' homes were presumed to be sheltered. Their parents were expected to protect their innocence as much as possible, for instance by keeping questionable reading matter out of their hands and monitoring their social encounters. In turn, the daughters would not only be kept pristine for their future husbands but would also retain a purity so refreshing that it would help to cleanse their fathers and brothers.

Such, at least, was the conventional line. In point of fact, of course, not all middle-class homes worked as convention dictated. Marguerite Radclyffe Hall, who under her final two names was to become internationally famous in the 1920s both as a novelist and as a lesbian, was born in 1880 to exceptionally unhappily married parents. Under the pressure of the couple's mutual recriminations and her father's infidelity, the marriage collapsed almost immediately after her birth. Far from being protected and petted as the light of the household, the child was abandoned by her father (who saw her only a handful of times before his death in 1898), rejected by her mother (who was inclined to treat her child violently), and sexually abused by her stepfather.[7] Consider also the large number of middle-class English children born in India and sent away from their homes at a young age to escape what was thought to be an unhealthy climate; like the children of John Lockwood Kipling in the early 1870s, they might be boarded with complete strangers, who were free to mistreat them more or less at will. But even in united and ostensibly functional homes, tension between middle-class parents and their daughters was by no means unknown. In the 1860s and 1870s, for instance, the *Englishwoman's Domestic Magazine* published various articles and letters noting that flogging was widely considered an appropriate method of disciplining female children and instilling in them a suitable respect for their mothers. Indeed, whipping would not have been seen as incompatible with the emphasis on sheltering gently reared girls, as both procedures were designed to produce dutiful children who adhered to the standards set by parents.

Yet duty could sometimes go hand in hand with a quiet iconoclasm. Some middle-class daughters managed to find not simply socially acceptable activities or useful domestic tasks to while away the time, but dynamic careers. Nightingale, for one, parlayed society's readiness to credit women with nurturing abilities into the revolutionizing of the nursing profession. Yonge, a devoted daughter who believed fervently in filial obedience, nonetheless maneuvered around her father's belief that women should not work for pay by donating her considerable literary earnings to an assortment of worthy causes. Elizabeth Barrett had to contend with ill health and a father who sought to prevent any of his eleven offspring from marrying, but she simultaneously became England's foremost woman poet; her father found her fame far more palatable than her elopement, at age thirty-nine, with Robert Browning. And Angela Burdett-Coutts, who remained single for the first sixty-seven years of her life, inherited at age twenty-three not only her grandfather's large fortune but also his banking business. She devoted both money and her organizational talents to philanthropic work so varied and so significant that she was raised to the peerage in 1871, the first Englishwoman to be granted this honor in her own right. Although such women were exceptional, they also demonstrate that it was possible for middle-class daughters to break out of the prison of social expectations—or, perhaps, to redefine convention in ways that would permit them considerable freedom.

THE MIDDLE-CLASS SON

In her 1852 essay "Cassandra," Nightingale contrasts the filial obligations of young women to those of young men. She notes that whereas daughters are expected to accede to their parents' wishes that they attend a particular social function or devote themselves to domestic duties, sons are permitted the freedom to insist upon their right to follow their own bent. In another sense,

however, the middle-class son who demanded time (and, probably, the expend-
ing of family resources) for self-cultivation was demonstrating his obedience
to Victorian family values as fully as was his sister who put aside her studies in
order to read aloud to her mother. For the role that Victorian society typically
assigned to young middle-class men was that of making their way in the world,
establishing themselves in a career so that they could earn enough money to
support a household. If the good bourgeois Victorian daughter provided her
parents with companionship or, perhaps, became a deputy "wife" to her father
and deputy "mother" to her younger siblings, her brother's function was to
prove that he was ready to take on a role similar, but ideally superior, to his
father's.

Within the home, this proof was to consist in part of consistent respect for the
values that parents were supposed to embody. Thus, for instance, Victorian sons
were frequently instructed never to do anything that they would be ashamed
to reveal to their mothers or sisters; the ability to maintain control (or at least
to seem to maintain control) over one's desires and behavior was a defining
trait of the domesticated male. Similarly, commentators took a dim view of
young men who addressed their fathers as "Governor" or "Pater" instead
of the more acceptable "Father"; the use of fashionable slang might betoken
excessive loyalty to one's peers, at the expense of deference to one's seniors.
Letters from fathers to sons at university often warn against going into debt or
devoting too much time to recreation and too little to study.

Yet although middle-class sons might remain inmates of their parents' homes
until, perhaps at around age thirty, they finally achieved the financial security
that would permit them to support a wife, a double standard was common. Many
Victorians who would have been adamant in their insistence that young women
avoid any experiences that might take the bloom off their innocence were
willing to grant tacit permission to young men to slip the leash occasionally.
Unlike their sisters, middle-class men of university age and beyond could go
out unchaperoned at night to spend a convivial evening with friends. If they got
drunk, or even became sexually intimate with a working-class woman—well,
many fathers felt, in the words of the popular adage, that young men must
sow their wild oats. As the feminist and social purity movements gathered
strength in the mid-Victorian years, objections to male license became more
and more heated, but there remained a large group of Victorian fathers who saw
no great harm in their sons proving their masculinity in venues outside polite
society.

There is an obvious inconsistency in the idea that an unmarried son might
indulge himself outside the home and still believe himself to be upholding
the precepts of Victorian domesticity within it. Nonetheless, some members
of the middle and upper classes pulled off this psychological sleight of hand.
They were assisted by the prevalence of the assumptions that private and public environments were ethical opposites and that the poor were the moral,
not merely the financial, inferiors of the privileged. Thus a young man who

would not have dreamed of drinking too much at home might feel that beyond the domestic boundary, overindulgence was his own affair. Similarly, a young man who would have treated his sisters' friends with the utmost respect might feel comfortable making sexual advances to a shopgirl, not least because, if the economic disparity was great enough, he would not be expected to marry her. But an additional factor here was that since middle-class parents' dreams for their sons so heavily stressed the achieving and maintaining of an appropriate level of economic success, the maintaining of a corresponding level of moral purity was not infrequently considered a goal more suitable for daughters.

> I can truly say, that the older my children grow, the more difficulty do I find in the discharge of parental duties. The best mode of attempting the formation of character occupies much of my thoughts. With respect to the girls, the path appears to me comparatively clear; but the boys, who must eventually mix with a variety of characters, occasion me much anxiety. They must be exposed to vice; how, in dependence on the divine blessing, they may be most effectually prepared to encounter it, is a deeply important question.
> —From an 1838 letter by J. G. Breay, included in *Memoir of the Rev. John George Breay Minister of Christ Church Birmingham, with Correspondence and Sermon* (5th ed., 1844)

Lacking the income-producing country estates that were a feature of life among the aristocracy, the sons of the bourgeoisie had a wider variety of career choices than did their social superiors. They too might enter the ministry, accept commissions as officers in the Army or Navy, or stand for Parliament. But they could also, without jeopardizing their social position, become businessmen, physicians, solicitors, chartered accountants, pharmacists, journalists, architects, civil engineers, bankers, police inspectors, educators, or creative artists, among other possibilities. Middle-class fathers typically considered that they had a duty to provide financially for their daughters, but provision for their sons worked somewhat differently; responsible fathers would see to their job training and placement in some suitable line of endeavor. As was the case in every social class, young men frequently entered their fathers' professions; for instance, even at the end of the century, four out of every ten clergymen were clergymen's sons. Yet simultaneously, the nineteenth century was an era in which many new ways of earning a living were devised and many old ones gained substantially in prestige. Like their economic inferiors, the middle classes were much more likely than the nobility and gentry to perform work that had not been hallowed by tradition.

Nevertheless, even within the middle classes, social levels existed and were defined to a substantial degree by the source from which a given family derived

By the third quarter of the nineteenth century, attendance at a public school was widely perceived as a particularly important marker separating the sons of gentlemen from their class inferiors. Above, a detail from an image of Weston's Yard at Eton College with a group of cricketers in the foreground, drawn by H. Railton and appearing in the *English Illustrated Magazine* for 1884–1885. [Courtesy Evans Library, Texas A&M University.]

its income, rather than the amount of the income. These distinctions were often exact. Doctors outranked dentists; whereas the former became increasingly professionalized over Victoria's reign, the latter remained "trade" and were expected to use the servants' entrance rather than the front door when making house calls. Bookkeepers were lower middle class, but accountants, who had to meet certain educational requirements, occupied a higher place on the social ladder. Farmers might not have much in the way of formal education, but were nonetheless middle class because they employed laborers to perform the lower-status agricultural jobs; a farmer's wife did not risk her standing if she fed her own poultry or ran the dairy, but a farmer might not want to be seen mucking out stalls or hedging and ditching. And so on. It was important for a son to be aware of the fine gradations among occupations so that he could maintain or improve the family's status. When in the 1870s Radclyffe Hall's father, the son of a successful physician, announced his intention of becoming an actor instead of a barrister, his father discontinued his allowance; when he became sexually involved with the daughter of a fisherman, his father threw him out of the house.

Nor was work necessarily the only standard by which families measured status. Some put culture and learning first, while others valued spirituality most highly. According to John Ruskin's 1889 memoir *Praeterita*, his father, a prosperous wine merchant, had no wish that young John should follow in his footsteps. Rather, he took pride in the boy's literary ambitions and sent him to Oxford (shepherded by his mother) in the hope that he would mingle with the aristocracy, win prizes for his poetry, and graduate at the top of his class. In contrast, Robert Louis Stevenson, who came from a line of lighthouse builders in Scotland, caused domestic consternation not only by marrying a woman of whom his parents disapproved, but also by insisting upon becoming an author rather than a civil engineer or an attorney. While his eventual success in his chosen field vindicated his choice, rebellion and status anxiety are recurring subjects in his fiction, a circumstance that many critics trace to his concern at flouting his father's will. Another factor in Stevenson's case—and, given the religious ferment of the nineteenth century, in the cases of many other Victorian sons as well—was his rejection of his family's religious doctrines, which likewise caused his parents considerable anxiety. A view widely held during the era, particularly in Nonconformist households (that is, families who, although Protestant, did not belong to the Church of England), was that parents were responsible not only for providing their children's religious education but also for fitting their offspring for Heaven.

The genteel Victorian expectation that adult sons would, in a sense, become their fathers by stepping into the roles of patriarch, provider, and in some cases high priest led to much anxiety in the cases of sons who, like Stevenson, rejected the pattern handed to them. Religious rebellion could be especially distressing, since parents might take it as a sign that they had failed in the weightiest moral duty of child rearing; religion thus had the potential to become crucial in either dividing or uniting the generations.

I was never at my ease in his company; I never knew when I might not be subjected to a series of searching questions which I should not be allowed to evade. Meanwhile, on every other stage of experience I was gaining the reliance upon self and the respect for the opinion of others which come naturally to a young man of sober habits who earns his own living and lives his own life. For this kind of independence my Father had no respect or consideration, when questions of religion were introduced, although he handsomely conceded it on other points. And now first there occurred to me the reflection, which in years to come I was to repeat over and over, with an ever sadder emphasis,—what a charming companion, what a delightful parent, what a courteous and engaging friend, my Father would have been, and would preeminently have been to me, if it had not been for this stringent piety which ruined it all.

—Edmund Gosse, *Father and Son* (1907), Epilogue

Conversely, the same assumption that sons would pattern themselves on their fathers often facilitated warm father–son relationships, or at any rate considerable paternal pride and interest, when boys were young. After his father's death, Edmund Gosse was to write *Father and Son* (1907), a memoir of his early years designed to show why his views on religion and evolution had come to diverge from his sire's in a way that greatly injured the comfort they took in one another. But Gosse recounts in the same work how his father taught him the basics of reading and geography, took him on outings, and, after the boy lost his mother at age seven, became his dear friend and boon companion. Guides to good parenting aimed at the middle classes encouraged fathers to spend time with their young sons, in particular. And if mothers were sometimes assigned the duty of providing sex education to nursery-aged children, the instruction in these matters of adolescent boys was more typically the province of the father—a practice that may presume a certain closeness and trust between the generations.

THE WORKING-CLASS SON

Among working-class families, the instruction that sons received from their fathers was often predominantly vocational. For much of the century, working-class people were likely to live out their lives within a few miles of their birthplace, unless they enlisted in the armed forces or were compelled to leave by economic necessity. If their homes were not in major metropolitan areas, the range of occupations open to them was comparatively limited: agricultural laborer, domestic servant, miner, tradesman, and so on. For a variety of reasons, then, it was common for working-class sons to enter the family business. If their fathers were self-employed, even quite young boys might be of material help as assistants performing basic tasks that needed little strength or skill; when the boys grew up, they would take on more and more responsibility until they reached the status of partner. A village might well contain only one blacksmith, say, and his son would clearly be in a better position than most outsiders to get the necessary training to take over the business in due course. Similarly, a father who was not self-employed might be eager for his son to get a job at the father's place of business. Not only would this move be convenient, since the father could furnish a reference, it would also afford the parents a measure of control. A father who was also a coworker would be able to monitor the son's conduct and wages, which many unmarried sons were expected to make over in their entirety to the parents.

To be sure, in many cases the changes brought by the Industrial Revolution interrupted this smooth transfer of livelihood from father to son. For one thing, the very poor might have no trade to pass on; an unskilled laborer might make his living by brute strength alone, so that a young child accompanying him to work would be a liability rather than an asset. In an urban setting, such a boy might instead stay with his mother. If she earned money by doing piecework (manufacturing at home items such as hats, toys, stockings, and so on that her employer then paid her for by the piece), she might enlist her children's help, both to give them something to do and because their assistance would be useful. An older boy living in the city might find employment outside the home that did not involve either parent, ranging from petty crime and begging to jobs held by youths at the higher end of the working-class spectrum, such as office boy and shop assistant.

Considering the case of a hypothetical cobbler provides an illustration of the potential effects of the Industrial Revolution on a trade that would once have been a likely candidate for transmittal from one generation of a family to the next. With the importation of the sewing machine from the United States in the 1850s, the manufacturing of shoes was gradually transformed from an operation performed entirely by hand into one performed entirely by machine. Gradually, one-man village shoemaking establishments closed their doors, driven out of business by the more efficient mass-production system. Even if our shoemaker's son decided to remain in his father's line of work, he would be performing this work under very different conditions and having to learn a different set of techniques in order to participate in the manufacture of his product. Moreover, he would no longer be a skilled artisan, but a factory hand. If the family could afford it, then, they would have been likely to perceive the need to fit their sons for another field of endeavor. Memoirist Siân Busby notes that her great-grandmother's brother Herbert Smith was the last in a five-generation dynasty of shoemakers, but that whereas Herbert's father, a master bootmaker, was able to cling to traditional ways and hold out against machine-made footwear, he was in the minority by the 1870s. In contrast, Herbert, joining the trade in 1883, was not a sole proprietor of his business but merely a member of a local assembly line. Subsequent generations left the business altogether.[8]

Among the respectable poor, education sometimes provided new opportunities. With the passage in 1870 of England's first major Education Act, known as the Forster Act after its proposer W. E. Forster, schooling was made more widely available for the working classes; in 1880 it became compulsory. Although children over the age of ten could get a certificate exempting them from attending school if they had attained a particular academic standard and/or if their families needed them as wage earners, theoretically, every child would spend at least a few years in a classroom, enough to achieve basic literacy and numeracy. While the education provided was often inadequate, it occasionally afforded children options that they might not have had before 1870; they could become clerks or teachers, for instance, and the highly gifted and motivated might even make their way to university. Strikingly, the rhetoric that Forster used in describing the Act translated to a national scale the sentiments that motivated many families to jockey for position through advancing their children.

> Civilised communities throughout the world are massing themselves together, each
> mass being measured by its force; and if we are to hold our position among men
> of our own race or among the nations of the world we must make up the smallness
> of our numbers by increasing the intellectual force of the individual.
>   —W. E. Forster, introducing the Elementary Education Bill
>   in the House of Commons (February 1870)

In some cases, the severing of continuity as a promising boy turned his back
on his father's livelihood and entered upon something new created a rift within
the family, the son considering his parents misguided or downtrodden or even
contemptible, the parents being baffled by the son's unfamiliar outlook. Novelist
H. G. Wells, born in 1866 to a father whose vocations included gardening,
professional cricket, and keeping a shop and a mother who had been first a
lady's maid and subsequently a housekeeper, left school in his fifteenth year to
be apprenticed to a draper. He nonetheless won a scholarship to study zoology
under Charles Darwin's great exegete Thomas Henry Huxley at the Royal
College of Science, began publishing works of popular science, and quickly
became a best seller as a writer of science fiction. His realistic novel *Tono-
Bungay* (1909) contains a scathing indictment of the outlook of people whose
experiences and social status recall those of his parents, as well as a moment in
which the narrator realizes, while attending his mother's funeral, the tragedy
of their alienation and estrangement from each other. The epiphany is one that
a number of upwardly mobile sons must have had.

> Suddenly as the service drew to its end, I felt something had still to be said which
> had not been said, realised that she had withdrawn in silence, neither forgiving
> me nor hearing from me—those now lost assurances. Suddenly I knew I had
> not understood. Suddenly I saw her tenderly; remembered not so much tender or
> kindly things of her as her crossed wishes and the ways in which I had thwarted
> her. Surprisingly I realised that behind all her hardness and severity she had loved
> me, that I was the only thing she had ever loved, and that until this moment I
> had never loved her. And now she was there and deaf and blind to me, pitifully
> defeated in her designs for me, covered from me so that she could not know....
>   —H. G. Wells, *Tono-Bungay* (1909), Chapter 2

Somewhat similarly, another future novelist, D. H. Lawrence, was born in
1885 to a father who was a miner and a mother who had been a teacher.
The social discrepancy between his parents put strain on the marriage, and
his mother committed herself to keeping her promising son out of the mines

and fitting him for a more intellectual and high-status occupation; success, in her view, would require him *not* to resemble his father. The young Lawrence, who was able to win a scholarship to Nottingham High School and eventually to Nottingham University College, strongly identified with his mother and repudiated his father, although he was to revise this stance in later life. As Lawrence's and Wells's cases both suggest, working-class sons whose careers diverged from their fathers' might face emotional barriers that made love and understanding difficult.

Victorian literature offers similar insights. In her 1859 novel *Adam Bede*, George Eliot adds that even when father and son share a line of work, a son's greater success may cause estrangement. Here, Adam's father's drinking causes him to miss deadlines and ultimately to drown; Adam's response to his wayward parent before the tragedy is impatient and even contemptuous, since he himself is strongly committed to the self-improvement, self-discipline, and upward mobility that Victorian social improvers prescribed for men of his class. Indeed, popular economic tracts such as Samuel Smiles's bestseller *Self-Help* offered young working-class men alternative role models to their fathers, inviting them to pattern themselves after men of higher social status and, it was implied, better character. In a sense, the Victorian ethic of optimism, which held out the possibility of higher wages and increased comfort for the industrious and thrifty members of the working classes, simultaneously expressed a willingness to see an increased emotional distance between the successful working-class son and what his father represented. After all, if the son succeeded in improving his economic, educational, and class standing, by some lights he had already done his duty by his parents.

THE WORKING-CLASS DAUGHTER

Like their brothers, working-class daughters typically expected to earn their way in the world, at least until they became mothers; the question that so bedeviled more affluent Victorian girls, namely how best to spend one's leisure, was less pressing among the poor because leisure was in considerably shorter supply. Nevertheless, the privileged frequently worried about it on their behalf. Were working girls reading the wrong kind of literature? Were they so eager for little luxuries, such as pretty clothes and chocolates, that they could be bribed to stray sexually? Were they relaxing instead of attending church? The anxiety with which some nineteenth-century observers viewed young unmarried female factory hands and shopgirls, in particular, manifests the same middle-class suspicion of working-class families that colored attitudes toward the girls' fathers and mothers. But more specifically, it also reveals bourgeois beliefs about what the daughter's role should be. The greater the girls' perceived deviation from this ideal, the greater the observer's concern.

For above all, bourgeois standards held that unmarried daughters should focus on fulfilling feminine duties, ideally in the home, and that they must embody purity and innocence. Girls away from a watchful mother's eye were vulnerable. Responsible employers of young female servants accordingly perceived a duty to supervise their charges closely. Free days would be kept to a minimum—perhaps an afternoon off every other week, or a day off once a month, as it was believed that girls of this class needed the structure that a rigid work schedule would provide. Servant girls might also be required to share sleeping quarters, and many employers stipulated that no "followers" (suitors) would be permitted. Clearly the employer's convenience was a major factor here, but these working conditions were also calculated to provide a version of the same sexual policing that was maintained over middle- and upper-class daughters. Concern for young female servants also gave rise to organizations such as the Girls' Friendly Society, a subspecies of district visiting that offered servant girls another layer of middle-class supervision.

Victorian culture, then, typically viewed with complacency a servant girl who worked in a sufficiently watchful environment. Indeed, such a girl might be considered safer and better off than one who remained with her parents. For one thing, she had been removed from a one- or two-room dwelling, where even if incest was not a threat (and the specter of working-class incest haunted concerned members of the more privileged classes in the nineteenth century), her parents would have been hard put to it to disguise the manifestations of their own sexuality. Conversely, social purity activists such as W. T. Stead held that working-class mothers might fail to warn their daughters against sexual predators, or to enlighten them about sexuality in any regard, so that an employer who discouraged "followers" was helping to preserve the innocence of a vulnerable group of girls. Yet a working-class daughter who entered domestic service in an irresponsible home was also considered to be prey to seduction because of the loneliness and cheerlessness of her position. As numerous commentators pointed out over the course of the period, the wrong kind of environment could destroy a girl's natural tendency toward virtue.

Thus despite the suspicion with which working-class homes were often regarded by the prosperous, they were nevertheless sometimes perceived as the best place for a daughter to remain. The various Victorian laws that sought to regulate child labor focused particularly on children working outside the home; girls laboring in their mothers' cottage-industry trades as seamstresses, lacemakers, and the like were less likely to attract official attention than children employed in more public venues. That these girls were presumed to be working under the watchful eyes of their mothers made even the most taxing conditions relatively acceptable to labor reformers. Similarly, after the passage of the Education Act of 1870, working-class parents were liable to punishment if they sabotaged their sons' chances to rise by removing them from school prematurely or encouraging truancy so that the boys could work. Yet historian Anna Davin has found that London School Board officials were prepared to wink at girls' truancy if mothers claimed that their daughters were needed to help with the housework.[9] While muckraking journalists such as Thomas

Archer (in his 1870 work *The Terrible Sights of London*) held up as horrific the sight of seven- or eight-year-old girls struggling to provide child care for one or more younger siblings, this form of child labor did not attract legislation.

Indeed, schools could in some cases facilitate child labor among girls. "Lace schools," for example, which gave industrial training in the craft to girls as young as five but offered reading and writing only as an afterthought, lingered on until the early twentieth century. The curricula of less specialized schools reflected this sense that boys were more in need than girls of skills that might help them to rise, and that the proper occupation of a daughter was housework. Historian of education Carol Dyhouse notes that elementary schools serving the children of the poor required girls, but not their brothers, to study needlework, cookery, and in some cases even laundry, while the boys received additional instruction in arithmetic or writing.[10]

> Girls . . . suffer from [absenteeism] more than boys; they are of use at home, are more handy in the household, and at a very tender age are trusted with the maternal duties of the family. Boys, however, are often sent to school, if only to be put out of the way. And more than this, the authorities of the School Boards are severer in the case of the boys absenting themselves from school than they are with girls. A sort of innate feeling, indeed, exists that school after all is more important to the boy than to the girl; so that if one must stay at home, it must be the girl.
> —G.C.T. Bartley, "Elementary Education"
> *Journal of Women's Education Union* (July 15, 1875)

One of the assumptions behind this sex-specific curriculum was that working-class daughters might not be learning crucial information about homemaking from their mothers. Recall that although a comparatively small proportion of married mothers of young children were employed in factories, Victorian journalists and other social observers frequently wrote as if the number were much larger. Samuel Smiles, for instance, reiterated over many decades his belief that industrialism had destroyed working-class family life by separating mothers from their child-rearing duties. By mandating the study of "domestic economy" as a school subject for girls, the government hoped not only to fill the place of mothers who might not be rearing their daughters properly, but also to create a new generation of better mothers for daughters yet unborn. A similar justification was used to urge job-seeking girls to accept positions as domestic servants rather than to look for what might be better paid work in factories or shops: a good mistress or housekeeper would provide invaluable training in maintaining a decent home, training that the girls' mothers might not have given them.

In short, Victorian discussions of working-class daughters often reveal a profound ambivalence toward home, a feeling that if the home were the right sort, the girl should certainly stay in it, but that it might easily *not* be the right sort. Working-class mothers, after all, so frequently seemed untrustworthy, incapable of guiding either their spouses or their children along the upward path. Observers worried about domestic violence, poor hygiene, alcoholism, and common class-specific practices such as sending one's youngsters to the local pub to bring home the family beer. In such cases, the ideal solution frequently appeared to be for some outside agency—the school system, the Church, the district visitor—to train up the daughter as a substitute who could serve as helpmeet to her father, mother to her siblings, and in due course wife and mother in a household of her own. In his 1883 series on "How the Poor Live," for instance, journalist George Sims assured his readers that hope was in sight, for slum girls who had attended board schools "have far tidier homes already than their elders. . . . These [older] people are irreclaimable, but they will die out."[11]

Commentary such as Sims's illustrates that although the daughters of the poor could expect to be wage earners for some portion of their lives, and might indeed be crucial contributors to the family coffers even as children, society's attention tended to focus not on how they might earn their way into a higher economic stratum but rather on their unpaid contributions to the domestic environment. In the laboring classes as in the middle classes and among the gentry, advancing the family financially was seen as a primarily masculine responsibility, for all that women and children typically accounted for a quarter of the earnings of a working-class family with a husband at its head. This perception meant that in a sense, and with all due respect, a son was encouraged to differentiate himself from his father, whether by expanding the family business or by taking up a new and higher-status line of work. In contrast, daughters were expected to conform to a maternal standard that the Victorian cult of domesticity did not consider subject to improvement. If individual mothers, particularly among the poor, did not meet that standard, their daughters were certainly urged to step into the breach. But their efforts to do so were frequently cast not as modern advances but rather as a return to a traditional norm that had been temporarily interrupted by industrialism or urbanization.

$$4$$

BROTHERS AND SISTERS

THE IDEAL

The Romantic writers of the immediate pre-Victorian period emphasized the emotional power of sibling relationships. The Romantic vision of love held that the perfect partner would be not merely one's complement but one's alter ego, and that successful couples would feel a deep affinity for one another because of the similarities that they shared. This stress on the importance of mutual understanding and spiritual kinship sometimes gave rise to households in which sibling ties were at least as important as marriages. For instance, biographical critics have typically regarded poet William Wordsworth's relationship with his wife, who bore him five children, as less significant than his bond with his sister Dorothy, who shared their home and contributed materially to his work. Meanwhile, Mary Lamb was not only literary collaborator to her brother Charles, but also his charge after she killed their mother during one of her periodic mental breakdowns.

While Valerie Sanders and other recent scholars have found that both the Wordsworths' and the Lambs' relationships had their troubled, ambivalent side,[1] in the nineteenth century the preferred view appears to have been that these bonds were notable for their purity, tenderness, and mutual sympathy. Mary Lamb's violence and her brother's instability, Wordsworth's illegitimate fatherhood, were largely absent from their public images in the Victorian period. Rather, the educated public focused upon the idyllic vision of brother and sister retreating from a difficult world to find happiness in one another. In other words, Victorian consumers of Romantic literature noted the importance of sibling ties to that literature and celebrated the preoccupation as a manifestation of the best—by which they often meant most domestic and respectable—qualities of genius.

Conversely, sibling bonds that did not enjoy this halo of innocence were deeply shocking to nineteenth-century sensibilities. Hounded by the all-too-plausible rumor that he was the father of his half-sister's baby, Lord Byron, who had earlier used his various sexual transgressions as a marketing technique to gain literary superstardom and boost the sales of his poetry, found it necessary to exile himself from England in 1816. Propriety-conscious Victorians of the genteel classes often forbade their daughters to read his works, which were considered to be too faithful a reflection of the depravity of their author to be suitable fare for innocent girls. Even so, when the American novelist Harriet Beecher Stowe published her treatise *Lady Byron Vindicated* as an *Atlantic* article, "The True Story of Lord Byron's Life," in 1869 and in book form in 1870, nearly half a century after Byron's death, it met with a cold reception.

Stowe's best seller *Uncle Tom's Cabin* had won many fans in England, Queen Victoria among them, and the treatise took a moral stance that one might suppose to be congenial to Victorian sensibilities, namely that Lady Byron was justified in packing up her infant daughter, returning to her parents' house, and securing a legal separation because her husband had committed incest. Many English readers were nonetheless deeply offended by *Lady Byron Vindicated*, in part because to discuss the subject of brother–sister incest among the privileged was itself to break a taboo. If Byron's contemporary the Prince Regent, himself no pattern of sexual virtue, had disapproved of the poet's behavior because his offenses against public morality were so overt, Stowe's airing of Lady Byron's grievances was similarly too outspoken for the dominant taste of her age. And many of her Victorian readers (her friend George Eliot, for instance, whose own sibling relationships will be examined later in this chapter) agreed that her discussion of Byron's relationship with his half-sister was her most serious lapse in judgment.

Victorians, then, and middle- and upper-class Victorians in particular, were powerfully influenced by the early nineteenth-century valorization of the sibling tie, which continued to be a feature of later nineteenth-century fiction, nonfiction, and poetry. But they had a precise vision of what this valorization both included and excluded. On the one hand, sibling relationships were supposed to be notable for the mutual support that they would afford. Sisters who helped their brothers make their way in the world or provided them with domestic comforts to offset their professional struggles, brothers who gave their unmarried sisters a home and a purpose, were clearly meeting the standards for family life that the cult of domesticity promulgated. So were older sisters who chaperoned younger ones into society so that they might meet prospective husbands, or older brothers who helped their juniors find gainful employment. Despite its title, for instance, Samuel Smiles's *Self-Help* is punctuated with anecdotes of notable men who owed their starts in life to such brothers. These exemplary tales functioned to remind ambitious readers of the importance not only of achieving individual success, but also of providing assistance to family members.

> [Lord Eldon] was the son of a Newcastle coal-fitter; a mischievous rather than a studious boy; a great scapegrace at school, and the subject of many terrible thrashings—for orchard-robbing was one of the favourite exploits of the future Lord Chancellor. But by this time his eldest [brother] William (afterwards Lord Stowell), who had gained a scholarship at Oxford, wrote to his father, "Send Jack up to me, I can do better for him." John was sent up to Oxford accordingly, where, by his brother's influence and his own application, he succeeded in obtaining a fellowship.
> —Samuel Smiles, "Industry and the Peerage," *Self-Help* (1859)

On the other hand, sibling relationships were also valued for what they were presumed to exclude. Because sexuality was a source of anxiety for many middle-class Victorians, any tie that held out the promise of the benefits of companionate marriage without its potential drawbacks had considerable appeal. A spinster or widow was encouraged to look to her brothers for financial advice and, if necessary, financial support, so that the husband's major domestic responsibility would be fulfilled in his absence. Similarly, a bachelor or widower was supposed to be able to call upon his sisters to provide some of what he might otherwise have expected from his wife: homely comforts, surrogate mothers for his children, and/or moral guidance for himself. Sampling data from the 1851 census on women living in households headed by a brother or brother-in-law, historians Leonore Davidoff and Catherine Hall report that in lower-middle-class families with this configuration, just over two-thirds of the men were either single or widowed. The arrangement was both more common and slightly different in the upper middle class, where just over half of the men were married.[2]

Perhaps in cases where more disposable income was available, sisters were taken in more as a form of charity than from the brother's need. Yet the latter was often a factor as well. When George Eden, Lord Auckland, became Governor-General of India in 1835, he took his younger sister Emily along with him to serve as his hostess, since his role required someone to act as first lady; she stayed with him in this capacity until his death in 1849, some seven years after his return to England. Moreover, the presence of an extra adult woman could be a benefit even in a household that already contained a wife, since the unmarried sister might be expected to repay the hospitality shown to her by helping to rear her nephews and nieces or sharing the burdens of housekeeping.

Indeed, she might function, like Dickens's sister-in-law Mary Hogarth (who made her home with the couple before her sudden death in 1837 at age seventeen), as an additional and idealized wife, an intimate companion who did not bring to the ménage the complications potentially engendered by sexual contact.

In Dickens's mind, claims his biographer Fred Kaplan, "The faultless Mary had been a better mother, a better sister, and a better Catherine [Dickens's wife], an alternate Catherine, a completion of Catherine, adding insight, sympathy, and intelligent understanding."[3] Mary's place in her brother-in-law's household was subsequently filled by her younger sister Georgina, who remained in it for the rest of Dickens's life, even after he and Catherine separated. Partly as a tribute to Mary and Georgina and partly as a way of representing the sanctified nature of a male–female love that excluded sexuality, a recurrent figure in Dickens's novels is that of the devoted sister who places her brother above other earthly considerations. The warmth with which Dickens's public responded to portraits of this sort suggests that the author's craving for the companionship of a perfect woman—understanding, loyal, pure, and bound to him by close family ties—was widespread, and that much of his audience may have shared the belief that this companionship might best be found in a sister.

The sibling bond also enabled the creation of all-female households. Although women who had not yet reached old age could not readily live alone without appearing alarmingly independent, sisters could set up housekeeping together and enjoy their freedom. Memoirist Geoffrey Robinson notes that such arrangements might endure even when sisters were incompatible, as in the case of his connections Annie and Olive Fisher, who shared a home in Nottingham in the 1890s. Olive was a dressmaker, while Annie, the older of the pair, "was lazy and lived on money inherited from her mother's family." According to Robinson, no love was lost between the sisters,[4] perhaps because of the discrepancy in their circumstances or Annie's relaxed attitude toward sexuality. Yet the awareness that society expected unmarried sisters to live together, or practical considerations such as economy, if not a combination of the two, dictated that this uncongenial household should endure. In other cases, sisterly love might serve as a socially approved rehearsal for romantic love. Here, for instance, is the eighteen-year-old Viola Taylor writing in 1900 to her thirteen-year-old sister, then a child prodigy enrolled at the Royal College of Art: "Your happiness, the happiness of your splendid young life is everything to me . . . I should be quite content to go softly all my years if you could live in a state of continual ecstatic joy . . . I pine to see you, I feel as if only half of me was alive without you . . . can't you draw me?"[5] Eight years later, Taylor would marry Maurice Woods, while her sister, the future Una Troubridge, was eventually to become the life partner of Radclyffe Hall and a champion of lesbian rights—yet it was the heterosexual sister who penned these ardent lines.

All these patterns between or among siblings could be said to mimic marriage, and in some cases potentially to improve upon it. After all, unlike the practice that governed middle-class couples before the passage of legislation governing married women's property, the law did not automatically give a brother control over his sister's money. Similarly, unlike many Victorian wives, most Victorian sisters did not need to fear that their interaction with their brothers would lead to the destruction of their health through venereal disease or excessive

The *Girl's Own Paper* story "Our Life in a Flat" describes two sisters keeping house together; in this illustration, published February 28, 1885, one tries her hand at making a plum pudding. [Collection of the author.]

childbearing. Conversely, internalizing a middle-class ethic of purity that could be taken to extremes, some men secretly feared that women (perhaps even their wives) who made their sexual availability apparent might not be "good women"; by definition, then, sisters were "good women" to their brothers. In other words, because sibling relationships were expected to exclude expressions of sexuality, the abuses and other sources of anxiety that Victorian feminists, reformers, and those who adopted the ethic of repression worried about in matrimony appeared to be absent from the brother–sister tie. As the Victorian sage Walter Pater wrote approvingly of Charles Lamb in an 1878 *Fortnightly Review* article, his closeness to Mary "[made] him content all through life, with pure brotherliness, 'the most kindly and natural species of love,' as he says, in place of the *passion* of love."[6]

Predictably, given this climate of esteem for close bonds of this type, Victorian England created its own sets of exemplary sibling relationships to hold up for praise, most famously that of the Brontë sisters. During and immediately after their lifetimes, the sisters' novels struck many propriety-conscious members of the reading public as unseemly, too unfeminine in their passion and their concern with sordid subjects such as infidelity, insanity, alcoholism, and cruelty to children or spouses. Yet as the early lives of their authors were gradually laid open to scrutiny, the Brontë family drama took on mythic qualities. The Victorian imagination was caught by the saga, revealed in Elizabeth Gaskell's 1857 *Life of Charlotte Brontë*, of the motherless children isolated even from their remote Yorkshire community, comforting one another in times of loneliness and privation, and maintaining sisterly devotion and intimacy throughout the span of their short lives. If Branwell Brontë failed his sisters by turning to drink and drugs, losing his teaching post when he became emotionally involved with his employer's wife, and dying young, the sisters stood by him and by each other in a manner that could only be considered admirable. Although this family was obviously unusual in any number of ways, Gaskell's biography of her friend focuses particularly on the ways in which Charlotte embodied virtues, such as self-denial, that the mid-Victorians held dear. And it is especially through the discussion of Charlotte as sister that Gaskell makes these virtues evident.

But the children did not want society. To small infantine gaieties they were unaccustomed. They were all in all to each other. I do not suppose that there ever were a family more tenderly bound to each other.... Charlotte's deep thoughtful spirit appears to have felt almost painfully the tender responsibility which rested upon her with reference to her remaining sisters. She was only eighteen months older than Emily; but Emily and Anne were simply companions and playmates, while Charlotte was motherly friend and guardian to both; and this loving assumption of duties beyond her years, made her feel considerably older than she really was.
    —Elizabeth Gaskell, *The Life of Charlotte Brontë*, Vol. I (1857),
Chapters 3 and 5

Victorian fiction frequently provided similar narratives. The devotion of brothers and sisters is a focus particularly of works that do not incorporate that favorite Victorian conclusion, the protagonists' marriage. In sentimental tales featuring pathetic and often dying children and in novels for juvenile readers (as well as in the separate genre of feminist fiction, which often viewed matrimony with a jaundiced eye), the sibling tie often substitutes for romance between unrelated adults. Sanders observes that in real life most of the famous nineteenth-century sibling bonds—Robert and Sarianna Browning, Elizabeth and William Sewell, Benjamin and Sarah Disraeli, Thomas and Hannah Macaulay, and so on—involved brothers and sisters rather than same-sex pairs.[7] But in sentimental and children's fiction, the question of whether the characters in question are boys, girls, or both does not appear to matter much. The emphasis is rather on the possibilities for selfless love when both parties are innocent of the promptings of sexuality and/or the desire for financial and social gain. Because they could readily be represented as disinterested and pure, ties between siblings were frequently showcased in literature aimed primarily at young women or children of the middle classes, upon whom unselfishness and purity were typically urged.

Tract literature is a good example of such a form. Best sellers such as "Brenda"'s Froggy's Little Brother (1875) and Hesba Stretton's Little Meg's Children (1868) idealize sibling bonds among the poor—partly to expose the inadequacy of the parents who fail to make adequate provision for their offspring, partly to establish the preternatural virtue of these narratives' small and ragged heroes. Froggy and his still younger brother, Benny, have lost both mother and father by the middle of Chapter 2. Nevertheless, they strive valiantly to keep together, Froggy earning a pittance as a crossing-sweeper and Benny comforting him through various catastrophes. Both boys retain their natural piety and their innate honesty in the face of considerable temptation to sin, and the implication is that in large part their virtue derives from (as well as being reflected in) the tenderness, concern, and willingness to sacrifice that they feel for one another. Similarly, Stretton's Meg is the oldest of the three children of a sailor and his wife, and must take over the care of the family when her mother dies during the father's absence on a voyage. Like Froggy, she exhausts herself taking care of the younger ones but never relinquishes her religious faith, her familial devotion, or her fidelity to her trust: although the family is desperately in need and the baby is dying, she keeps intact a nest egg that she has been asked to safeguard. Although Meg is a girl and Froggy a boy, they exhibit strikingly similar character traits and have nearly identical family responsibilities, in each case the combination of breadwinner and homemaker that would be normally be vested in two adult parents instead of in a single child. Such works seek to illustrate for their readers that whether one is a brother or a sister, ideal sibling love is marked by a one-size-fits-all set of qualities whose ultimate exemplar is Christ.

Narratives about wealthier children are understandably less likely to represent their protagonists as providing financially for smaller brothers and sisters

An idealized vision of a working-class brother (in clean but picturesquely ragged garb) tending his twin siblings, from a drawing entitled "Twins" by Dorothy Tennant in the *English Illustrated Magazine*, 1884–85. [Courtesy Evans Library, Texas A&M University.]

or to emphasize that one should be prepared to endure privation for one's family. Nevertheless, here too sibling love is frequently used as a measuring stick for virtue. Domestic novels such as those of Charlotte Yonge celebrate the pleasures of family life but also praise brothers and sisters who make sacrifices for one another. Representative of Yonge's exemplary youths is Felix Underwood in *The Pillars of the House* (1873), who plays a father's part toward his twelve younger siblings, remaining a bachelor to the end of his short life because one of his brothers has fallen in love with the woman of Felix's choice. Yonge herself was a spinster who provided a home over nearly a quarter-century for her brother's invalid sister-in-law; her biographers Margaret Mare and Alicia Percival view this arrangement as motivated by her desire to suit her brother's convenience. And indeed, Yonge holds up for readerly condemnation characters who fail to demonstrate a willingness to make similar accommodations because they put their own desires first. To Yonge as to many Victorian moralists, self-denial is crucial both to spiritual growth and to successful family life.

Even when a protagonist is careless, erring, and a source of grief to the surrounding adults, his or her ability to love a sibling may be a redeeming virtue. In Florence Montgomery's *Misunderstood* (1869), for instance, the high-spirited Humphrey Duncombe has a regrettable tendency to lead little Miles into danger; nevertheless, Humphrey's unfailing affection for Miles is an important way in which Montgomery compels our esteem for her protagonist. Conversely, in Frederick Farrar's didactic school story *Eric, or Little by Little* (1858), an early sign of the title character's falling away from virtue is his brusque treatment of his younger brother. Later, one of the most emotionally intense moments of the narrative is Eric's agonized sobbing over the corpse of the smaller boy, whom he has repeatedly failed to protect and cherish. As these examples suggest, the moral tale focusing on privileged children may show siblings as inattentive, whereas its counterpart about the poor is more likely to emphasize the preternatural care with which quite small children treat their juniors. But the essential point in both cases is the same, namely that whether they live up to it or not, siblings bear enormous responsibility for one another and should take this responsibility very seriously indeed.

There are a number of reasons why Victorian domestic fiction and religious tracts were so concerned with making this point. First, while the business ethos of the age often stressed individual success and autonomy, domestic life offered another kind of outlook, one that emphasized cooperation and altruism. Since the family was frequently perceived as analogous to the Christian community and/or as the most natural environment in which to learn about God's love for humankind, fiction that illustrated how siblings should feel and behave toward one another was teaching an important moral lesson. Simultaneously, it is significant that such fiction typically does not show siblings doubting their emotions toward their brothers or sisters. Farrar's Eric or Montgomery's Humphrey may not behave wisely toward their little brothers, but they nevertheless love them deeply. Such works thus lay out for readers the attitudes approved by society. A literature that only rarely acknowledges the possibility that siblings may feel indifference, jealousy, or hatred for one another is a powerful tool in encouraging readers to repress such feelings in their own lives. Then too, in a culture in which well-to-do children might have comparatively little daily interaction with their parents but a great deal with their siblings (unless and until boarding school intervened), sibling bonds would not uncommonly have been the strongest ties of a young person's existence. Among the poor, as social observers endlessly pointed out, siblings would typically share beds (both space and furniture being in short supply), take responsibility for each other's well-being, and often go into the same line of work; here too, fellow feeling would often have run strong. Although the intensity of sibling relationships in Victorian fiction may strike readers today as overblown, an outdated convention of an era addicted to sentimentality and melodrama, this intensity mirrors the lived experience of any number of nineteenth-century children.

Finally, the emphasis on the element of sacrifice expected in sibling relationships helped to teach middle-class girls, in particular, behaviors expected of them within Victorian society. Sacrifice was a manifestation of selflessness, a virtue greatly prized within the middle-class cult of domesticity because it facilitated the smooth running of a household that was likely to contain a sizable number of inhabitants. Girls capable of sacrifice, of subordinating their desires to others' good, were demonstrating their purity, which in turn was considered to be a potent source of moral influence. And just as mothers were credited with the power to strengthen their sons against the temptations that freewheeling masculine society might hold out, sisters were exhorted to exert the same power over their brothers. Mothers had proven their capacity for self-sacrifice by bearing children, since bringing a child to term requires a woman to undergo considerable discomfort and danger for the sake of her offspring. In contrast, the moral power of an unmarried sister was typically traced to her sexual inexperience. Presumed to be above contamination by the animal world of sensual gratification, sisters were considered to be in a position to preserve their brothers from the fate to which men's allegedly stronger sex drive might otherwise lead them. Thus purity reformer Ellice Hopkins, writing in 1899, notes that sisters are second only to mothers in their ability to guide young men to virtue.

SIBLING SACRIFICE

The requirement that a good sister sacrifice for her brother might have to do not with the salvation of his soul but rather with his convenience, of course, as ideal sisterhood might take practical forms as well as ethical ones. To return to the case of Charlotte Yonge, her brother Julian, and Julian's sister-in-law Gertrude Walter: Walter, also a spinster, had formerly made her home with Julian and his wife, an arrangement that itself illustrates the requirements of the sibling bond. In 1873, however, Walter moved in with Charlotte, who had

> There rises up before me the vision of a young girl ... who in her young days was the very embodiment of all that I have been urging that our girls might become to their brothers. She was a daughter of the great French preacher, Frederick Monod, and had an only brother who was all in all to her. She knew enough of the evil of the world to know that a medical student in Paris was exposed to great temptations; and she was resolved, so far as she could, to make her womanhood a crystal shield between him and them. She entered into all his pursuits; she took an interest in all his friends and companions; she had always leisure for sympathy and counsel in his difficulties and troubles. . . . Years after, when he was a married man, with boys of his own, he said to her: "You little know all that you were to me as a young man. My temptations were so maddening that I used sometimes to think that I must yield to them and do as other young men did all round me. But then a vision of you used to rise up before me, and I used to say to myself: "No; if I do this thing, I can never go and sit with her in her own little room; I can never look into her dear face again."
>
> —Ellice Hopkins, "Of Sisters," *The Power of Womanhood* (1899)

lived alone since the death of her mother five years earlier. Yonge was poorly suited to the role of nurse, whether her patient was her mother or her friend, as she found others' suffering difficult to witness; she was also a highly successful and busy writer and enjoyed an active social life. According to Mare and Percival, the arrival of an invalid who was frequently in discomfort meant that Yonge's interaction with her friends was curtailed, since being guest or hostess had to take a back seat to attending to Walter's needs. Moreover, they consider that even though there was no great diminution in quantity, the quality of her literary output suffered.

Writing in the mid-1940s, these biographers are outraged on Yonge's behalf and view Walter's death in 1897 as long overdue. After all, they belong to a generation that came of age in the postwar period, when novelists such as May Sinclair (*Mary Olivier*, 1919) and Radclyffe Hall (*The Unlit Lamp*, 1924) were condemning the practice of immolating daughters on the altar of their siblings' careers and their elderly parents' needs. But Yonge was a product of a different era, and Mare and Percival provide no evidence to suggest that the author herself ever expressed dismay over the situation or considered Walter's advent an imposition. Moreover, Yonge's disciple and connection Christabel Coleridge reports in her 1903 biography of her mentor that the author valued Walter's companionship, and that Walter, who described herself as "Char's wife," provided useful secretarial assistance and literary feedback. Apparently Yonge and those in her circle took it for granted that middle-class women should not live alone, that a brother's wife's sister counted as kin and could make claims on one correspondingly, and perhaps above all that a sister should do her utmost to make her brother's life easier.[8]

A sister makes common cause with her brother's wife; notice the vertical line suggesting the emotional obstacles that they are having to overcome. [Illustration by Kate Greenaway for Charlotte Yonge's *Heartsease* (London: Macmillan and Co., 1895); collection of the author.]

Yonge's case was by no means unique, even among the relatively small subset of middle-class female writers for children. Annie Keary, now best known for the collection of Norse mythology that she and her sister Eliza produced in 1857, relinquished her fiancé (Eliza's report leaves ambiguous whether he died or ended the engagement) in order to move in with a recently widowed brother who needed help raising his three children. As she never married, she could be called upon later in life to nurse her ailing mother and to take care of four small cousins when their parents moved to India, a place that many Victorians considered unhealthy for children. Similarly, when Flora Shaw's mother descended into invalidism and eventually death, the teenage future author of *Castle Blair* (1878) became responsible for her eleven younger siblings. When her father remarried some years after losing his wife, and Shaw no longer had to be the surrogate mother to her brothers and sisters, she soon replaced this duty by taking on the raising of other children and subsequently the care of the elderly parents of a rejected suitor. Although she eventually emerged in the 1880s as a respected foreign correspondent and authority on the colonies, and in the 1900s, after a late marriage, as the wife of the governor of Northern Nigeria and (subsequently) Hong Kong, Shaw's early life was typified more by sacrifice than by glamour.[9] And it was her role as sister that primarily facilitated this pattern.

Such cases remind us that girls and young women were presumed to be mothers in training, in a society that saw the maternal and quasi-maternal role as characterized, ideally, by the unselfish relinquishment of one's individual aspirations. Hopkins's *The Power of Womanhood* (quoted at the beginning of this section), which devotes a chapter to the sister's moral responsibility toward her brother, is subtitled "Mothers and Sons, a Book for Parents and Those in Loco Parentis." That the latter category explicitly includes sisters is clear, as Hopkins notes that "one of the great shaping influences of a boy's life, which certainly comes next to the mother's . . . [is] the influence of sisters."[10] A clichéd piece of advice among those exhorting young men to virtue was, "Think of your mother and sisters," a line that assumes, à la Hopkins, that at least as far as purity is concerned, there is little difference between these categories.

The principle that a young woman was appropriately seen as her mother's understudy where her father and siblings were concerned applied on a practical level as well. If a girl's mother died, she might legitimately be expected to bring up the younger children of the family. If a working-class mother had to absent herself from her family in order to support them financially, the task of looking after one or more toddlers, and perhaps the neighbors' children too (this time for pay), would often fall to a sister herself not far removed from infancy. And if child-care responsibilities kept the girl from attending school, so be it. Accounts of urban slum life by Victorian sociologists or reformers frequently include portraits of girls in their teens or younger who appear to be wholly responsible for caring for a flock of smaller siblings, if not for the adults of the family as well.

She had been out selling a few "creeses" [watercress], she informed us, and had now returned to look after the children, and to finish washing a few "things" of theirs, and some of her papa's. But for her mentioning the children in this maternal manner, I might have foolishly mistaken her for being one of them herself. My guide, however, with due deference, addressed her as "little Mother," which she apparently accepted as her rightful title. Being delicately questioned on the subject of her age, she owned to being sixteen, but confessed the age was counted from her birthday in next August. . . . I put a shilling in her hand, just wet out of the wash-tub, and asked if she could read what was impressed upon the coin. She frankly answered, "No," for she had "never gone to school. Never had the time," she added with some briskness, to which her father by a nod in silence signified assent.

—[Walter Austin?], "Travels in the East, Part VI," *All the Year Round* (April 5, 1884)

Even among working-class families with two surviving parents, grown children, but daughters especially, might be asked to take younger brothers and sisters into their homes if the parental budget was overstretched. And an adult spinster was likely to find herself at the service of any married sibling, and perhaps of a throng of nieces and nephews as well, just as she would commonly relieve her brothers and married sisters of the burden of caring for their aging parents. These duties were assigned to brothers both less frequently and less stringently, partly because males were not considered to have a natural turn for child rearing or for nursing the aged, but partly also because Victorian society acknowledged that men might legitimately pursue other callings beyond the family.

This is not to say that sacrifice was no part of the Victorian ideal where brothers were concerned. Female authors in particular constructed visions of virtuous brothers who devote themselves to their sisters, sometimes at considerable cost. The job of these exemplary brothers, however, is not to raise their sisters' children or to stand by an erring sister in a time of moral need, as Harriet Carker does for her embezzler brother in Charles Dickens's *Dombey and Son* (1847–1848). Rather, it is to make financial provision for a sibling who has no husband to support her. As George Eliot notes in her 1859 novel *Adam Bede*, a spinster sister's unwritten right to claim her brother's support may prevent him from contracting a marriage himself. And again, under the Victorian middle-class family code, a good brother was not to air his feelings of resentment over what family might have caused him to give up. In fiction as in life, however, the assumption was more commonly that sisters would sacrifice for their brothers, and later for their brothers' offspring, than the reverse.

And if that handsome, generous-blooded clergyman, the Rev. Adolphus Irwine, had not had these two hopelessly-maiden sisters, his lot would have been shaped quite differently; he would very likely have taken a comely wife in his youth, and now, when his hair was getting grey under the powder, would have had tall sons and blooming daughters—such possessions, in short, as men commonly think will repay them for all the labour they take under the sun. As it was—having with all his three livings no more than seven hundred a year, and seeing no way of keeping his splendid mother and his sickly sister, not to reckon a second sister, who was usually spoken of without any adjective, in such lady-like ease as became their birth and habits, and at the same time providing for a family of his own—he remained, you see, at the age of eight-and-forty, a bachelor, not making any merit of that renunciation, but saying, laughingly, if any one alluded to it, that he made it an excuse for many indulgences which a wife would never have allowed him.

—George Eliot, *Adam Bede* (1859), Chapter 5

Such sacrifice was manifested in different ways at different socioeconomic levels. Among the respectable working classes, a boy who had reached the age of usefulness was more likely to be employed outside the home than his sister of the same age. Because the family might be reluctant to risk alienating him and losing the income that he brought in, and because of the respect that Victorian society typically meted out to males who were living up to the masculine role by earning wages, his need for leisure time was often acknowledged. When not on the job, then, he might spent his time reading newspapers, attempting self-improvement through attendance at public lectures at Workingmen's Institutes, or socializing with friends, among many other activities. In contrast, his sister would probably be expected to devote herself to household labors—a time-consuming task in an era in which the poor made their own clothes from socks and underwear on out, did laundry without the convenience of washing machines or electric dryers, kept houses clean without piped-in hot water, plucked their own chickens, and so on through a seemingly unending series of time-consuming and often physically exhausting tasks. It was a rare family of modest means whose womenfolk had the luxury of entertaining themselves. In other words, sisters were often expected to perform for their brothers the domestic tasks that would eventually be taken over by these young men's wives, thus benefiting the family exchequer by delaying as long as possible the time when grown sons would leave to start families of their own.

Even among the middle classes, girls commonly carried out a goodly number of chores of which their brothers were the beneficiaries. If a boy tore his clothes or wore holes in his stockings, his sister, in training to run her own household later on, was likely to do his mending. She might also assist him with his studies (many Victorian girls picked up a substantial portion of their education by helping their brothers memorize Latin declensions or mathematical theorems), run his errands, make him the beneficiary of her home handicrafts, and provide any number of other demonstrations of her devotion and his superiority. A growing middle-class boy would probably not be called upon to assist his father at work if an employee became unavailable. A growing middle-class girl was quite likely to be used as backup to her younger siblings' nanny, not only providing valuable help to her mother but also, and simultaneously, being trained in the ethic of sibling sacrifice. And if a mother fell ill, again, married daughters and unmarried sons might be exempt from doing much to fill the void, but an unmarried teenage girl could find her education suddenly ended and her role transformed into that of her mother's nurse and her father's companion. This fate could befall even the most intellectually promising; when her mother developed breast cancer in 1835, the fifteen-year-old who would later become famous as George Eliot was removed from school and turned into sick-nurse and housekeeper. Like Charlotte Yonge, she appears to have expressed no complaint.[11]

As for the upper-class girl, if her domestic responsibilities were slighter than would have been the case among her social inferiors, she would still normally have been aware of a substantial gulf between herself and her brother. That he had a much better chance than she of being sent to boarding school typically had a substantial impact upon their relationship. His curriculum included prestige subjects such as classics and higher mathematics, whereas boys and girls alike often assumed that fields of study associated with femininity were only fit for inferior intellects. Although girls' schools became more plentiful toward the end of the century and started to experience a push toward academic reform in the 1870s, the desire for increased rigor was not always fulfilled, whether among the upper classes or among those who might eventually teach others. Schoolmistress Amy Barlow, for one, considered that in the 1890s "one taught or did nothing" as a preceptor of girls.[12] As the lower-middle-class Tom Tulliver says scornfully to his sister, Maggie, in Eliot's *The Mill on the Floss* (1860), "I should like to see you doing one of *my* lessons! Why, I learn Latin too! Girls never learn such things. They're too silly."[13] Tom has access to an education approximating that of a gentleman; Maggie's schooling is primarily described in terms of what it omits—Latin, geometry, and logic—but she nevertheless later earns her living as an educator.

Moreover, the major public schools advertised themselves as turning out leaders of men; graduates of Eton and Harrow were to make their marks in the army, in Parliament, or in the Church, if they did not become dominant figures in county life, with their landed estates as their bases. Girls were not trained to exert such authority; if anything, they were required to subordinate themselves to it. This subordination was frequently evident in the deference that a sister might show a brother, which is recalled in any number of accounts by women who grew up in the Victorian era. Anne Jemima Clough, for instance, experienced the death of her older brother Arthur as a major emotional loss, but

Teaching older girls to take care of their younger siblings was both a convenience to mothers in the absence of a nanny and useful training for the girls in later life. The above illustration by Muir from *The British Workwoman* (1874) shows a girl helping to prepare her little brother for his sponge bath. [Reprinted in *Children: A Pictorial Archive from Nineteenth-Century Sources*, selected by Carol Belanger Grafton, Dover Publications, Inc.; used by permission.]

only in his absence could she establish herself as a leading figure in women's education. Even the redoubtable Harriet Martineau, who, as we shall see below, was destined to develop the strength of mind sufficient to distance herself from her favorite brother, James, reports that she embarked upon a literary career because her oldest brother, Thomas, told her to do so—and adds that she turned down a promising post as editor of a magazine on economics in 1837 because James advised her not to take the post.[14]

> [Thomas] then laid his hand on my shoulder, and said gravely (calling me "dear" for the first time) "Now, dear, leave it to other women to make shirts and darn stockings; and do you devote yourself to this." I went home in a sort of dream, so that the squares of the pavement seemed to float before my eyes. That evening made me an authoress.
>
> —Harriet Martineau, *Autobiography*, Vol. 1 (1877)

If sibling (and especially sisterly) sacrifice worked differently from class to class, individual reactions to the cultural expectation that such sacrifice would take place varied as well. Historian Carol Dyhouse cites a number of women who recalled having felt that their brothers' lives were easier than theirs and resented the discrepancies between male and female gender roles within their families. Suffrage worker Hannah Mitchell, for one, wrote in her autobiography about her childhood on a Derbyshire farm in the 1870s and 1880s that "I think my first reactions to feminism began at [age eight] when I was forced to darn my brothers' stockings while they read or played cards or dominoes . . . the fact that the boys could read if they wished filled my cup of bitterness to the brim."[15] Many women whose experiences resembled Mitchell's, however, accepted the discrepancies between their household responsibilities and their brothers' as natural, indeed divinely ordained. God had created man to lead and woman to support him, and that decision was not to be appealed. As Yonge wrote in her nonfiction work *Womankind* (1877), "I have no hesitation in declaring my full belief in the inferiority of woman, nor that she brought it upon herself" when Eve's weakness led to humankind's expulsion from Eden.[16] Clearly, it was the duty of the inferior being to serve, and many Victorian sisters did so as a matter of course.

SIBLING ESTRANGEMENT

Sisters who were not convinced of their responsibility to relinquish their desires, ambitions, and views when such expressions of personality were not conducive to sibling harmony might jeopardize their relationships with their brothers. Let us return to political economist Harriet Martineau, who wrote in an 1859 *Daily News* article that only the unobservant could believe that British women were still financially supported by their fathers, husbands, or brothers—a state of affairs, she claimed, that had not been current since the Napoleonic Wars.[17] While in 1859 one could have found any number of women, from the respectable working classes on up, whose money derived from their menfolk, the theme of women's enforced economic independence from men, and perhaps specifically brothers who are failing to support their sisters, had echoes in Martineau's life. After the death of her once well-to-do father in 1826, the family fortunes waned dramatically, and Martineau, then in her mid-twenties, had to earn her own living, initially by her needle and subsequently by her pen. The success of her writings on economics and other social and political matters gave her confidence. Increasingly, she made her own decisions, which ultimately included embracing agnosticism and establishing herself not as spinster sister in the home of one of her assortment of brothers, but rather as a head of household in her own right, with an admiring niece to serve as companion-help. Martineau's religious infidelity and feminist leanings were important factors in her deteriorating relationship with her younger brother James, a theologian, to whom she had been particularly close in childhood.

Sanders, who has written extensively on Martineau, traces the escalating quarrel between this sibling pair. She suggests that it stemmed from two intertwined sources. First, James was unsympathetic to a number of ideas dear to Harriet, from abolitionism and feminism to agnosticism to mesmerism and phrenology. But in addition, he sought to retain a fraternal authority over her that was conventional in Victorian society, long after she had repudiated conventionality in other areas of her life. Her anger at her brother is evident in comments contained in her correspondence with her friend Fanny Wedgwood, to whom she wrote, "The truth is that James has been injuring and wounding me in every possible way since my illness in 1839," and again, "Considering the intervals of 4, 6, and 7 years when he has not even *seen* me,—that he despises my books, knows none of my friends, or my habits, and very few of my opinions, and has never seen me for 20 years without insulting me,—he is not exactly the person to write my life."[18] Clearly Martineau is responding to what she perceived as her brother's lack of respect for her, his assumption that her ideas, experiences, and work are insignificant compared to his own.

Given the disparity between the treatment of boys and girls in many nineteenth-century homes, a belief in male superiority would have been ingrained in any number of Victorian brothers. For that matter, sisters would often have shared it. Even Martineau, in her early novel *Deerbrook* (1839), focuses not on hostility between brother and sister but on the jealousy that divides two sisters in competition for male attention. The narrative traces the lives of Margaret and Hester Ibbotson; Margaret, the younger, attracts the love of the local physician, Mr. Hope, and of the eligible Philip Enderby. Hope altruistically leaves Margaret to Enderby and marries Hester instead, upon which

Margaret, not yet engaged, comes to live with the newlyweds. The situation is a difficult one for both husband and wife, as Hope still loves Margaret and Hester is aware of his feelings. After many vicissitudes, the novel ends with family harmony restored. The emotional dynamics on display here may have affinities with those of the Martineau clan, however, since Martineau notes in her *Autobiography* her own jealousy of her sister Rachel, who, being less than two years her senior, would always have been her most immediate rival. James's marriage in 1828 introduced yet another female rival into the fold. And however great Martineau's resentment of James's slighting treatment of her, she seems never to have stopped regretting the gulf between them. As Davidoff and Hall note, their separation remained such a source of unhappiness for her that she left posterity no record of what precipitated their falling out. Instead, she only remarks wistfully in her memoirs that "brothers are to sisters what sisters can never be to brothers as objects of engrossing and devoted affection."[19]

George Eliot is perhaps the best-known example of a Victorian sister estranged from a much-loved brother after ceasing to hold views congruent with his. Born Mary Anne Evans in 1819, Eliot was the third child of her father's second marriage—the rest of the family consisted of a half-brother and half-sister born in 1802 and 1805; a full sister, Chrissey, born in 1814; and a full brother, Isaac, born in 1816. (Twin boys were born, and quickly died, in 1821.) Eliot seems to have begun hero-worshipping Isaac in her fourth year, a feeling memorialized in the opening chapters of *The Mill on the Floss* and in her 1869 sonnet sequence "Brother and Sister." Both texts trace a childhood bond in which the brother is decidedly the dominant partner, quick to police his sister's behavior and to punish any failure in carefulness or feminine propriety, while the sister longs for signs of his approval or benevolent attention. Like Harriet Martineau, Eliot diverged from her brother's religious faith, initially embracing a fervent Evangelicalism that was nearly as uncongenial to his High Church Anglicanism as her later agnosticism; their disparity of belief caused a corresponding friction between them. And like Martineau, she embarked upon a career that brought her considerably more under the public eye than did her brother's. At the time of Eliot's death, she had become the most admired English novelist of the day, whereas although Evans managed to raise his social status (partly through a profitable marriage), his was hardly a name to be conjured with.

But in Evans's eyes his sister's chief sin was to live as man and wife with George Henry Lewes without benefit of the marriage ceremony. When Eliot wrote to Evans in 1857 to inform him of the step that she and Lewes had taken almost three years earlier, the brother's reaction was to end direct communication with his sister, addressing her only through his solicitor. He also forbade his other sisters to have any contact with Eliot. Not until in 1880, when, after Lewes's death, Eliot married John Walter Cross, did Evans write to her again.

He received in return a letter expressing joy at her brother's "kind words of sympathy, for our long silence has never broken the affection for you which began when we were little ones." Tellingly, this conciliatory spirit did not extend to Eliot's feelings toward her half-sister, Fanny; in 1874 the author had rejected a proposal from her oldest brother's son that she and Fanny meet, noting that "some (perhaps eight or ten) years ago, she spoke of me with dislike and unkindness."[20] The difference in Eliot's response to the two overtures would seem to reflect her different perceptions of the two relationships. The hostility of a half-sister fourteen years her senior was ground for continued resentment; that of the brother closest to her in age, who had been the moral arbiter of her childhood, was to be lamented.

Of course, estrangement between brothers and sisters was not invariably traceable to differences in opinion. But even when it did not, male–female inequities might still be discerned as a root cause. Consider a less dramatic rift within the Evans family, that between Isaac and his older full sister, Chrissey. When in 1852 Chrissey's husband, Dr. Edward Clarke, died, leaving his widow £100 a year on which to bring up the six survivors of their original brood of nine children, her brother seems to have resented the convention that made him responsible for supporting his impoverished sister. In sharp contrast to the generosity of the Rev. Irwine in *Adam Bede*, Isaac Evans made minimal provision for Chrissey. He allowed her rent-free housing (in an abode that had once belonged to her before her husband sold it to his father-in-law in an attempt to keep bankruptcy at bay) but otherwise did little to alleviate her anxiety about her family's welfare. Dying at forty-five, Chrissey may be seen as representative of the breakdowns, surely common if unacknowledged, in the system of mutual brother–sister dependence that ostensibly existed at need among the Victorian middle classes. But she might also be considered an illustration of the dangers of being too stereotypically feminine. Orderly and biddable, the young Chrissey had duly acquired a small roster of "accomplishments" and married a man who seemed like a good catch for the daughter of a land agent. As a widow with half a dozen children under the age of fifteen, however, she was not prepared to earn a living, unlike her childless and brilliant younger sister or her upwardly mobile brother, who had always anticipated the need to make his own way in the world.

Same-sex siblings had their own sources of disharmony. The practice of primogeniture among the landed classes, for example, could certainly lead to ill feeling. Victorian inheritance novels such as Yonge's *The Heir of Redclyffe* (1853) and Mary Elizabeth Braddon's *John Marchmont's Legacy* (1863) hinge upon the resentment that one family member might feel for another who, by an accident of birth, is placed above him in status and wealth. Significantly, both these novels locate this resentment not in brothers but in cousins, a literary device likely to be less disturbing to the sensibilities of readers conditioned to revere the sibling tie—yet in reality, such jealousy seems at least as likely to involve members of one's immediate family. Similarly, sisters might find themselves in competition for recognition as "most beautiful" or "most accomplished." And in an era of large families, rivalry for a parent's attention might be intense, each child vying with the next for marks of esteem.

In the Victorian era as today, then, sibling tensions might be manifested in a variety of arenas. Economics, personality, perceptions of inequitable treatment by parents and/or society, and personal preferences for one sibling above another are only a few entries on a list that may become longer with each family that one examines. To consider even a single well-documented family in detail is to uncover a host of cross-currents and complexities, as may be illustrated by the experience of Virginia Woolf, born Virginia Stephen in 1882. Her parents had produced eight children between them; as the marriage of Leslie Stephen and Julia Jackson Duckworth was the second for both, the family was intricate with half- and full-sibling relationships. Feelings ran high in the Duckworth-Stephen ménage. The young Virginia was a staunch ally of her immediate seniors in the family, her sister Vanessa (born 1879) and her brother Thoby (born 1880), and on more neutral terms with her youngest brother, Adrian (born 1883). Her father considered his daughter Laura (born 1870), by his first wife, Minny Thackeray, "mentally deficient," "backward," "perverse," a factor that strongly affected the emotional undercurrents in a family that placed a premium upon intellectual achievement.[21] Julia's oldest daughter, Stella, became her younger siblings' substitute mother (in the familiar Victorian pattern) upon Julia's death in 1895 but married within two years of that event and promptly died of appendicitis. And Woolf's feelings toward her older half-brothers, Gerald and George Duckworth, were complicated by episodes in which each of the young men sexually abused her—Gerald when she was a young child, George for at least the years between their mother's death and the death of Virginia's father.

In an essay written about 1921 but detailing events of 1897 and earlier, Woolf speaks caustically of George's paradoxical blending of "God, faun and pig," his oscillation between the kind of brotherly devotion that moved him to spend hours coaching his four youngest siblings at cricket and the kind that moved him, a few years later, to try to force Vanessa and Virginia into a social round entirely uncongenial to these aspiring artists. Woolf dryly notes George's invoking of the Victorian sibling ideal as a justification of his efforts to dominate his sisters, not only socially but, ultimately, sexually as well.

George's behavior brings us full circle. Within middle-class Victorian orthodoxy, the sibling tie was supposed to be a shield against illicit sexuality. Indeed, in Woolf's rendition of his viewpoint (quoted below), he sees his sisters' role in this light. But it was precisely the function of the idealized Victorian sister as an appropriate object for the homage of her adult brother that enabled George to give rein to his incestuous urges. His obsession, unlike Lord Byron's, seems to have been fueled not by a wish to be as badly behaved as possible, but by a perversion of Victorian recommendations about how to remain virtuous.

His two sisters were the most precious things that remained to him. His home had always meant more to him—more than he could say, and here he became agitated, struggled for composure, and then burst into a statement which was at once dark and extremely lurid. We were driving Gerald from the house, he cried—when a young man was not happy at home—he himself had always been content—but if his sisters—if Vanessa refused to go out with him—if he could not bring his friends to the house—in short, it was clear that the chaste, the immaculate George Duckworth would be forced into the arms of whores. Needless to say he did not put it like that; and I could only conjure up in my virgin consciousness, dimly irradiated by having read the "Symposium" with Miss Case, horrible visions of the vices to which young men were driven whose sisters did not make them happy at home. . . .

Yes, the old ladies of Kensington and Belgravia never knew that George Duckworth was not only father and mother, brother and sister to those poor Stephen girls; he was their lover also.

　　　　　　　—Virginia Woolf, "22 Hyde Park Gate" (composed c. 1920)

THE DECEASED WIFE'S SISTER

Between the mid-seventeenth and the early twentieth centuries, England had no law against incest, and when the Punishment of Incest Act was finally passed in 1908, the twenty-five-year legislative campaign that brought it about had focused primarily on father–daughter incest. Sex between brother and sister (or mother and son or grandfather and granddaughter) was criminalized as well, but pre-1908 efforts to prosecute incest under laws against rape or laws prohibiting sex with girls under a certain age typically put fathers rather than brothers in the dock. Sibling incest, like homosexual incest, was evidently not a matter that even purity reformers felt comfortable contemplating. One way to measure this discomfort is to contemplate the opposition—which spanned the entire period of Victoria's reign—to a bill that sought to permit a man whose wife had died to marry her sister.

Entering English law only in 1907, the Deceased Wife's Sister's Marriage Act provided that such unions were not to be annulled solely on the basis of the kinship tie already existing between the participants; it also provided that if such a union had already been annulled, the annulment would stand. These stipulations were necessary because until the passage of the Marriage Act 1835 (also known as Lord Lyndhurst's Act, after the Lord Chancellor who introduced it into Parliament), canon law had held that a widower could marry his sister-in-law but that the marriage might be voided at any point during the couple's lifetime. The Marriage Act had addressed this ambiguity by permitting all such marriages contracted before August 31, 1835, and forbidding all contracted after that date. But this type of union was not the primary focus of the law, which embraced not merely marriages between a man and his deceased wife's sister but *all* unions violating a set of parameters laid down by Henry VIII, who had lived to regret his own marriage to his deceased brother's wife; these parameters specified permissible degrees of consanguinity (relationship by blood) and affinity (relationship by marriage). And at the time that the Marriage Act 1835 was being debated, a number of Members of Parliament who eventually voted for the new law expressed their hope that another law would follow to allow marriage to a deceased wife's sister. After all, supporters observed, this was a style of union that seemed eminently practical in cases where there were young children, as an aunt would make a better stepmother than any stranger could.

But while a deceased wife's sister bill was introduced as early in the Victorian period as 1842, and replaced as often as it was defeated, and while the Marriage Act was frequently violated,[22] the feeling against it was too potent to permit its enactment. An 1849 novel by Felicia Skene, polemically entitled *The Inheritance of Evil, Or, the Consequences of Marrying a Deceased Wife's Sister*, illustrates the extent of the distaste that some Victorians felt for such marriages. The novel represents the guilty couple at its center as being cast off by right-thinking family members, shunned by the local peasantry, and subject to unremitting retribution from Providence. The results of the husband's rash act in marrying his sister-in-law (for which his ostensible motivation is the seemingly innocuous desire to preserve the health of his frail younger child by enabling his wife's sister to remain in their home as caregiver) are legion. By the end of the novel, the first wife's younger child is no more and the older one has been reduced to idiocy; the second wife's son has been brought to the grave by a lifetime of uninhibited selfishness and excess; the remarriage has been voided, to the second wife's great shame, by an aspirant to the hand of the older daughter who wants her to inherit money that would otherwise go to her half-brother;

Elizabeth had . . . the instinctive delicacy of feeling with which a pure mind must revolt from a transaction so opposed to all that is just and holy. What a horrible shade was now cast over the past intercourse of her husband and sister, and the happy familiarity she had herself loved to promote between them! It maddened her even to think of the result which would probably follow on her own death. Instead of living to watch over her children and remember her with unchanged affection, they would remain together in a union condemned of God, and reprobated even by the world itself. . . . A new horror rose out of the idea of this unhallowed marriage. Was Agnes, the gentle Agnes, so fair and joyous, thereby to become a being unworthy of the favour of heaven, and an outcast even from society? Was the sister for whom she had indulged in so many a bright ambitious dream, reserved for such a fate as this?—a wife disowned both by the laws of God and man!
—Felicia Skene, *The Inheritance of Evil* (1849), Chapter 3

and the husband has dropped dead, unable to withstand any further shocks. Only the second wife is left functioning, to expiate her crime by nursing the stepdaughter whom she has so grievously wronged.

Skene's novel will seem wildly overblown to most readers today, the heaping up of catastrophe so exaggerated as to be comic. And it has its counterparts on the other side of the question, such as Dinah Mulock Craik's almost equally polemical *Hannah* (1871), in which the admirable heroine moves in with her widowed brother-in-law to be a mother to his newborn child, learns to love him, and finally, after waiting in vain for the Deceased Wife's Sister Bill to pass Parliament, renounces England for France, whose more enlightened marriage laws permit her to marry the man she loves. But clearly, Skene's novel dramatizes a point of view widely held at the time that it was written. Although the royal commission formed in 1847–1848 to investigate the question generally supported legalization of such marriages, public distaste for them was sufficiently great as to represent a significant bar to reforming the national policy. The law's proponents spoke of the deep revulsion that right-thinking people should feel for unions so clearly unnatural and inappropriate. The list of those supporting the prohibition included Roundell Palmer, first Earl of Selborne and Lord Chancellor under Gladstone; Gladstone himself; Victorian sage Matthew Arnold; William Hale, the Archdeacon of London; purity advocate Theodora Chapman; and the Bishop of Oxford. Toward the end of the period, they also included George Duckworth, who forbade Vanessa Stephen to marry her half-sister Stella's widower, on the ground that it would cause too much talk.

Conversely, advocates of legitimating marriages to deceased wives' sisters tended to fall on the more Bohemian side of the Victorian moral spectrum. Poet and parliamentarian Richard Monckton Milnes, an aficionado of the works of the Marquis de Sade and a close associate of A. C. Swinburne (viewed by many mid-Victorians as the most scandalous poet of the day), was an outspoken supporter of the bill, as was the unconventional journalist Eliza Lynn Linton. Painters William Holman Hunt, who subsequently headed up the Marriage Law Reform Association formed in 1851 to advance the bill, and John Collier went abroad so that they could marry their sisters-in-law. Hunt's sister-in-law and future wife, Edith Waugh, took Craik along to Switzerland as her chaperone before the wedding, which took place four years after the publication of *Hannah*; as Sally Mitchell notes, Craik's novel reaches "an essentially radical conclusion" in that it rewards its heroine's willingness to question "patriarchal authority" by granting her lasting happiness.[23] In short, both in intensity and in rhetoric, the Victorian debate over legitimating marriage to one's deceased wife's sister is analogous to the discussion of gay marriage in contemporary American society.

Historian Nancy Fix Anderson, whose 1982 article on the deceased wife's sister controversy remains one of the best sources on this subject, argues persuasively that the anxiety and taboos surrounding this topic were as strong as they were because "the Wife's Sister Bill forced Victorians to confront the difficult matter of incest." As she notes, the passionate attachments that Victorian society promoted among siblings had their erotic dimension, inevitable in a culture that discouraged intimacy between young men and women who did not belong to the same family. Typically, of course, this erotic dimension was rigorously repressed. It is precisely this repression that interests Anderson, who suggests that the agitation against the bill "can be seen as evidence of Victorian society's need for more safeguards against repressed but intensified incestuous feelings."[24] In repudiating the concept of marriage with a deceased wife's sister, a concept that had not aroused anything like this level of anxiety in earlier centuries when family was differently conceived, the Victorians who took this stance saw themselves as safeguarding the purity of the family overall, and the brother–sister tie in particular.

The deep feeling stirred up by discussion of the bill helps to illuminate the extent to which the perceived innocence and self-sacrifice of sibling relationships were crucial to the dominant Victorian culture's image of itself. If siblings— even siblings by affinity rather than consanguinity—could marry, and indeed wanted to marry, then, to borrow Woolf's phrase, "the old ladies of Kensington and Belgravia," and perhaps even George Duckworth himself, would be forced to acknowledge that the middle-class Victorian home was not what society demanded that it be. Similarly, the tensions and resentments memorialized in many volumes of Victorian memoirs and letters, as siblings record feelings of anger, jealousy, and resentment aimed at a brother or sister, appear comparatively seldom in Victorian fiction, which frequently sought to illustrate for the reading public the qualities associated with virtue. Identified as distinct from both the marital bond and the parent–child bond, but as sharing the better traits of both, the sibling bond was in some ways the foundation stone of the vision of the ideal Victorian family.

5

THE EXTENDED FAMILY

In American society today, middle-class households typically consist of a married couple and any minor children belonging to one or both of the partners. We often assume that children being raised by grandparents or an aunt and uncle, say, signal some family problem, perhaps a broken home, a teenage mother, or a drug-addicted parent. The rising number of adult children who continue to reside with their parents after completing their education is attracting the bemused and mostly disapproving attention of the media, and we do not expect to see the pattern continue after marriage. If an elderly person shares a home with his or her married son or daughter, we usually perceive the arrangement as temporary, a brief stop on the road between widowhood and the nursing home. The dominant mode in our contemporary society, in other words, is to equate the household with a nuclear family of a fairly narrowly defined sort. But in Victorian England, the nuclear family was rarely the end of the matter—a fact that often worked well in practice but that nonetheless gave rise to cultural anxiety on a variety of fronts. Many Victorians existed in a complicated web of extended family and, potentially, surrogate family, a system of practical and emotional ties that could and did shift back and forth between blessing and burden.

"JUST LIKE ONE OF THE FAMILY": SERVANTS AND THEIR EMPLOYERS

For one thing, households in the middle classes and above, and some working-class households as well, contained live-in servants. At least in the establishments of the landed gentry, since there were fewer employers to choose from in rural regions, a maid or manservant might pass the years from adolescence

The lady of the house with one of her servants. The paraphernalia on the table is for flower arranging, a domestic activity that was viewed as the mistress's purview. [Wood engraving from the 1890 edition of *Mrs. Beeton's Cookery Book and Household Guide* (London: Ward Lock & Bowden, 1890); collection of the author.]

to old age working in the same home. (This, at least, was the pattern often desired by employers, who placed a premium upon faithfulness; employees reserved the right to "better themselves" by migrating to greener pastures if such could be found.) The proportion of the population engaged in domestic service rose during Victoria's reign, cresting at around 1.4 million in the final decade of the nineteenth century, and was heavily female. Focusing on Birmingham, Essex, and Suffolk, historians Leonore Davidoff and Catherine Hall find that in the mid-nineteenth century, women made up 82 percent of the servant force working for middle-class families.[1]

Among the lower reaches of families employing domestic workers, Di Cooper and Moira Donald report, it was not unheard of for mistress and maid to be related by blood or marriage—for instance, they might be aunt and niece.[2] And even when a clear status difference existed, servants often functioned as surrogate family members for the children of their employers, in some cases because of a similarity in age (about one-third of all female servants were in their teens), in others because child care was among the household duties most likely to be relegated to an employee. Hence many memoirs recounting Victorian childhoods speak of comradeship between the affluent young and their social inferiors. Because male domestics typically worked outside the house in the gardens or stables, servant boys often received less supervision than did indoor servants and so could find time to socialize. The children of employees such as gatekeepers or housekeepers also made readily available playmates and, for young children, occasional surrogate siblings. While such bonds often did not survive the departure of a higher-status child for boarding school, say, or the requirement that a lower-status child enter the working world in a serious way, they could be of real emotional importance while they lasted.

The intimacy of the master–servant relationship worried many Victorian commentators, particularly since servants were so disproportionately young, female, and unmarried. Fiction frequently explored this question. Anne Brontë's *The Tenant of Wildfell Hall* (1848) shows the heroine's dissolute husband bringing one of his mistresses into the home, ostensibly to serve as his small son's teacher. Becky Sharp, the ambitious governess in W. M. Thackeray's *Vanity Fair* (1847–1848), has to refuse her titled employer's proposal of marriage because she has already clandestinely married his son. Jane Eyre, both better born and more virtuous than either Thackeray's or Anne Brontë's creation, not only marries but also reforms her employer. And if governesses were a special case because of their equivocal status—they were often gentlewomen by birth, though not by fortune, and thus occupied an uneasy middle ground between their employers' social class and that of the lower servants—Victorian fiction concerned itself with other sorts of liaisons as well. Marriage between a clergyman's son and his parents' erstwhile housemaid figures in Samuel Butler's *The Way of All Flesh* (written 1885, published 1903), and sensation novels such as those of Wilkie Collins, whose two primary sexual relationships were with working-class women, not infrequently feature romantic interest across class lines. Housemaid Rosanna Spearman's love for the wealthy and dashing Franklin Blake in *The Moonstone* (1868), former maid Lydia Gwilt's vamping of the two Allan Armadales in *Armadale* (1866), are only two examples of Collins's preoccupation with this theme, which he shared with other writers in this genre.

Such literary visions hit home because these relationships were not simply the stuff of fiction. For one thing, the middle classes tended to view servants' sexual morality as somewhat suspect in any case. In London, reports historian Michael Mason, servants were considered particularly likely to bear children out of wedlock and/or to moonlight as prostitutes. Around two out of three women who sought assistance from the London Foundling Hospital were servants; conversely, shelters for unmarried mothers attempted to find their clients positions as servants after the birth, heightening the association between service and being a "fallen woman."[3] While many of the liaisons that produced illegitimate children involved partners on the same socioeconomic level, some entailed the crossing of class lines.

Similarly, it was not unheard of for widowed or single employers to marry their housekeepers, motivated partly by a desire to maintain the stability of a domestic environment that the men felt incapable of supervising themselves; Augustus Meredith, father of future novelist George Meredith, took this step shortly after going bankrupt in 1838. Alternatively, the title of housekeeper might be used to justify an irregular union, as in the case of playwright and novelist Charles Reade, who lived with actress Laura Seymour for the quarter-century before her death in 1879, officially designating her his housekeeper so that the liaison would not be too obvious. Radclyffe Radclyffe-Hall, father of another future novelist, settled £200 on his legitimate daughter and the same sum on the child of his housemaid when he separated from his wife in 1882, a gesture that implies that the two youngsters may have been half-siblings.

Geoffrey Robinson's gossipy account of the lives of his grandparents and their associates in rural Lincolnshire in the nineteenth century is punctuated by anecdotes about the sexual arrangements that existed between members of the middle class and their employees. In short, sexual connections between female domestics and male householders were as much a feature of life in Victorian England as they were of the antebellum American South.

Certainly some of the dismay that master–servant sexual contact engendered had to do with the crossing of class boundaries, in an era in which many people still deemed it only seemly to remain in the sphere in which it had pleased God to call one. But the issue was more complex than mere class transgression. The purity of the middle-class home was of enormous importance to dominant Victorian culture. If the innocence demanded of wives and children was sullied by the knowledge that husband and father, or perhaps son and brother, was defiling that purity, not safely outside the bounds of the domestic space but within the very confines of the home, surely the family itself was under threat. And when servants were not directly implicated in the master's sexual wrongdoing, they might pose another sort of problem to family stability, as they could be, and were, called as witnesses in divorce, separation, and child-custody cases. The suspicion with which young female servants, or their male employers, are often regarded within Victorian fiction thus illustrates a number of points: the extent to which such anxiety might prove well founded in reality; the extent to which the middle- or upper-class household depended upon a blending of the nuclear family with ostensible outsiders who were nonetheless intimately bound up with the family's personal lives; and the extent to which family, supposed to be the bedrock upon which Victorian society was built, nonetheless appeared vulnerable.

A key area in which servants were often presumed to threaten the innocence of the Victorian family was that of child rearing. Although sexual contact between servants and masters is likely to have been considerably more common than the sexual debauching of young children by nursery maids, again and again nineteenth-century child-rearing manuals warn the Victorian mother about the latter possibility, while remaining tactfully silent about the former. The fear that a servant might provide her small charges with sexual information or even sexual experience reflects middle-class stereotypes of the poor as profligate. The working classes were presumed to be morally inferior, a trait furthered by the overcrowded conditions in which they lived, since a large family would probably have to share not only one or two small rooms but also one or two beds. But the warnings reiterated by the experts also reflect awareness of the degree to which the day-to-day tasks associated with raising children were undertaken not by the mother but by hired surrogates—the nursery maid, the nanny, the governess. The concern that our culture today now directs toward day-care providers (what are they doing when a parent isn't around to supervise?) has its antecedent in the cautions that nineteenth-century commentators directed toward households containing both servants and young children. Servants, that is, had taken over many of the responsibilities of the middle-class mother without necessarily sharing her commitment to her children's well-being.

> To think that whatever the man may become, learned or great, worldly or wicked, he is at present only the child, courting [the nurse's] smile and coming to her for kisses, or hiding from her frown and sobbing on her neck, "I will be good, I will be good!" That, be she old or young, clever or ignorant, ugly or pretty, she has, next to the mother—sometimes before the mother, though that is a sad thing to see—this all-powerful influence over him, stronger than any he will afterwards allow or own.... And what a reward there is in this, beyond any form of service—to a woman! Respect and gratitude of parents; consideration from all in the house; affection, fresh, full, and free, and sweet as only a child's love can be. Trying as the nurse-maid's life is, countless as are her vexations and pains, how many a childless wife or solitary old maid has envied her, playing at romps for kisses, deafened with ever-sounding rills of delicious laughter all day, and lying down at night with a soft sleepy thing breathing at her side, or wakened of a morning with two little arms tight round her neck, smotheringly expressing a wealth of love that kingdoms could not buy.
>
> —Dinah Maria Mulock, *A Woman's Thoughts about Women* (1858)

In other words, surely some of the fear surrounding servants' influence over the younger members of the household arose from the recognition of the depth of the emotional bond that might exist between the two groups. In the upper reaches of society, servants bathed, dressed, and fed children; they got them up in the morning and put them to bed at night; they took them for walks and provided entertainment and discipline back at home. In short, they frequently spent considerably more time with their employers' progeny than the employers themselves did, and this intimacy offered servants substantial influence. As Dinah Mulock (later Craik) notes, a servant might wield her power over a child "wisely and tenderly, for the guidance and softening of his nature, or harshly and capriciously, after a fashion which may harden and brutalise him, and make him virtually disbelieve in love and goodness for the remainder of his existence."[4] A mother inclined to be jealous of her prerogatives might feel little happier about the former alternative than about the latter.

Mulock identifies here a very real phenomenon. Many writers of memoirs speak lyrically of the love that they felt in their youth for a nanny or cook. Robert Louis Stevenson's childhood nurse, Alison Cunningham, was a major influence upon his later writings, in that the stories that she told or read to him profoundly shaped his imagination. His collection *A Child's Garden of Verses* (1885) is dedicated to her. The nanny of future bishop William Streatfeild remained in her employers' home long after her youngest charge (born in 1868) and his nine siblings had grown up; she became "Gran-Nannie" to the next generation of children, dispensing comfort, recounting family stories, and eventually being carried to her grave on the shoulders of the family's sons.[5] Agatha Christie, born in 1891, recalled of her early years that "Our various servants are far more real to me than my mother's friends and my distant relations." She writes with particular affection of her parents' cook, Jane Rowe, who stayed with the family for forty years and left, weeping, only because her brother needed her.[6] The women who occupied positions as nannies and cooks would in many cases have been the primary sources of nurturing in the lives of middle- and upper-class children, sometimes—as Mulock notes— generating warmer feelings than the biological parent. The very success of such relationships could also have signaled to sensitive observers the imperfections of parent–child ties. Above all, they remind us of the need to see the Victorian family as potentially stretching beyond ties of blood or class affinities.

BEYOND THE FAMILY? THE ELDERLY

Although servants' lives were often unenviable, they at least had an income and a roof over their heads; moreover, it was considered appropriate for the wealthy to provide pensions and sometimes housing for long-time employees who had become too old to work, although servants in middle-class establishments were by no means guaranteed financial support in their declining years. Again depending on the family's economic and social standing, other individuals connected to it might be less fortunate. Victorian England afforded little in the way of a safety net for the elderly members of poor families, and the questions of how best to provide for this segment of society, and who might properly be responsible for making such provision, were vigorously debated over the course of Victoria's reign. That this debate took place at all illustrates the tension between two schools of thought, one holding that blood ties entailed a sacred responsibility, the other that when money was short, the well-being of the younger generation trumped the needs of older people, especially when the latter were aunts or uncles rather than parents.

Memoirist Siân Busby's account of two aging women in her family allows us to examine one common scenario illuminating the "blood tie" position on this question. Busby's great-great-grandmother Lou Warner Smith was born in 1842, the daughter of a farm laborer. When he died in 1891, Lou offered a home to her elderly mother, Martha Warner. Lou's four younger children, ranging in age from six to sixteen, made space for their grandmother in the room that they shared in the family cottage, and the family retrenched to accommodate the financial setback represented by the extra mouth. Warner's sixteen-year-old granddaughter and namesake relinquished her teacher training, which required the payment of fees and reduced one's earning capacity for the three years spent as a pupil-teacher, and found work in the post office, a career considered appropriate for women with yearnings toward respectability but without much hope of upward mobility. Twelve-year-old Beth left school and found work, first as a "daily" (nonresident) servant in a modest home in the neighborhood and soon thereafter as live-in help with a somewhat wealthier family. The arrival of a penniless and needy elderly relative—Busby reports that Warner was rapidly losing her eyesight and succumbing to dementia—affected not only the family's comfort but also its aspirations.[7]

Warner died in 1894, but the drama was shortly to recur in the next generation. In 1895 or 1896, Lou's husband, Joe, was incapacitated by a stroke and could no longer ply his trade of shoemaker. By this time all but the youngest child had left home, but over the years of invalidism that preceded his death in 1899, which also witnessed Lou's increasing fragility, the couple was dependent upon the largesse of their offspring. Lou died in 1902, aged sixty, in a five-room home that also housed two of her daughters, a son-in-law, her sixteen-year-old youngest son, and a female tenant, taken in to help ends meet. (Renting out rooms, and often providing occupants with meals, housekeeping services, and clean laundry as well, was a common method of generating income among widows at this time.) With the possible exception of the tenant and the sixteen-year-old, these individuals were probably present in this domicile not so much because they needed a home as because they recognized Lou's need. No longer able to generate an income herself, Lou would have been wholly reliant upon the younger generation's contributions to the housekeeping money.[8]

At that, Lou Smith and her mother were fortunate: they continued to receive support from younger members of their family, and neither had to enter the workhouse, a form of welfare that carried a considerable social stigma and that was consciously designed to be both penitential and humiliating so as to foster self-sufficiency on the part of the poor. Under the English Poor Law Reform Act of 1834, also known as the Poor Law Amendment Act and the New Poor Law, England was divided into 643 districts called "unions." Each union was responsible for maintaining a public institution to house dependent members of society—defined as those for whom the workhouse seemed the only alternative to starvation. Such individuals might include young orphans (Charles Dickens's Oliver Twist spends his early years in a workhouse before being apprenticed to an undertaker), the mentally and/or physically disabled, and the able-bodied unemployed. These inmates were segregated by sex and age, with husbands being separated from wives and parents from children, and set to complete tasks that might be as meaningless as they were laborious.

But by the 1890s about a third of the population of workhouses consisted of elderly men and women, with this figure substantially higher in London and other cities; workhouse infirmaries, which housed the incapacitated poor, were the public nursing homes of the era and thus held a substantial proportion of senior citizens. The elderly were exempt from some of the punitive rules that governed their younger fellows (after 1847 married couples over sixty could stay together, for example), while old or disabled people who could count upon some support from their families were the only groups eligible under the New Poor Law to receive "outdoor relief." This form of assistance consisted of meals and a small allowance from the union and was designed to permit people classified as "deserving poor" to remain in their own homes when family circumstances made it feasible for them to do so. The comparatively privileged treatment given to the elderly poor under the workhouse system suggests an official recognition that family support might be expected to wear thin in one's old age. Charles Booth, for one, began in the late 1880s to urge the establishment of state-funded pensions for the elderly; as he put it in the third edition (1903) of the final volume of his magnum opus, quoting an unidentified source, "'The great loss of the last twenty years' is asserted to be 'the weakening of the family ties between parents and children. Children don't look after their old people according to their means. The fault lies in the fact that the tie is broken so early,'" as many working-class boys left home as soon as they became self-supporting in their teens.[9] To be sure, blood ties saved countless individuals from entering the workhouse, as for many members of the working classes, family pride militated against anything smacking of charity.

Yet charity was often, in the end, the only option, whether the donor was the taxpayer or a private individual. Speeches such as that of Anthony Trollope's fictional archdeacon Dr. Grantly, quoted below, suggest why charity would have been unpalatable to those who could avoid it, since it was often administered with an admixture of contempt for its objects, who were considered to have failed in their responsibility to provide and preserve a home. Nevertheless, avoidance was often not possible. Although a few trades provided their members with retirement plans in connection with trade unions or Friendly Societies, it was otherwise rare for members of the working classes to save enough disposable income to account for their old age. The respectable poor generally considered that they owed it to their honor to "put something by" toward their funerals so as to avoid the ignominy of a pauper's burial, but seeing oneself— or depending on support from relatives—through any extended retirement was more difficult. Many members of this class thus hoped instead to drop in harness. To be sure, it was recognized that staying employed until one's death was not always possible, particularly for those whose family duties might have precluded the acquisition of marketable skills. Before the 1870s, elderly women, at least, were often eligible for forms of government assistance that did not carry with them the shame associated with the workhouse. But in that decade new laws dramatically reduced the number of pensions available, transferring to working-class families the responsibility for the well-being of members too old or infirm to support themselves.

The families, however, did not inevitably accept this duty, and the numbers of the aged as a proportion of workhouse inmates climbed. By the 1890s, public anxiety about the proliferation of the destitute elderly resulted in a variety of official actions. For instance, the government convened in 1893 a Royal Commission for the Aged Poor, whose members included Victorian sociological luminaries such as Charles Booth, and formed in 1898 an Old Age Pensions Committee, whose efforts culminated a decade later in the Old Age Pensions

Act of 1908. Like the special treatment afforded to elderly people resident in workhouses, the existence of these bodies signals an underlying anxiety that working-class families were not providing adequate help for their senior members. The need for help from the government or the church or the trade union or some benevolent individual often appeared to reveal the absence of similar help forthcoming from sons or daughters.

"When John Hiram built a hospital for worn-out old men, worn-out old labouring men, infirm old men past their work, cripples, blind, bed-ridden, and such like, do you think he meant to make gentlemen of them? Do you think John Hiram intended to give a hundred a year to old single men, who earned perhaps two shillings or half-a-crown a day for themselves and families in the best of their time? No, my men, I'll tell you what John Hiram meant: he meant that twelve poor old worn-out labourers, men who could no longer support themselves, who had no friends to support them, who must starve and perish miserably if not protected by the hand of charity; he meant that twelve such men as these should come in here in their poverty and wretchedness, and find within these walls shelter and food before their death, and a little leisure to make their peace with God." [. . .]

Not a sound came from the eleven bedesmen, as they sat listening to what, according to the archdeacon, was their intended estate. They grimly stared upon his burly figure, but did not then express, by word or sign, the anger and disgust to which such language was sure to give rise.

—Anthony Trollope, *The Warden* (1855), Chapter 5

The situation of the elderly was somewhat less desperate among the middle and upper classes. Here both houses and financial assets were larger, so that if a householder found himself accommodating his parent or a superannuated aunt or uncle, the new arrival generally would not strain the house to bursting point or, as with Martha Warner, require the rising generation to make less ambitious career decisions. Mary Hodgson, born in 1782, moved in with her son's growing family in the 1850s. There were to be five children in all—including the future novelist Frances Hodgson Burnett, who would famously chronicle love between grandfather and grandson in her 1886 best-seller *Little Lord Fauntleroy*—but although this middle-class household was modestly circumstanced after the son's death in 1853, the presence of an extra person does not seem to have added materially to the Hodgsons' difficulties. Among families a financial step up from the Hodgsons, it was comparatively likely that old people could remain in their homes, looked after by servants and funded not by their children's sacrifices but by their own bank accounts, marriage settlements, insurance policies, and/or pensions or investment income derived from the business with which a man had been occupied during his working life. Households that mingled the old and the young at this socioeconomic level were thus more likely to be responding to a need for companionship or tender nursing than to a need for food and shelter.

But if the financial circumstances of the elderly were comparatively secure among the middle and upper classes, the anxiety surrounding them could be as great as in the case of the poor. Aging spinsters were a particular source of concern. Not only did the 1851 census reveal that England and Wales contained 355,159 more females than males, it was also the first census to inquire into marital status, an investigation that revealed the presence of 204,650 women aged forty-five and up who had never been married. The gender gap, and consequently the number of single women, expanded disproportionately over time. In 1901, when the combined English and Welsh population, at just over 32.5 million people, was not quite double the almost 18 million that it had been fifty years earlier, women outnumbered men not by the 700,000 that might have been projected from the 1851 figures, but by more than a million, and there were 421,549 spinsters over forty-five years of age. They were considered problematic or pitiable not only because most were not obeying the promptings of what Victorians deemed the strongest drive in a woman's nature, the instinct to bear children, but also because they might face a lonely and impoverished old age. Historian and critic Martha Vicinus notes that when the Governesses' Benevolent Institution made available an annuity of £20 (a tiny sum when viewed as a year's income), it "drew 150 applicants over fifty years old, of whom 83 had not one penny in the world."[10] When needy elderly women belonged to the genteel classes, the slip in status occasioned by the lack of a marriage portion or other provision made by a husband was particularly alarming to middle-class commentators, who found that the situation of such women hit close to home: with bad luck, "decayed gentlewomen" might be their sisters, or even themselves.

Accordingly, middle-aged and elderly spinsters of the affluent strata of society are frequently represented in Victorian writings as unnatural and alien. Partly this convention existed because such difference from the feminine norm was often considered to be the inevitable result of failing to fulfill woman's maternal function, but we may also see it as a technique that writers used to distance such figures from themselves and their families. The eccentric spinster, desiccated, domineering, and laughable, signified both the perils of not being incorporated into a family and the embodiment of qualities that women, at least, *should* not bring into the family. To quote Eliza Lynn Linton, a writer who built her pioneering career as a journalist on savaging women who (like Linton herself) strayed from traditional ideals of femininity, "Painted and wrinkled, padded and bedizened, with her coarse thoughts, bold words, and leering eyes, [the wrong kind of spinster] has in herself all the disgust which lies around a Bacchante and a Hecate in one. . . . Such an old maid as this stands as a warning to men and women alike of what and whom to avoid."[11]

Rhetoric aside, of course, elderly spinsters—and other aging relatives—were often valued members of the extended Victorian family. Schoolmaster Cecil

Botting, father of novelist Antonia White, was devoted to his two maiden aunts, memorialized in White's fiction as charming late-Victorian countrywomen who turned their poverty into a game and who, far from being repellent, seem to have afforded the most positive examples of womanhood to be found in the clan. The many Victorian children who, after being orphaned, found substitute parents in husbandless aunts could hardly have done without this care; households such as that headed by the three unmarried Hudleston sisters, who in the 1890s were bringing up their deceased brother and sister-in-law's three younger children, were both common and necessary. Grandparents, too, formed a significant part of the Victorian family landscape, whether or not they shared a home with a grown child. Many are the accounts of coming of age in Victorian England that identify a grandparent as a major source of stability and warmth for a youngster whose relations with his or her parent might be flawed.

Yet for every portrait of a beloved and respected elder, comfortably established in the world and an integral part of a multigenerational family, there exists in counterbalance a portrait of an aging solitary, alienated from kin or lacking them altogether. The elderly eccentrics who populate the works of authors such as Wilkie Collins and Charles Dickens are horrifying at least as often as they are endearing, and a substantial bank account could not guarantee that one's relations would consider one's presence desirable. As Teresa Mangum observes from the vantage point of a literary scholar who has published extensively on old age in the nineteenth century, Victorian responses to aging varied considerably, running the gamut from fear to contempt to admiration to love.[12] The diversity of attitudes toward the old, and the corresponding diversity of the roles that such people might occupy within the Victorian family, reminds us that the strength of kinship ties was by no means constant from household to household.

THE WEB OF COUSINHOOD: MARRIAGE AND MORE

In some clans, of course, kinship ties that stretched beyond the immediate family were both powerful and extensive. Particularly before the coming of the railroads and other changes associated with the Industrial Revolution, the denizens of the English countryside often remained in hamlets that their ancestors had inhabited for centuries. According to sociologist Robin Fox, for much of the Victorian period "the radius of the average isolate, or pool of potential spouses, was about five miles, which was the distance a man could comfortably walk twice on his day off, when he went courting."[13] Consequently, England was full of villages in which generations of intermarriage had resulted in a community tied together by a complex network of blood relationships. Robinson reports that in his ancestral home of Hedingham, Lincolnshire, "practically all the farmers and master-craftsmen . . . were closely enough related to my grandfather to be regarded as his cousins," resulting in a social system that had "no place . . . for a labourer, nor for a journeyman who worked for a master other than his father."[14] Such communities might be insular, resistant to change, and suspicious of strangers, but they also had built-in emergency backup systems. In times of crisis, the inhabitants of villages in which one's neighbors were also one's cousins knew that they could find help.

English people became more likely to leave their home counties as a result of forces such as the economic downturn of the early nineteenth century, the decline of certain local industries, and the shift toward an urban rather than an agrarian economy. Increasingly, cities became population magnets. Among the working classes, the extended kinship networks that continued to flourish in many rural areas might be considerably less significant in urban centers, since those who migrated to London or Birmingham often did so as individuals rather than as part of a large family move. While a family might continue to correspond across the miles if its members were literate, distance and the vastly increased pool of eligible mates made repeated intermarriage, with its concomitant strengthening of family ties, less common.

The attenuation of the sense of kinship associated with urban life was a source of regret for Victorian commentators such as Thomas Carlyle and William Pulteney Alison, who saw sympathy as painfully absent from a changing Britain. Citing Alison, Carlyle famously wrote in *Past and Present* (1843) of a destitute widow who, turned away from the doors of charity after charity, died of typhus in the street, fatally infecting seventeen fellow citizens and in this way "prov[ing] her sisterhood; her typhus-fever kills *them*; they actually were her brothers, though denying it!"[15] The use of the language of blood relationship in this passage is nostalgic; Carlyle's work contrasts what he considers to be the excessively individualistic Britain of his day with his romanticized vision of a more unified past. But it is also as characteristic of the imaginative power of the extended family during this period as it is of the nineteenth-century rhetorical tendency to invoke family as a metaphor for amity among people divided by class, religion, and/or race.

Closely knit extended families were not only a feature of small rural communities in which relatives might occupy adjacent farms or run businesses down the street from one another, however. Among the nobility and gentry, cousin marriage was again quite common; Queen Victoria's ostentatiously blissful marriage to her first cousin was part of a wider pattern within the upper tiers of society. One factor here was that the upper class was a comparatively small segment of the Victorian population. Although some concern about the potential negative effects of inbreeding existed, xenophobia often outweighed it. To a group that considered it important to marry within one's own circle, first and second cousins sometimes seemed more rather than less desirable than nonrelatives as prospective marriage partners. When in 1875 George Darwin conducted a study of cousin marriage that drew upon information provided by *Burke's Peerage*, the wedding news in the popular press, the central marriage registry kept at Somerset House in London, and a survey disseminated among 800 well-to-do Britons, he found that cousin marriage was more frequent the higher one went in the social scale. His data showed that 4.5 percent of aristocratic marriages involved first cousins, followed by 3.5 percent of marriages among the gentry and upper middle classes, 2.25 percent in the countryside, and 1.15 percent for unions contracted across the social spectrum in the capital.[16] A twenty-first-century study conducted by anthropologist Malcolm Smith and dealing with all classes in the 1890s, arrives at a figure comparable to the latter, namely 1.12 percent—declining precipitously to .32 percent by the 1920s.[17] By the standards of their descendants, it would seem that Victorian cousins were unusually affectionate.

George Darwin's interest in cousin marriage was an outgrowth of his membership in the endogamous Darwin–Wedgwood clan. His parents, Charles Darwin and Emma Wedgwood Darwin, were first cousins; moreover, Charles's sister was the wife of Emma's brother (for siblings to marry siblings was also by no means uncommon in Victorian England). Another of Charles's cousins, Francis Galton, was a well-known eugenist who contended that genius tended to run in families and that the talented owed it to posterity to marry other members of talented tribes, an argument that could in some cases turn cousin marriage into a social duty. Historian Adam Kuper notes that upon George Darwin's publication of his findings that cousin marriage was not only widely practiced among the well-to-do but also without significant risk to the offspring of such unions, Galton "wrote enthusiastically to George Darwin that he had 'exploded most effectually a popular scare.'"[18]

There are, say, 200,000 annual marriages in the kingdom, of which 2,000 and more are between first cousins. You have only to print in proportion, and in various appropriate scales of cheapness or luxury:

WORDS of Scientific COMFORT
and ENCOURAGEMENT
To COUSINS who are LOVERS

then each lover and each of the two sets of parents would be sure to buy a copy; i.e. an annual sale of 8,000 copies!! (Cousins who fall in love and don't marry would also buy copies, as well as those who think that they *might* fall in love.)
                    —Francis Galton, letter to George Darwin (1875)

Victorian literature, too, is full of cousin marriages. In Emily Brontë's *Wuthering Heights* (1847), young Cathy Linton marries two of her first cousins in succession. Charles Dickens includes cousin marriage in *Bleak House* (1852–1853) in the union of Richard and Ada, and even (adoptive) aunt–nephew marriage in *Martin Chuzzlewit* (1843–1844) when the title character marries his grandfather's foster daughter. In Elizabeth Gaskell's *Sylvia's Lovers* (1863), Sylvia's devoted cousin, Philip, suppresses a message from her preferred suitor, Charley, so that Sylvia will believe Charley dead and turn to Philip instead.

Wilkie Collins incorporates cousin marriage into *No Name* (1862), *The Moon-stone* (1868), "Miss or Mrs?" (1871), and "A Shocking Story" (1878), in which the well-born heroine crosses class lines to marry a groom employed by the aunt and uncle with whom she lives, and later discovers that her attraction to her husband is partly based on blood: he is her aunt's illegitimate son. Aurora Leigh, the title character of Elizabeth Barrett Browning's 1857 novel in verse, marries her cousin; Clara Amedroz in Anthony Trollope's *The Belton Estate* (1866) becomes engaged to hers; Charlotte Brontë's Jane Eyre rejects a proposal from hers, while the same author's Caroline Helstone nearly dies of love for yet another cousin in *Shirley* (1849) before he finally proposes. Thomas Hardy traces a tragic cousin marriage in *Jude the Obscure* (1896), whereas in Oscar Wilde's play *The Importance of Being Ernest* (1895), the happy ending requires the revelation that Ernest is the long-lost legitimate first cousin of his future wife and thus not a social nobody. Meanwhile, the prolific novelist Margaret Oliphant serves as an example of a Victorian writer whose cousin was also her husband.

The nineteenth-century preoccupation with this trope, whether in fiction or in life, tells us much about the Victorian family. Like marriage to a deceased wife's sister, which as we have seen in Chapter 4 was a tempting if forbidden prospect to many Victorian men, cousin marriage was a way of safeguarding the domestic circle against change. As potential life partners, cousins would in many cases have seemed desirable because of their familiarity. The rules governing propriety were such that young people of the middle and upper classes often had few opportunities to form friendships with members of the opposite sex who were not somehow connected to them by blood; cousins, however, were exempt from the need for chaperonage, so that one could get to know them well outside the context of courtship. In a society that prized companionate marriage and tended to be suspicious of the outsider, keeping matrimony within the family helped to ensure that partners would understand each other and get along with their in-laws. Moreover, as Davidoff and Hall point out, among the well-to-do classes, in which marriage settlements were a fact of life, cousin marriage meant that money would not move into the control of an alien clan.[19] If these motivations sound more practical than romantic, their down-to-earth quality may have been part of their appeal for some. Victorian sensation fiction, to name only one genre, tends to present obsessive love as *excessive*, indeed dangerous; Mary Elizabeth Braddon's *John Marchmont's Legacy* (1862–1863) details a woman's passion for her cousin, which is disastrous not because of the blood tie but because her feeling is so strong that it swamps her better nature. Ordinarily, perhaps, a cousin well known from childhood onward might be considered an unlikely object for this variety of uninhibited passion.

Nor, of course, were cousins only important to one another when marriage was a possibility. Emily Eden's *The Semi-Attached Couple* (1860) follows a family in which the titled and cadet branches remain close; both Lord Beaufort and his cousin Colonel Beaufort stand for Parliament, coming in first and second in their polling district and thus being elected as a team, in an illustration of the ties of loyalty and common interest that often helped to make the aristocracy a coherent unit. And the circumstances of novelist Charlotte Yonge provide an example of the potential emotional significance of cousinhood even when distance was a factor. Yonge was raised in Hampshire as the older of only two children. As her brother was six years her junior and she was educated at home in a village that contained few families on her social level, she was a comparatively solitary child whose chief companions were her dolls and the characters in a family saga of her own imagining, ten boys and eleven girls who supposedly lived in the Yonge garden. Visits to her many cousins in Devonshire, her father's native county, were thus a high point of her childhood, although they occurred no more than once a year. Literary scholar Alethea Hayter identifies these cousins as an important inspiration for the many large families that populate Yonge's published fiction and quotes Yonge as commenting that she regarded her visits to the lively Devonshire cousins as "Elysium."[20]

The point here is that Yonge's situation was by no means unusual in her social circle. When in 1859 Yonge's friend and relation Mary Coleridge suggested that Yonge sponsor for the rising generation of teenage girls a combination of writing group and mutual improvement society that became known as the Goslings, most of the members belonged to what Yonge christened "the cousinhood."[21] If they were not blood kin of Yonge herself, they were her cousins' cousins or friends, a network that spread out from the south and west of England (London, Torquay, Winchester) as far north as Lancashire and Scotland. The Goslings created a magazine, the *Barnacle*, that circulated among them in manuscript and thus both required that the members stay in touch and capitalized upon what was already their inclination to do so. Tied together by a similarity of age and background (Yonge's protégées were bright, upper-middle-class Anglicans, often the daughters of clergymen or educators), "the cousinhood" seems to have found cousinship as important as Yonge had considered it a generation earlier.

One could point to a number of similar constellations elsewhere in Victorian England. As an eight-year-old child in 1866, Edith Nesbit was sent to a boarding school in Stamford, Lincolnshire (a considerable distance from her home in London) because the school already housed her nine-year-old second cousin; later, she made an extended stay with the family of a cousin of her deceased father. Nesbit's uncle Edward had emigrated to Australia but remained in contact with his brother's family, corresponding with his teenaged niece Mary and, fifty-odd years after leaving his native country, paying the fare so that one of his great-nephews could join him in Adelaide. Davidoff and Hall note that male cousins sometimes occupied the same advisory role for an unmarried or widowed woman that was at other times filled by a brother, and add that the ties uniting extended family were not limited to a single generation. They instance the case of Essex farmer John Bunting, whose will, probated in 1858, named as executors two men who were simultaneously Bunting's "daughter's husband's brothers [and] his son's wife's brothers."[22]

The devoted aunt was a staple figure in late-Victorian fiction. This illustration to Rosa Nouchette Carey's *Aunt Diana* is captioned, "She took a great interest in his work." [*The Girl's Own Paper* (September 5, 1885); collection of the author.]

SECOND PARENTS AND EVIL GENIUSES: UNCLES AND AUNTS

The closeness expected to exist among siblings tended also to foster warm ties both among the children of those siblings and between the generations along uncle or aunt lines. If a young woman had made her home before marriage with an older brother or sister and acted as an extra mother to the latter's children, the children would presumably take a more active interest in their aunt, and she in them, than might otherwise have been the case. If a man stationed in India wanted to send his son or daughter to be raised in England, he might well call upon a brother or sister back home for child care during school vacations or even year-round, so that cousins would grow up in the same household as foster siblings and regard their aunt and uncle as foster parents. People who died while their offspring were young were likely to name their own brothers or sisters as guardians, as is reflected (albeit with unfortunate consequences) in Elizabeth Barrett Browning's *Aurora Leigh*. Future novelist Richard Blackmore was raised by a maternal aunt and retired from teaching on the strength of a legacy from an uncle, and George Eliot's *The Mill on the Floss* (1860) contains an uncle who understands himself to be in some measure responsible for his nephew Tom upon the incapacitation of the young man's father.

Indeed, even when parents were still alive and functional, uncles and aunts could be of material help to a young person starting out in life. Among the working classes, many fathers held jobs that required them to be absent from the family for extended periods of time; they might be soldiers or sailors, migrant farm workers, or engaged in one of any number of other occupations that would take them on the road. As Leonore Davidoff and her coauthors note in *The Family Story*, "when 'natural' fathers were not available to provide and protect, father figures often stepped in," commonly uncles or grandfathers (although benevolent clergymen or kindly employers might also occupy this role).[23] Rhoda Broughton published her first two novels by enlisting the help of an uncle, Sheridan Le Fanu, himself a successful writer of tales of the supernatural. In other families, uncles took in nephews as apprentices and, if childless, might designate these younger relatives their heirs. More rarely, aunts might be in a position to aid nieces professionally, as in the case of Anne Jemima Clough, whose niece Thena succeeded her as principal of Newnham College, Cambridge. Close bonds between spinster aunts and nephews occur in a number of Victorian family novels, perhaps most famously Dickens's *David Copperfield* (1849–1850) and Butler's *The Way of All Flesh*. In the former, the lovable eccentric Betsey Trotwood rescues the title character from his cruel stepfather and gives him a home; in the latter, the admirable Alethea, motivated by "a woman's love for children, and her desire to find someone among the younger branches of her own family to whom she could become warmly attached, and whom she could attach warmly to herself,"[24] identifies her oldest nephew as someone worth saving from his tiresome and domineering parents.

She never gave him a syllable of good advice, or talked to him about everything's depending upon his own exertions, but she kissed him often, and would come into the workshop and act the part of one who took an interest in what was being done so cleverly as ere long to become really interested.

What boy would not take kindly to almost anything with such assistance? . . . His aunt was happy and grateful for his happiness, the improvement she saw in him, and his unrepressed affection for herself. She became fonder of him from day to day in spite of his many faults and almost incredible foolishnesses. It was perhaps on account of these very things that she saw how much he had need of her; but at any rate, from whatever cause, she became strengthened in her determination to be to him in the place of parents, and to find in him a son rather than a nephew.

—Samuel Butler, *The Way of All Flesh* (composed 1885, published 1903), Chapter 34

Uncles, too, might be represented in fiction as powerfully benevolent forces. The orphaned title character of Yonge's *Countess Kate* (1862) moves from the home of the clergyman uncle who has reared her to the more aristocratic abode of two spinster aunts when she inherits a title. Unlike her widowed Uncle Wardour, who has a large number of progeny, her aunts are unused to children and make a poor job of bringing her up, so that her chief pleasure is in interacting with the family of a second uncle, Lord de la Poer. The story's denouement involves her transplantation to the home of yet another uncle and his wife, where Kate will benefit from a combination of intelligent guidance, the training appropriate to her station, and the chance to see her original foster family on a frequent basis. In this story, aunts tend not to be particularly potent influences for good; one is dead, several others are minor characters, and the two with whom Kate lives are each in their separate ways ill equipped to understand the child—as we see magnified in Charlotte Brontë's *Jane Eyre* (1847), a novel in which the guardianship of an aunt and the nursery companionship of cousins prove singularly unpleasant. In contrast, in Yonge's text, at least, uncles can be relied upon to make good substitute fathers, and even in Brontë's the absent uncle John Eyre leaves Jane the money that she needs in order to be independent.

Yet while it is possible to find pro-uncle texts in Victorian literature, and while such texts reflect a society in which many uncles were of considerable use in getting nephews and nieces well established in life, the concept of the wicked uncle clearly had a powerful hold on the Victorian imagination. Figures such as the Princes in the Tower, widely believed to have been murdered in the early 1480s at the behest of their uncle and guardian Richard III, or the Babes in the Wood, folk-tale characters who die of exposure owing to the cruelty of another guardian uncle, were the stuff of paintings and pantomimes that had wide appeal among nineteenth-century consumers. The list of heartless uncles in Victorian fiction is also a long one. Consider the works of Dickens, which include (among other examples) the usurer Ralph Nickleby in *Nicholas Nickleby* (1838–1839), who maneuvers his nephew into accepting a disastrous job and attempts to maneuver his niece into a disastrous marriage; Ebenezer Scrooge in *A Christmas Carol* (1843), another bachelor who, before supernatural forces intervene, thinks only of his own gain and cares nothing for either family or employees; and John Jasper in *The Mystery of Edwin Drood* (1870), an opium addict and arch-hypocrite who nurtures a murderous hatred for his nephew, Edwin. Le Fanu's *Uncle Silas* (1864) is another drug-taker, this time of laudanum; when he is named guardian of his niece and next heir to her fortune, he first tries to marry her to his son and subsequently imprisons her, preparatory to attempting her murder. Collins offers Frederick Fairlie of *The Woman in White* (1860), a hypochondriac whose interest in himself is so consuming that he expends no energy on safeguarding his niece and ward. In Brontë's *Shirley*, Caroline Helstone's clergyman uncle and foster father forbids her to seek employment, enforcing a stultifying idleness that contributes to Caroline's near-fatal decline. And a Scottish example, Uncle Ebenezer in Robert Louis Stevenson's *Kidnapped* (1886), has usurped the family estate and engineers the shanghaiing of his indigent nephew to the Carolinas when the latter comes to ask for his help.

The presence in Victorian texts of these deeply flawed uncles, who occupy a parent's place but betray this responsibility owing to an overweening selfishness and/or lack of sympathy, and of similarly unprepossessing aunts, who provide food and shelter but not love and understanding, is suggestive. Most Victorian novelists were born into and were writing for the middle classes, in which the cult of domesticity was especially powerful. Although some authors, as we have seen in Chapter 2, were prepared to hold their protagonists' parents up to scorn, others seem to have believed that criticizing middle-class parents directly could pose problems. Doing so might induce feelings of guilt in the author, might alienate the reader, or might encourage unfilial sentiments in society at large, thus betraying what many Victorian writers considered to be their responsibility to further the moral improvement of their audience. But as Chapter 6 will further explore, figures who occupied a parental space without actually being parents, including uncles and aunts who functioned as guardians to their brothers' or sisters' children, could safely be pilloried.

ROOTS: THE IMPLICATIONS OF THE PREOCCUPATION WITH EXTENDED FAMILY

It should by now be apparent that the presence in so many works of Victorian literature of servants or collateral relations who play an important role in the lives of the major characters, or of penniless elderly members of the working classes, has a number of causes. The simplest of these causes is the widespread Victorian admiration for realism in art. If the protagonists of novels are frequently reared by relatives other than their parents or become romantically involved with cousins, this is partly because such scenarios were common in life. Many children lost one or both parents in infancy and were transferred to the care of grandparents or parents' siblings or their own older brothers or sisters. Servants were in many cases part of the family—not just part of the household—in a number of significant ways. Cousins married cousins in the nineteenth century at a rate many times higher than would prevail in the twentieth. Moreover, the building of the railways in the 1830s, the inauguration of the penny post in 1841, the spread of literacy over the course of the period, even the advances in photography (by the 1870s photographs had declined substantially in price and had become easier to produce), all contributed to the preservation of ties among extended family, as both written communication and visiting became speedier, partly compensating for the increased likelihood that individuals might not remain in their native neighborhoods.

But Victorian authors' preoccupation with family beyond the constellation of husband, wife, and children surely has psychological roots as well. Take the idea, present in many Victorian texts, that the mother–child bond could be replicated in any number of relationships in which biological motherhood was not a factor—in, say, teacher–pupil situations (Jane Eyre and her beloved teacher Miss Temple, for instance), or aunt–nephew connections such as Butler's Alethea and

Ernest Pontifex, or between older and younger cousins, as in Yonge's *Countess Kate*. The belief that the mothering instinct was present in all women, or at any rate all good women, whether or not they had ever given birth, was an article of faith for any number of Britons during this period, and was used to justify anything from allowing women to run for elective office as school board members to discouraging them from entering the realms of higher education. But in addition, the thought that motherless children could be provided with a surrogate mother who would be just as effective as their original one would have quieted the anxieties of many bereaved husbands at a time when women not infrequently died in early middle age.

Or consider the cousin marriages with which Victorian fiction teems. In a society in which brothers and sisters were expected to feel an attachment for each other not very different in kind or intensity from the attachment felt between husband and wife, marrying off one's protagonist to his or her cousin permitted the invoking of a common fantasy (romance between close relatives) in a socially sanctioned way. Symbolically, it could also be a means of asserting a key element of the cult of domesticity, namely that the family circle was proof against intrusions from outside because it could provide all that one might want or need—up to and including romance. To be sure, not all marriages or proposed marriages between fictional cousins are presented as happy or desirable, a circumstance that permits authors to make the converse point: although finding a spouse outside the family may involve more risk, taking this risk is sometimes desirable. Although Jane Eyre's cousin and suitor St. John Rivers is handsome, upright, and self-sacrificing, superficially a better choice than her errant employer, the bigamous Mr. Rochester, in fact despite his checkered past Rochester will make the more desirable husband. For if St. John marries Jane the union will not, as St. John's sister hopes, keep the newlyweds at home within the bosom of their family; rather, he will take her off to India to live out her (short) life as a missionary, away from all that is familiar. Against the odds, Rochester turns out to be the more domestic choice.

Such paradoxes are characteristic of Victorian attitudes on the family. On the one hand, as nineteenth-century discussions of extended families frequently suggest, families were exceptionally strong at this time, bound together beyond the small circle of immediate kin both by society's fiat and by their own inclination. Many working-class families sacrificed considerably to preserve the dignity of grandparents or other older members by keeping them out of the workhouse; others made it a priority to offer assistance to young nephews starting out in the world of employment. Letters traveled back home from émigré brothers and uncles, nephews and cousins, who remained committed to their long unseen families and wanted to remain in contact and, if possible, to offer help to relatives back in England who might need a bequest or a start in a new country. Some servants identified so strongly with their employers' families that they spent their lives in the families' service. In the upper reaches of society, aristocratic households tended to be connected to one another by blood and marriage in a multiplicity of ways; in the early twentieth century, Victoria's grandsons occupied the thrones of England, Germany, and Russia, while her granddaughters were married to the rulers of Greece, Norway, Romania, Sweden, Spain, and (again, because of another cousin marriage) Russia. This genealogical spider's web merely recapitulates at the highest level what was also the pattern among the English aristocracy, namely a genetically tightly knit society in which cousinhood featured prominently.

On the other hand, nineteenth-century discussions of extended families also indicate that the Victorian family was often perceived—and with justice—as being under siege, threatened by a number of factors having to do with the rapid pace of modernization. Families were increasingly likely to be separated by distance as younger members moved to the city to find jobs or, perhaps, took up the task of empire building abroad. The work of artisans was increasingly likely to be done by machine, so that crafts once handed down within the family and providing apprenticeships that might be filled by one's younger relatives were disappearing as the sources of livelihoods. Older people brought to the end of their earning capacity by physical frailty, the obsolescence of their traditional ways of making money, or other causes frequently found themselves penniless, and their juniors were not always willing or able to intervene between them and destitution or the workhouse. Even cousin marriage could be seen as a threat to the family, inasmuch as some observers warned that inbreeding would sap the vitality of the stock.

Small wonder, perhaps, that Victorian fiction oscillates to such a pronounced degree between representing members of the extended family as guardian angels like Betsey Trotwood, reaching down benevolent hands to help their collateral relations, and representing them as hypocritical monsters aided in their plots by their privileged position as kin. The conflicting quality of such images stamps them as stand-ins for closer relationships still.

6

STEPFAMILIES AND FOSTER FAMILIES

While both the cult of domesticity and the Victorian science of eugenics made much of the blood tie, in practice many nineteenth-century children were raised by people other than—or in addition to—their biological parents. The complicated household formed by the marriage of Leslie Stephen to Julia Duckworth, with its competing systems of half, full, and stepsiblings, is merely one example of a blended family, a phenomenon that seemed no more strange during an era when many people died in early middle age than it does in our own era of high divorce rates. Foster care, whether provided by relatives, family friends, or other individuals paid or unpaid, was also common, although before the passage of the Adoption of Children Act of 1926 adoption was a private and often informal matter. A look at Victorian demographics reveals why the constructed family should have been so widespread; historian George Behlmer cites studies from the mid- and late century showing that in Lancashire and East London respectively, nearly one-third of the population would lose a parent, and nearly one-tenth be orphaned altogether, by age fifteen.[1]

Consequently, stepparenting and fostering, and to a lesser extent single parenting, were the subjects of lively discussion in the Victorian era. Some of this discussion consisted of advice and encouragement to brides who found themselves thrust into the role of stepmother. Some, for example discourse exposing the connection between "baby farming" (paid foster care for young children, usually working-class and often illegitimate, who for whatever reason could not share their parents' homes) and infanticide, or publicizing child-placement efforts such as those of Thomas Barnardo, was part of the extensive literature of Victorian reformism. A small part of the discussion advocated a system of legal adoption for England, which might be modeled after the adoption laws that, from 1851 onward, were enacted by various American states. And a large part took place within Victorian fiction, which chronicled a broad range of stepparenting and adoptive situations of greater or lesser desirability.

Like the novels about aunts and uncles examined in the preceding chapter, fiction about families constructed by marriage or adoption rather than by birth often functions as a way of critiquing other sorts of family relationships. Literary stepparents may embody flaws of inattention, lack of sympathy, or outright cruelty, identifying for the reader in a noncontroversial fashion flaws that might also mark biological parenting. Literary adoptive parents may prove preferable to a child's blood kin, thus emphasizing that good parenting cannot be taken for granted, or may function as markers of a secrecy that may characterize other aspects of domesticity as well; literary single parents may demonstrate that fathering and mothering can go beyond gender. In short, the phenomenon of the constructed family and its representation in fiction and nonfiction provides us not only with information about atypical (but not uncommon) demographic patterns in the Victorian era, but also with further insight into the anxieties surrounding Victorian families of all kinds.

SERIAL FATHERS AND ENDANGERED CHILDREN: CONCERN ABOUT THE WORKING CLASS

Sociological commentators on the lives of the poor were particularly likely to remark, whether fairly or unfairly, on the fragility of their family bonds. Cohabitation by unmarried couples was much more prevalent in slum settings than it was among those who could afford the luxury of respectability, and people explaining the lower orders to a middle-class audience often found common-law marriage of compelling interest. In his 1883 series of articles in the *Pictorial World* entitled "How the Poor Live," for example, journalist George Sims remarks on the rarity of wedding ceremonies in London's East End. And although he concedes that most partners are reasonably monogamous, he also provides anecdotes to the opposite effect, such as the story of the child who came to school wearing a pair of secondhand footgear instead of being barefoot as usual. When asked where she got her shoes, the girl responded, "One of my fathers gave 'em to me, mistress; the one what's at home this week." Sims turns the particular into the general by adding, "This 'father' was evidently a better fellow than most of the nomadic husbands who wander about from family circle to family circle, ready to replace its absent head at a moment's notice."[2]

The language used to describe such situations reflects how alien these practices were to the dominant moral code of middle-class Victorian England. Like the quasi-anthropological title of Sims's series, which implies that the poor live in a manner so different from the bourgeoisie that newspapers need to provide guided tours of their domestic arrangements, words such as "nomadic" convey a breath of the exotic. This rhetorical strategy was fashionable in the sociological commentary of the mid- to late nineteenth century. Sims's articles, subsequently published in book form, were sufficiently popular to inspire two columns in the rival *Daily News*, "Evenings with the Poor" and "Homes of the London Poor," which like Sims's work represented the poor as aliens after the fashion of "the Zenanas, the Aborigenes, and the South Sea Islanders."[3] In the same vein, the popular magazine *All the Year Round* published yet another series of articles as "Travels in the East" in 1884, a title chosen to link the explication of inner-city London to travel narratives about Baghdad or Damascus. In such a framework, middle-class writers could contend that working-class families were fundamentally unstable without implying that the families of the more affluent members of society might also have their weaknesses.

The "nomadic" men of the lower strata of society were typically represented as more or less devoid of feelings of protectiveness or responsibility toward their partners' children. Whereas social investigators such as Sims, Walter Austin, and Henry Mayhew note the existence of affectionate relationships among biological fathers and children, the expectations for stepfathers—particularly when no marriage has been solemnized—seem lower. In 1851, for example, Mayhew quotes a child watercress seller as explaining, "I ain't got no father, he's a father-in-law [stepfather]. No; mother ain't married again—he's a father-in-law. He grinds scissors, and he's very good to me. No; I dont mean by that that he says kind things to me, for he never hardly speaks."[4] The reader is free to conclude that "very good" treatment in this context merely means that although the stepfather evidently pays little attention to the child, he does not actively mistreat her. Writers who were themselves born into the working classes, such as Thomas Hardy (son of a stonemason), might also reproduce this stereotype of the stepfather of humble origins who is at best indifferent to his partner's child. Thus the title character of Hardy's *The Mayor of Casterbridge* (1886), who mislays his wife for eighteen years because in a fit of drunkenness he has sold her and their child for five guineas to a passing sailor, is a loving father when his wife returns to him, as he supposes that the daughter she brings with her is the daughter who went away. When he discovers that his own child has died and that his wife's living daughter, who shares her half-sister's name, is the offspring of the sailor, his paternal feelings are buried in hostility; moreover, although stepfather and child later establish a workable relationship, she leaves him when her biological father reappears. Again, the biological tie triumphs.

Working-class stepparents of a more malevolent sort than Hardy's Michael Henchard were not infrequently associated with crime. Mayhew's interviews with female tramps identify tense relationships with stepparents, and particularly stepmothers, as a major factor influencing young women to become vagrants. His subjects describe their fathers' second wives as violent troublemakers whose much-resented intrusion into the family destroyed domestic peace. Stepparents are said to drink too much, to beat their partners' children, to tell lies about the children to the biological parents, and to alienate parent from child. "George Egerton" (Mary Chavelita Dunne) details a complex

Child street sellers were often considered to be particularly in need of middle-class benevolence to compensate for the protection that their parents were evidently not providing. Here, a motherly looking woman in a fur-trimmed coat distributes largesse to a flower vendor (who has only a scanty shawl over her dress) in a snowstorm. [Detail of illustration from *The Girl's Own Paper* (December 27, 1884); collection of the author.]

domestic situation in her short story "Wedlock," published as part of *Discords* in 1894; here a stepmother's drinking problem is connected to her separation from her illegitimate three-year-old, Susie, who is being raised by an aunt because the new husband refuses to incorporate another man's child into his family. When, jealous of his wife's love for her daughter, the husband prevents her from attending Susie's deathbed, the woman cuts the throats of his three children. The story implies that the bond between mother and biological child is far more potent than that between husband and wife, let alone stepmother and stepchildren. Such family dysfunction was sometimes confirmed by the felony crime news, as in the London *Times*'s coverage of the murder of Sarah Redhead on May 30, 1870 by her eighteen-year-old stepson, who reportedly had much resented his father's remarriage and who stated to the divisional police superintendent that he had shot his victim because she "had behaved very cruelly to him and his sister."[5]

The prospects for working-class abuse of the parent–child bond, especially in the absence of a marriage license or a blood tie, were increasingly evident to Victorian reformers over the course of the period. Concerned about the alarmingly high infant mortality rate—even by the end of the century, in some desperately poor urban neighborhoods only half of all babies survived their first year—commentators were convinced that the problem was not merely overcrowded living conditions, inadequate sanitation, epidemic disease, and malnutrition, but infanticide as well. If an illegitimate baby died, the death was often (and sometimes correctly) seen as a purposeful act on the part of a mother who might not be able to retain her job or her place in her parents' home if she

---

This wretched woman's cruelty and her terrible doom are, in truth, the natural result of a wide-spread immorality, and there are many men and women whom the sentence pronounced yesterday ought to afflict with a bitter remorse. They have given way to the most devouring of human passions; nature has compelled them to encounter the usual consequences of their acts; they have been overwhelmed by a fear of shame only to be measured in its intensity by the passion to which they have yielded; and, for the sake of evading their own punishment, they have acquiesced in the murderous treatment of their innocent offspring. It is frightful to what an extent even actual infanticide prevails among us. We yesterday reported four inquests held on the previous day upon the bodies of newly born children found in the neighbourhood of the Regent's Park and the Edgware-road. One of them had been thrown into the canal with a brick tied to its neck, like a dog. A conviction for MURDER will, it may be hoped, strike terror into all who share the responsibility of these shocking barbarities, and will teach the licentious and the cruel that "he that hateth his child is a murderer."

—"The So-Called 'Baby Farming Case' Has Ended"; London *Times* editorial on the murder conviction of Margaret Waters (September 24, 1870)

had a child and who could not count on financial support from the baby's father. Writing in 1870, Thomas Archer quotes Dr. Edwin Lankester, the coroner for central Middlesex (London), as remarking that for every 15,000 members of the population at large, one murder verdict was handed down in inquests on newborns.[6]

Although some well-publicized cases of infanticide involved defendants who were not related to their victims, such as the baby farmers Charlotte Winsor in 1866 and Margaret Waters in 1870, when the dead child was less than two weeks old the accused killer was typically the mother. Nor were such mothers invariably young, unmarried, and abandoned by their partners. The phenomenon of postpartum psychosis as something that might afflict even women of secure social standing was familiar to Victorian jurisprudence, and according to Siân Busby, at the end of the century some 60 percent of the inmates of the Broadmoor hospital for criminally insane women had been committed to that institution for killing their children. As Busby notes, citing the case of Elizabeth Agar in 1883, middle-class child murderers might be permitted to evade both Broadmoor and the death penalty; it was working-class mothers who appeared to judges to constitute the real social threat.[7]

In other instances, murders of children by their parents were said to be motivated by the desire to benefit from life insurance policies taken out to cover funeral costs. Thomas Carlyle begins his work of social criticism *Past and Present* (1843) with an account of a newspaper report of the arraignment in a town near Manchester of an Irish-born couple for poisoning three of their children in order to collect a total of £11 in payouts. That child life insurance could be a temptation to evildoing came up again and again over the remainder of the century, attracting the efforts of such reformers as sanitation pioneer Edwin Chadwick and Benjamin Waugh, first head of the National Society for the Prevention of Cruelty to Children. Reformers' efforts to ban insurance policies on children or to ensure that payouts were made only to undertakers and not to parents continued, even in the absence of concrete evidence that death benefits amounting to a few pounds were statistically significant as a factor causing the impoverished to exterminate their offspring.

In a climate in which it was widely believed that working-class parents might readily be brought to kill the children born to them, it is hardly surprising that concern about the potential callousness of foster parents unrelated to their charges ran still higher. Starting in the 1860s, newspaper accounts uniformly treated baby farming as a national shame; the publicity given to this subject resulted in the Infant Life Protection Act of 1872, which required individuals who received money for fostering two or more infants to register with the state. The difference in the terms used from one social group to the next is significant. The working classes spoke of "adoption"; the pejorative "baby farming" was used by muckrakers and reform organizations, who saw the practice of boarding other people's sons and daughters for pay not as a potentially workable solution

A women's dormitory at Broadmoor, as shown in the *Illustrated London News* on August 24, 1867. [Courtesy of Evans Library, Texas A&M University.]

to child-care needs but rather as a criminal attempt to turn children into sources of profit.

Thus on the one hand, some commentators noted that mothers seeking foster care for their small children might genuinely want to do the right thing by youngsters whom they could not look after because of the need to earn their livings. Yet on the other hand, the foster parents were usually represented as monsters rather than as a mixed lot of individuals who might run the gamut from abusive to nurturing. Investigative journalist James Greenwood's chapter on baby farming in *The Seven Curses of London* (1869) is typical. He begins by providing some sample advertisements placed in periodicals aimed at working-class women.

NURSE CHILD WANTED, OR TO ADOPT—The Advertiser, a Widow with a little family of her own, and a moderate allowance from her late husband's friends, would be glad to accept the charge of a young child. Age no object. If sickly would receive a parent's care. Terms, Fifteen Shillings a month; or would adopt entirely if under two months for the small sum of Twelve pounds.

ADOPTION—A person wishing a lasting and comfortable home for a young child of either sex will find this a good opportunity. Advertisers having no children of their own are about to proceed to America. Premium, Fifteen Pounds. Respectable references given and required.

—Baby farmers' advertisements quoted in James Greenwood,
The Seven Curses of London (1869), Chapter 3

Subsequently, Greenwood teaches his audience how to interpret such seemingly innocent texts: having secured their victims, and the money that accompanies them, the baby farmers will either kill the children by neglect and slow starvation, or abandon them in the street, where they may find a home in the workhouse or with benevolent strangers. Toddlers left to fend for themselves in the slums, Greenwood adds, are likely to become dependent on the kindness of prostitutes and thieves—who, he warns, comprise the entire population of some parts of London. Consequently, they will embark upon a life of criminality themselves, in which some of them may be all the more successful because of the intelligence inherited from their unwed but well-born fathers. (Charles Dickens's Oliver Twist avoids precisely this fate only because of his unusual and innate virtue.) In Greenwood's formulation, then, baby farming and abandonment both reveal and further the most troubling aspect of class division, namely the potential for an attack from below. Moreover, even foster parents who are not paid for their efforts might be identified as socially dangerous, in that the environment in which they raise an adopted child to adulthood is considered so corrupt as to make decency impossible.

To be sure, the informal adoptions that occurred among the poor were sometimes represented in a positive light. One of a number of works dated 1884 that focus on life in London's tenement districts, the Reverend D. Rice-Jones's *In the Slums*, contains a chapter titled "The Adopted Child," which recounts how a poor family with seven children of its own takes in a neighbor child who has suddenly been orphaned. The adoption is characterized as motivated not by greed but by charity, and Rice-Jones frames it in religious terms by praising the practical Christianity of the kindly adopters. Somewhat similarly, the final chapter of *Travels in the East* describes a cramped and squalid two-room dwelling, one room occupied by a family of three, the other (thirty square feet in area) rented to the wife's mother and an orphan for whom she is caring. Again, because no money has changed hands between the child's original parents and the new mother, the adoption is not framed as a murder waiting to happen, but rather as a rare sign of humanity in a household that otherwise offers us little to admire. And the title character of Dickens's "Doctor Marigold" (1865) is an itinerant salesman ("Doctor" is his first name, not his profession) who rescues a deaf and dumb child from her abusive stepfather and raises her as his own. In educating her and making sacrifices for her, he illustrates for Dickens's middle-class readers the tenderness of an ideal father–daughter relationship, especially in the absence of a mother.

Because English law made no provision for registering adoptions before 1926, it is impossible to tell how many Victorian children might have lived in quasi-adoptive situations in working-class households. Some nineteenth-century writers on the lives of the poor indicate that informal adoptions were relatively widespread, whether they involved the orphaned children of neighbors, the children of living people seeking boarding homes for their inconvenient infants, or the children of one's connections by blood or marriage. In describing the situation of a representative family from the lowest social class, Victorian sociologist Charles Booth notes that Alexander Grant's wife told a welfare worker in 1883 that "her husband was a drunken, good-for-nothing fellow, who spent all he could get in drink. He had taken the boots of an orphan boy who lived with them, and spent the money he got for them in drink." Another impoverished couple described by Booth had a childless marriage until a woman abandoned her baby on their doorstep; they kept the child a year, "when one day he was taken off and a little girl (his sister) left in his place." The biological father was identified but died shortly thereafter, and the girl remained in her new home even after the death of her adoptive father. Whether these adoptions were motivated by compassion, the children's potential usefulness, or some other factor is not recorded, but Booth adds later in his work that "if the family tie [among the lower working classes] is not strong, neither is it exclusive.... adoption is common."[8]

Similarly, Rice-Jones reports an interview with a printer who notes that after the early death of his mother, his father remarried and promptly died. His stepmother then took another husband before dying herself, leaving the child to the care of the new husband. He too remarried and died. Because this man's widow was abusive, the eight-year-old left home and grew up under the patronage of a clergyman.[9] In a population with a relatively low life expectancy, the inheritance of children along a chain of serial caretaking was hardly inconceivable, especially since children past the toddler stage could be turned into financial assets; Rice-Jones's interviewee remarks that his first stepfather, at least, saw their arrangement as a business deal in which the child would get room and board and the adult would gain an assistant in his work as market porter. In contrast, the clergyman's acceptance of responsibility for the boy was presumably charitable in nature.

Middle-class readers would probably have been more comfortable once the clergyman entered the picture, although he lacked even the shadowy parental claim to the child possessed by the stepmother's second husband's widow; Victorian social commentators tended to be happier with institutional or at least quasi-professional solutions to the problem of displaced poor children than with private ones. Indeed, while foster care arranged by the biological parents of the poor was viewed with deep suspicion, foster care arranged by the state or by a philanthropic organization might be seen as essential to the child's moral development. Of course, some Victorians were also suspicious of institutional solutions, and exposés of flaws in various charitable practices were very much a part of public discourse—but overall, the middle and upper classes believed that society would benefit if their emissaries could take charge of the children of the poor. Even Dickens's worthy Doctor Marigold surrenders his adopted daughter, Sophy, for two years so that her education may be completed, a process that prepares her to marry a man who shares her deafness but is better situated in life, being a clerk in a mercantile establishment in China. While Sophy retains a fitting love for Marigold, she also assimilates into the middle class, as is symbolized by her giving birth to a hearing daughter whose speech is not marked by the working-class peculiarities that characterize her grandfather's.

In part this comparative comfort with the idea that poor law unions, orphanages, and charitable concerns might be trusted to determine the fate of destitute young people arose from a belief that the institution did not profit from the children's labor and that its motives must therefore be disinterested. Another source of confidence, however, appears to have been that such institutions usually did what they could to sever any remaining ties between the child and its biological parents, who were often still in the picture. (The problem with baby farming was not that the child was distant from its mother, but rather that the caretaker was presumed to be immoral, cruel, venal, and deliberately neglectful—in other words, the antithesis of the maternal ideal.) Workhouses separated family groups if these were intact upon admission, housing parents and children in different areas of the building and reserving the right, which by law would normally have belonged to the father, of apprenticing the child to a trade. After 1870, local Poor Law Guardians were also authorized to place young orphans or waifs in foster homes, not because such homes would provide the best socialization for eventual reunion with kin but because they could train the children for work as domestics more readily than could the less home-like institution. The Poor Law Acts of 1889 and 1899 gave Poor Law Guardians rights over certain classes of children that superseded those of the birth parents; although parents retained the right to appeal, Behlmer notes that "these appeals must have been either few in number or else singularly ineffective."[10] Once children came under the control of the Guardians by entering a workhouse, they would remain under that control until age sixteen (for boys) or eighteen (for girls).

Likewise, the London Foundling Hospital accepted illegitimate infants on the application of their mothers. When admitted, the child was assigned a number, which the mother might use later on for the purpose of inquiring about her offspring's health; however, she would not be told the child's new name or given visitation rights, since the child was presumed to be better off without her. Like the workhouse, the Foundling took over parental functions vis-à-vis its charges, apprenticing boys at age fourteen, placing girls in servant positions at age fifteen, and providing counsel to any of its alumni who might ask for it in later life. Similar patterns may be found in many other institutions as well—preserving family relationships among the poor was generally not a priority, although child-savers often complained that the law did all too much to protect the parental rights of the unfit.

Children trained in the midst of vicious or criminal surroundings almost inevitably become criminal or vicious, whilst the wholesome influences of a well-ordered home produce good citizens.... What hope is there ... of securing attention to the pressing need for legislation on behalf of the waifs and strays of our streets, and the children of our criminals and paupers? Yet here it is that we can reach the very roots of the tree which produces such a fruitful crop of criminals. And, surely, the conscience of the nation cannot slumber much longer over this great question. We are, nowadays, too enlightened to recognize "the right divine of kings to govern wrong," but the divine right of vicious and brutal parents to make their children brutal and vicious like themselves is still guarded with scrupulous care.

—Assistant Commissioner of the Metropolitan Police Robert Anderson,
"Morality by Act of Parliament," *The Contemporary Review* 59 (January 1891)

Given their belief that the law was inappropriately biased in favor of the biological father, child-savers were not above bending it to circumvent that father's authority. The Church of England Waifs and Strays Society devised a contract in the 1890s that would require blood relatives who sought to reclaim a child to pay the substantial sum of £10 to £13 for each year that the child had been in care; although in fact this agreement was not legally binding, it could be intimidating to people who did not know that fact. Meanwhile, Barnardo was charged on a number of occasions with infractions relating to his practice of "philanthropic abduction" in cases where, in his view, a parent was abusive or criminally neglectful. The degree to which this challenge to working-class paternal rights struck lawmakers as justifiable may be gauged by the 1891 passage of the Custody of Children Act, known among Barnardo's detractors as Barnardo's Relief Act.

This piece of legislation abrogated parental rights over children who had been abandoned or had subsisted at the expense of someone other than the parent, including workhouses and charitable organizations, and established that the child's good (as determined by the courts) took precedence over the rights of parents who could not convince a judge of their fitness. In other words, the Act gave the legal system leeway to transfer custody rights from parents to child-savers. It thus ratified the work of aid workers such as Barnardo, who often saw their mission not merely as providing shelter for destitute children who requested help, but also as actively recruiting needy young people whether their parents liked the idea or not. Barnardo's clients might enter one of the 112 Barnardo Homes that dotted Great Britain by his death in 1905 or might be among the approximately 18,000 adolescents for whom he arranged emigration to Canada or Australia, where they would be placed with new families—usually as farmhands or domestic servants rather than as adopted children in the modern sense of the word.

Barnardo's was only one of many emigration schemes run by such organizations or individuals as the Children's Friend Society (founded 1830); the Scottish-born Annie Macpherson, who conducted more than 3000 children to Canada in her first ten years of resettlement endeavor through the Liverpool Sheltering Homes; Maria Rye, who, in addition to establishing the Female Middle-Class Emigration Society in 1861 as part of an attempt to solve the problem of "superfluous women," also relocated child inmates of workhouses; the National Children's Homes and Orphanages; the Salvation Army; the Nugent Society Care Homes run by the Roman Catholic Father Nugent; the Church of England Waifs and Strays Society; and any number of others. Canada was the most common colonial destination, but British children were also sent to Australia, South Africa, the West Indies, and New Zealand. To be sure, there were occasional outcries when cases of abuse came to light, and placements did not always "take." The Children's Friend Society dissolved in 1841 after publicity surrounding a police inquiry gave rise to a widely held belief that the Society was facilitating the sale of white English-born children as slaves in the Cape Colony. An 1874 report by Poor Law inspector Andrew Doyle, criticizing some aspects of the Canadian child-resettlement efforts of Macpherson and Rye, led to an 1875 ban on emigration from workhouses and reformatories, though that from privately run institutions continued. And it was not unheard of for Canadian or Australian families to return as incorrigible the children they had been sent.

Nevertheless, the belief that poverty could be alleviated through the exporting of poor children to new environments, and particularly to new families, continued well into the twentieth century. As the Rev. John Macpherson wrote in a foreword to an 1882 book about Annie, through emigration "A child [who] is snatched from pinching hunger, fluttering rags, and all the squalor of gutter life; from a creeping existence in the noisome pool of slum society is lifted up into some taste for decency and cleanliness; from being trained in the school whose first and last lesson is to fear neither God nor man, is taught the beginnings of Christian faith and duty."[11] Similar points were made about officially sanctioned foster care that took place in England. Foster mothers who were deemed to be themselves too close to destitution came off badly in inspection reports, but those who appeared to be in a position to convey the rudiments of respectability to their charges were applauded. Likewise, the before-and-after photographs of children that Barnardo used as fund-raising devices had captions such as "Once a Little Vagrant . . . Now a Little Workman," thus assuring potential supporters that the charity was redirecting youngsters toward economic self-sufficiency. When facilitated by certified child-savers, in other words, foster care and "wholesome" farm or industrial labor were often deemed considerably better than remaining in one's native environment, even when one's parents were still available.

Like the publicity given to baby farming during the final third of the century, arrangements such as these reveal the distrust with which many Victorians regarded impoverished and/or illegitimate parents. Far from endeavoring to make it possible for families under social and economic stress to remain together, the system was increasingly set up so as to remove children from their families and transfer them to what was presumed to be the more responsible care of the institution or the financially solvent colonial or rural household. While workhouses, in particular, had high child mortality rates and were notorious for their inadequate food (memorialized in Dickens's *Oliver Twist* in 1837–1838), they were nonetheless officially regarded as *morally* safer than life with an improvident parent. And while "Barnardo children" were often subject to abuse in their new settings, since there was little or no oversight once they had been placed in homes, emigration was presumed to offer them a better chance than their original families could have afforded them.

CONSTRUCTED FAMILIES AND THE MIDDLE CLASSES

The faith that many Victorians placed in placement schemes that sought to insert destitute children into more affluent families (albeit usually on a highly unequal footing) might seem to imply the existence of a widespread assumption that middle-class parents could be trusted to behave well by children not born to them. In fact, however, the assumption was more that the general moral tone of the bourgeoisie was better than that of the working classes—less domestic violence, joblessness, alcoholism, and criminality, for example—than it was that social standing would necessarily assist people to feel tenderly toward their stepchildren or foster children. Advice manuals such as T.E.G.'s *The Etiquette of Love, Courtship, and Marriage* (1847) could go so far as to state flatly that the instinct of the genteel stepmother, which she should endeavor to repress, might well be to neglect or abuse her husband's children.

The situation of a Step-mother is somewhat peculiar and difficult. It cannot be expected that a wife can love the children of a former marriage, so well as her own, but she ought to discharge the duties in which she is placed towards them as a mother. The lady well knew the responsibilities of such a situation before she entered upon it, and consequently she has no plea for neglecting to discharge them. A harsh and cruel treatment will be fatal to the happiness of your husband, and productive of domestic quarrels and discord.

—T.E.G., "Step-Mothers," *The Etiquette of Love, Courtship, and Marriage* (1847)

T.E.G.'s viewpoint seems incompatible with the middle-class cult of domesticity, which valorized the image of the gentle, giving wife and mother whose freedom from selfish impulses should have the effect, one would suppose, of causing her to love all her husband's children equally, whether she had any biological part in them or not. Yet the assumption that some sort of genetic tie was necessary for love was also found in the widespread belief that if a man's wife died, the best thing that he could do for his children was to recruit her sister to move into the family home in order to bring them up—the implication being that stepmothers were chancy matters.

But love, as it happened, was not always the top priority. When John and Alice Kipling decided in 1871 to send their six-year-old son, Rudyard, and his three-year-old sister, Trix, to be reared in England instead of remaining in India with their parents, they found a foster home for the pair—a move that members of the middle classes could accomplish without being considered complicit in baby farming. The Kiplings placed their youngsters not with relatives (although there were a good many suitable family connections who might have been called upon for this purpose, Mrs. Kipling felt that such arrangements usually "led to complications"[12]) but with a paid caregiver, evidently chosen from the advertisement columns of a newspaper. The children were thus handed over, with no advance warning, to a Southsea couple whom neither they nor their parents had met before, Sarah and Pryse Holloway, after which the elder Kiplings vanished from their lives for six years.

Unsurprisingly, perhaps, the episode had "complications" of its own. Trix experienced a number of breakdowns later in life, possibly schizophrenic in nature, which clinical psychologist Cora de Chumaceiro attributes to the separation. Meanwhile, Rudyard, whose relationship with his foster mother and her son was one of mutual loathing, revisited his "six years in hell" in bitter autobiographical tales that included "Baa Baa Black Sheep" (1888) and *The Light That Failed* (1890).[13] When the children's parents made another brief stay in England in 1877, they removed their traumatized son from the care of the recently widowed Mrs. Holloway and sent him to boarding school instead.

Trix, however, remained in the home, occasionally visited by her brother, for several additional years.

The point here is not to criticize John and Alice Kipling's judgment in making this particular arrangement for Rudyard and Trix (although their action may well strike today's readers as remarkable), but rather to note that their decision to hand over their two small children to be brought up by strangers would have seemed normal to middle-class Anglo-Indian society during and after the 1870s. The practice is memorialized in fiction such as Frances Hodgson Burnett's *Sara Crewe, or What Happened at Miss Minchin's* (1888, later expanded as *A Little Princess*), to name one well-known example, while other narratives, such as Juliana Ewing's *Six to Sixteen* (1872), contain Indian-born protagonists who are housed not with relations but with family friends. In Burnett's story, as in the Kiplings' experience, the father's decision to leave his daughter with a schoolmistress of whom he knows very little turns out badly; when the father dies an apparent bankrupt, Miss Minchin turns Sara into the school drudge until Captain Crewe's business partner appears, adopts the child, and showers her with expensive presents. Yet, again, the narrative does not invite readers to question the idea that English children should not remain with their parents if this means being reared in India. The reason commonly advanced for the quite typical practice of sending one's Indian-born progeny to be raised at "Home" was that the Indian climate was detrimental to the health of the ethnically English. But as de Chumaceiro notes, white parents may additionally have feared the moral and social effects on the young of being cared for by Indian servants, have wanted to ensure that their children identified as English, and have found it convenient to evade the investment of time that parenting involved even when a nanny was employed.

On the one hand, foster placements such as the Kipling children's suggest that even among the middle classes, the group most heavily invested in the cult of domesticity, the preservation of the family circle was not invariably the highest priority. On the other hand, members of the middle class also used stepparenting and adoption as a means of creating such a family. Eliza Lynn appears to have felt real reluctance to marry William Linton, whom her fiction depicts as effeminate or even physically repellent to her and who was ill equipped to support a wife and family. Yet his seven children clearly needed a mother. Their biological mother (sister to Linton's first wife, and so perhaps not in fact his legal wife because of the barriers to marrying a deceased wife's sister) had been a friend of Lynn's and, Lynn claimed, had begged her to look after her family. The last Linton daughter, Lizzie, aged two when her mother died of tuberculosis, was Lynn's namesake. Well before she married their father in March of 1858, Lynn had accepted responsibility for bringing up Lizzie and her next older sister, whom she instructed in the rudiments of reading, sewing, and speaking with a proper accent. Of Lizzie, she wrote to her future husband, "Baby has become one of the most straightforward truthful little darlings you can imagine. She is so beautiful! She is a dear little thing, and is so like my own child... that I don't think I could let her be taken away from me now, even by papa if he wanted to do so!"[14] Lizzie's death shortly before the marriage greatly grieved her would-be stepmother.

Lynn's biographer Nancy Fix Anderson theorizes that through her marriage she sought to re-create and heal the damaged family of her own childhood experience, as well as to fulfill middle-class Victorian society's expectations that women should engage in marriage and motherhood. Certainly Lynn's action in becoming stepmother to the Linton brood excited at least some approving commentary from observers. Upon hearing of the marriage, George Eliot, for one, noted that the deed was "something to admire and love her for."[15] Eliza Lynn Linton was to achieve success in her journalistic career by critiquing women who did not measure up to approved standards of womanliness. In embracing stepmotherhood even if it meant taking on a husband toward whom she felt distinctly ambivalent (the marriage broke up six years later, after the death of her favorite stepson), she could be said to be living up to those standards herself.

Adoption could serve a similar function, whether or not marriage was part of the picture. After marrying George Craik when she was almost forty, Dinah Mulock adopted a daughter from a foundling home in 1869, affectionately writing little Dorothy into her children's story *The Little Lame Prince* (1875) and becoming an advocate of American-style legal adoption in her late novel *King Arthur, Not a Love Story* (1886). Reformer Mary Carpenter was fifty-one and unmarried when she adopted five-year-old Rosanna in 1858, subsequently preventing the biological mother from making contact with the child whom she had relinquished. Educator Constance Maynard became a foster mother in 1888 to a six-year-old girl, Stephanë Anton, whom she found in a Paris nursery run by the Salvation Army and rechristened Effie. While the adoption failed and Maynard sent Stephanë/Effie back to France, she maintained a connection with the younger woman until the latter's death in 1915. As Martha Vicinus points out and as the actions of women such as Eliza Lynn Linton suggest, the Victorian world placed substantial pressure on middle-class women to prove their capacity for mothering. Single career women such as Carpenter and Maynard, whose energies were expended in ways not particularly compatible with child rearing, might use adoption as a way "to fulfill themselves in ways society would approve."[16]

Even in the United States, where legal adoption was increasingly possible in the nineteenth century (its availability depended upon the state in which one lived), adoption came in a number of forms and arose from many different motivations: the longing to become a parent, the hope of replacing a biological child who had died, the need for household help. The same range of attitudes could be found in Victorian England. Behlmer quotes turn-of-the-century adoption advertisements from a large-circulation periodical, the *Bazaar, Exchange and Mart*, that range from a request for "an orphan girl [to be] one of the family, for general domestic work" to a plea for an attractive three-year-old girl to be adopted by a "lady of position" in Staffordshire.[17] (In an era of high infant mortality and unreliable baby food, would-be parents whose desire for an adopted child was rooted in emotion often specified that they wanted a toddler, as children of two or three were considered young enough to bond readily with their new family but old enough to be past the stage of greatest danger. Older children were more likely to be "adopted" as servants.) Similarly, individuals might become foster parents in order to bring in some extra income or because they wanted the experience of raising a child; middle-class foster parents, in particular, might waive payment so that what they saw as an emotional and/or charitable act would not be tainted by commerce.

To be sure, parents on the receiving end of the adoption would sometimes pay for the privilege of securing a child. Baby farmer Waters defended herself by testifying that the child for whose murder she was standing trial was taken as a commercial speculation; she had, she claimed, been commissioned by a comfortably situated husband and wife to procure them a son for adoption. Paraphrasing an officer of the court, a London *Times* editorial on the case conceded that "such transactions do occur," although the writer added that "it is not credible that they can be sufficiently frequent to render the adoption of children at such a rate as WATERS admits [forty or more infants fostered over the preceding four years] a remunerative business."[18] To the *Times* writer, apparently, middle-class adoption looked comparatively unusual. And indeed, while it is possible to find advertisements placed by middle-class people seeking to become foster or adoptive parents, as well as accounts in the records of charitable organizations discussing child placements made in middle-class homes, overall the historical record has less to say about this issue among the middle classes than among the poor. Or perhaps there was merely less anxiety. After all, when the children of affluent parents were orphaned, they did not risk ending up in the workhouse or on the streets, nor was it assumed that they were criminals in the making. Nevertheless, adoption features in a number of nineteenth-century novels aimed predominantly at middle-class readers—and here again, it serves a variety of narrative functions.

THE VICTORIAN ADOPTION NOVEL

One important role that adoption plays in Victorian fiction is to suggest that families may be the repositories of secrets. Adoption is thus a frequent device in sensation fiction. Mary Elizabeth Braddon's first novel, *The Trail of the Serpent* (1861, initially serialized in somewhat different form as *Three Times Dead*), features a foundling deserted by his criminal father, who was in turn abandoned by his own father, an equally murderous French marquis. The boy, known as Slosh, is rescued from the mud by a mute investigator who has for some time nurtured a wish "to bring a child up from the very cradle in the police detective line." Slosh's adoption breaks the chain of wrongdoing by transforming him from potential malefactor into a successful excavator of his family's insalubrious history. The ruthlessness inherited from his biological father and grandfather combines with the training received from his adoptive father, so that the "undercurrent of his father [will] make him the glory of his profession. Soft-heartedness has been the ruin of many a detective as has had the brains to work out a deep-laid game, but not the heart to carry it through."[19] Adoption is figured as a means simultaneously of saving society from its outlaws (by moving members of the underclass into the ranks of the superior working class) and exposing the discreditable secrets of the seemingly respectable—in this case the titled aristocrat and his son, who has risen to become a wealthy banker.

An equally successful sensation writer, Wilkie Collins, returned to the figure of the adopted child in novel after novel. His last completed work, *The Legacy of Cain* (1888), hinges on the question of which of two sisters is her clergyman father's adopted rather than biological child, since it is known that one is the offspring of a husband-killer and may have inherited her mother's murderous propensities. (In fact, Collins wishes to debunk the idea that criminality is necessarily inherited; while one of the sisters is indeed a would-be poisoner, she is not the adopted child.) Similarly, Collins's much earlier work *The Dead Secret* (1857) derives its title from its heroine's birth: unbeknownst to herself, she is the illegitimate daughter of a servant, brought into the wealthy Treverton family so that Mrs. Treverton can cement her husband's love by persuading him that she has given birth to his child. *Hide and Seek* (1854), like Dickens's "Doctor Marigold" (which it clearly influenced; the two authors were close friends), features a deaf daughter adopted by a benevolent artist from a circus in which she was abused. The girl, known as Madonna, attracts the interest of a free-spirited young man whose father strongly disapproves of the idea that his son might ally himself with a bride whose biological parentage is unknown and whose adoptive father follows the frivolous occupation of painter. Inevitably, it turns out that Madonna is the natural daughter of the censorious father, who as a young man shared his son's wild streak. In these and similar texts, Collins uses adoption as a way of attacking the hypocrisy that he saw as the besetting sin of the respectable middle class. By permitting birth to be a matter of mystery, adoption as a literary device suggests that kinship is only one of many hidden aspects of a family's past, and that the upright domesticity fetishized by Victorian culture may have its dark sides.

In the hands of other authors, adoption could serve as a mechanism for meditations on both naturalization and alienation. As Marianne Novy observes in *Reading Adoption*, adoption seems to have been a particular interest for such major Victorian novelists as Charlotte Brontë (in *Jane Eyre*, *Shirley*, and to a lesser extent *Villette*), Dickens (in more novels and short stories than may readily be listed here), and George Eliot (in *Felix Holt*, *Romola*, *The Spanish Gypsy*, *Daniel Deronda*, and *Silas Marner*).[20] For instance, in *Daniel Deronda* (1876), Sir Hugo Mallinger has adopted Daniel and given him the upbringing conventional for an English gentleman. In adulthood, Daniel discovers that he is the son of a famous singer of Jewish descent, who could not reconcile motherhood with her career. The revelation creates in him an increasingly powerful yearning toward his ancestral people; he marries another Jewish singer and becomes a fervent Zionist, turning his back on the Christianity that many of Eliot's original readers would have defined as essential to Englishness. Eliot's early novel *Silas Marner* (1861) follows the adoption of a strayed toddler, Eppie, by a miserly and hermitlike weaver. Here, adoption not only gives Eppie a name and a place in the community, it also unites Silas to his fellow beings. When Eppie's biological father finally identifies himself to her after many years of self-protective silence (she is the product of a disgraceful secret marriage to a working-class woman) she politely declines to see herself as part of his family, since her loyalties belong entirely to the man who has brought her up. Eppie Marner and Daniel Deronda, who represent very different personality types, thus reach different conclusions about the relative importance of origins versus nurture. While Eliot had a personal interest in this subject because of her role in raising the sons of her partner George Henry Lewes, as a writer she parlays this interest—characteristically—into a way of meditating on larger issues of personality formation, the social web, and human destiny.

> "But I have a claim on you, Eppie—the strongest of all claims. It is my duty, Marner, to own Eppie as my child, and provide for her. She is my own child—her mother was my wife. I have a natural claim on her that must stand before every other."
>
> Eppie had given a violent start, and turned quite pale. Silas, on the contrary, who had been relieved, by Eppie's answer, from the dread lest his mind should be in opposition to hers, felt the spirit of resistance in him set free, not without a touch of parental fierceness. "Then, sir," he answered, with an accent of bitterness that had been silent in him since the memorable day when his youthful hope had perished—"then, sir, why didn't you say so sixteen year ago, and claim her before I'd come to love her, i'stead o' coming to take her from me now, when you might as well take the heart out o' my body? God gave her to me because you turned your back upon her, and He looks upon her as mine: you've no right to her! When a man turns a blessing from his door, it falls to them as take it in."
>
> —George Eliot, *Silas Marner* (1861), Chapter 19

Consider also an earlier novel, Emily Brontë's *Wuthering Heights* (1847), which introduces into a well-born Yorkshire family the wild waif Heathcliff, whose background is never explained. Heathcliff's passion for his adoptive sister, Catherine, coexists with his hatred for his adoptive brother, Hareton, whose son Heathcliff coopts. The embodiment of a passion and violence already present in the family, Heathcliff is the primary vehicle for Brontë's complex discussion of class, cruelty, and the interplay of love and the desire for vengeance. Although like the novels by Eliot mentioned above, *Wuthering Heights* is not generally classed as a sensation novel, and although Brontë's novel and the assortment of adoption works by Eliot all take different approaches to adoption, in each case we again see adoption marking areas of domestic discord and raising questions about which matters more, nature or nurture. Quite clearly, these issues preyed on the Victorian mind.

Wuthering Heights, as critic Tess O'Toole has pointed out, is one of a number of Victorian novels that use adoption to express concern about the disruption of standard inheritance practice.[21] Among other texts, O'Toole instances Charlotte Yonge's *Hopes and Fears* (1859), in which an unmarried adoptive mother inherits an estate from a cousin but hesitates to bequeath it to her son since there is no blood tie linking him to its source, and Craik's *King Arthur*, which after prolonged discussion finally identifies the adopted son as the ideal heir to the family property—and symbolically to the nation. The presence in Victorian literature of the mini-genre of texts in which adoption functions to dramatize inheritance anxiety is suggestive. We may connect it to Victorian science's eventual preoccupation with eugenics, which was similarly fixated on preserving good blood and keeping bad blood at bay, and to the xenophobia that animated many Britons in the nineteenth century. In an age punctuated by revolutions against established authority in various Continental countries, and in an empire in which Anglo-Saxons maintained a sometimes tenuous rule over supposedly uncivilized and inferior non-European peoples, anything smacking of otherness could look threatening. Conversely, representations of adoption that identify the adoptee of dubious background as someone who may readily be assimilated into the world of the gentry—Collins's *The Dead Secret*, for example—simultaneously reassure middle- and upper-class readers that the lower orders are not out to get them and interrogate the social system that draws lines of privilege between one group of people and the next.

It is also worth recalling our earlier discussion of the parental duties frequently undertaken by aunts and uncles. Narratives about children raised by family members other than their parents are particularly common in Victorian literature. To name only a few instances: Jane Eyre spends her first ten years under the resentful care of her uncle's widow. Elizabeth Barrett Browning's Aurora Leigh is also reared by her aunt, as is Esther Summerson in Dickens's *Bleak House* (1852–1853). Pip in *Great Expectations* (1860–1861) falls to the care of his shrewish older sister and her kindly husband, although in the pairing of Estella and Miss Havisham the novel also explores single-parent adoption by a nonrelative, here motivated by a desire for revenge rather than a hankering after motherhood. The children in Flora Shaw's *Castle Blair* (1878) live with an elderly bachelor uncle and the title character of Juliana Ewing's *Jackanapes* (1886) with an elderly spinster great-aunt, while Charlotte Yonge's Countess Kate moves around from one uncle or aunt to another. There are, of course, many additional examples.

While Novy notes that within the nineteenth-century adoption fiction that she examines, aunts and sisters who function as adoptive mothers are treated more harshly than uncles, brothers, and unrelated men who take on a paternal role,[22] this pattern tends to dissipate as we increase our sample size. The large number of unpleasant or self-involved uncles in Victorian novels who fail the nieces or nephews who depend on them calls to mind the anxiety often felt during this period about the emotional distance that separated many Victorian fathers from their children. The fictional presence of cold-hearted aunts who seek to dominate and thwart their charges both distinguishes the woman who is not a genuine mother from the maternal ideal and allows authors to critique the failings of mothers without seeming to attack the sanctity of motherhood. Conversely, when a relative takes on a parental role in a positive way, the reader is led to conclude that family—any family—is a blessing and that perhaps merely occupying the role of father or mother is enough to bring out the best in a person, both messages that help to advance nineteenth-century domestic ideals.

Another frequent preoccupation of the Victorian literature of adoption is the "lost heir" motif, in which the adoptee is revealed to be not an emissary from the social underworld but a rightful member of the upper classes. Because this device is a stock plot twist of melodrama, it was sometimes used for comic effect. Consider, for instance, W. S. Gilbert and Arthur S. Sullivan's operetta *The Pirates of Penzance* (1880), whose respectability-craving hero has been brought up by a band of pirates because his nanny misheard instructions issued by his biological parents. Equally over the top is Oscar Wilde's play *The Importance of Being Earnest* (1895), in which the hero's foundling status is traced not to illegitimacy but to the carelessness of a nurse who left him in a piece of luggage at a train station when he was a baby.

But lost heirs appear as well in works intended seriously. Despite an extremely disadvantageous start in life, Dickens's Oliver Twist, who moves from a workhouse to an unpromising and short-lived apprenticeship and subsequently to a nest of thieves, is consistently incorruptible, apparently a sign of what turn out to be his aristocratic bloodlines. The heroine of R. D. Blackmore's historical novel *Lorna Doone* (1869) similarly triumphs over her upbringing by the clan of bandits who killed her biological parents. Although she wrongly believes herself to be closely related to the lawless Doones, Lorna escapes both them and the worldly demands of her title and lineage in order to settle down with an upstanding young farmer in a peaceful and idealized country life, a denouement that suggests that the bourgeoisie is the true nobility of England. Even Kipling's Mowgli stories, about an Indian boy raised by wolves who eventually must take his place among humans, may be considered a variant of the lost heir tale type, while they simultaneously illustrate the nineteenth-century interest in the feral child—who, in being reared by forest animals, sometimes seemed to readers of the time to shed light on children "dragged up" in the worst urban slums.

The lost heir narrative considerably predates the Victorian period; we may find it in texts from earlier centuries, such as the French romance *Valentine and Orson* (translated into English in 1550) and Shakespeare's *The Winter's Tale,* among many other examples. The popularity of the device in the nineteenth century, however, speaks not only to the era's love of melodrama but also to other preoccupations of the day, including the frequent desire to see the well born as naturally, not merely environmentally, different from the poor. Raise a human child among wolves (or the supposedly subhuman poor), some authors suggest, and he will still grow up to be human. Yet just as various Victorian writers contradicted Kipling by producing accounts of feral children who had proved unreclaimable, there is considerable dissent among nineteenth-century tellers of adoption tales over whether heredity or upbringing is more important. This debate reminds us of the degree to which understandings of the meaning of "family" varied from individual to individual in the nineteenth century—as, indeed, they continue to vary today.

STEPMOTHERS AND STEPFATHERS IN VICTORIAN FICTION

Adoption fiction may be divided between works in which the adoptive parent is a considerable improvement over the biological one (*Silas Marner* is a good example of such a text) and works in which the adoptive parent is distant or abusive. The fiction of stepparenting contains the same split. Yet because stepparents were more common than adoptive parents in Victorian England, there are many more texts to choose from, and the proportion of unfavorable portraits of stepparents may seem rather higher. Somewhat counterintuitively given the era's interest in the blood tie, Victorian adoption fiction is more likely to take a negative view of the new parent when he or she is already related to the child by birth or marriage; strangers tend to get the benefit of the doubt. Stepparents, however, are often presumed to see their partners' children as more or less inconvenient encumbrances, accepted as the price of a desirable marriage. This literary trope permitted Victorian novelists to explore a number of issues relating not merely to blended families but also to families more generally: the feeling shared by many children that their parents are more interested in each other than in their offspring; the jealousy that one spouse, in Victorian fiction commonly the husband, may feel about the other's sexual past; the extent to which family life may be governed by convention rather than by sincere affection. While some literary stepparents are fully as admirable as the exemplary adoptive father Silas Marner, many offer their creators an opportunity to critique parenthood. And if the wicked uncles of Victorian fiction are usually motivated by the desire for financial gain, the unpleasant stepparents may simply dislike children—arguably a still worse sin against the cult of domesticity.

For many readers, Mr. Murdstone in Dickens's *David Copperfield* (1849–1850) is the archetype of the nasty Victorian stepfather. He is cold, domineering, and entirely without sympathy; he overawes his childlike wife and refuses to do his duty by his stepson. His first step is to oust David from the family by exiling him to a dreary boarding school, away from his mother's love. After Mrs. Copperfield's untimely death (attributable to her husband's harshness), and with the support of his equally unprepossessing sister, he seeks to sabotage David's membership in the middle classes by consigning him to a life of menial labor. David's solution, apparently the only remedy possible, is to defy his stepfather's authority and sever the relationship by running away to his paternal aunt, Betsey Trotwood.

Dickens was much influenced by the fairy tales that he loved as a child, and in the traumatic substitution of the rejecting false parents, Mr. and Miss Murdstone, for the affectionate widowed mother entirely absorbed in her son, we may perceive a pattern familiar from stories such as "Snow White": the attentive mother is suddenly removed and replaced with an evil witch. Following the lead of the pioneering fairy-tale interpreter Bruno Bettelheim, psychoanalytic critics have seen in tales of this sort a veiled exploration of the young child's resentment that the parent, formerly responsive to the infant's needs, becomes less responsive as these needs become too complex to be subject to quick fixes such as a feeding or a diaper change. Within the specific contexts of Victorian England and Dickens's own experiences, however, *David Copperfield*'s project may be somewhat different. For one thing, the novel's indirect comments on Dickens's life appear to have less to do with his infancy than with the trauma that he underwent at age twelve, when his father was jailed for debt and the family accompanied him to prison—with the single exception of young Charles, who was sent to work in a blacking warehouse. Dickens's deep resentment of his sudden exile from childhood and from parental care informs not only *David Copperfield* but also the portraits of neglected children that feature in many of his other works.

In other words, one element that makes Mr. and Miss Murdstone so horrific is that they demonstrate the failure of the biological father and mother to fulfill their parental duties, a failure that Dickens blamed in his own parents as well. The dead Mr. Copperfield is not present to protect or provide for his wife and child; the living Mrs. Copperfield can be prevented from making a home for her son. The role of stepparent is thus an aperture through which something malevolent may enter the family to fill an emptiness that is already there. Moreover, since stepparents lack the ties of blood that may encourage sympathy and understanding between parent and child, they may demonstrate in exaggerated form the negative side of the fatherly or motherly role. Mr. Murdstone prides himself on his firmness and mastery, qualities that many Victorians deemed essential to the good father. Miss Murdstone, like the good Victorian mother, considers it her duty to look to David's moral training. In both cases, however, from the standpoint of the child in their power, these apparently promising qualities are disastrous.

Yet detestable as he is, Mr. Murdstone may nonetheless be preferable to stepfathers such as Dr. Roylott in Arthur Conan Doyle's "The Adventure of the Speckled Band" (1892), who kills one of his wife's daughters by means of a poisonous snake. This unusual murder weapon seems symbolic of Roylott's treachery and evil, and hints at unpleasant sexual overtones as well. Moreover, its associations with the Garden of Eden appropriately suggest the destruction of the innocence of the home environment with the intrusion of the new parent, which is followed by the death of the girls' mother. The doctor's crime has financial roots, as he seeks to secure the daughters' inheritance to himself; this motivation helps to establish him as the antithesis of the good Victorian father, who was expected to bring money into the family rather than siphoning it off. Dr. Roylott thus demonstrates that the stepparent tale could manifest the same anxiety about inheritance that characterizes many Victorian adoption narratives: here too, the lack of a blood tie proves dangerous and unsettling, causing money to flow from the second generation to the first instead of the other way around. Yet he may also be a manifestation of another form of anxiety, namely the concern that many middle-class Victorians felt about masculinity itself, and particularly the deleterious effect that masculine sexuality and selfishness might have on the home.

"Our mother died [in Ceylon], when we were little children. We have had a wretched existence. She made [her husband] our guardian, and he was a miserly wretch who grudged us food to eat, and clothes to wear. . . . This stepfather of ours was a cruel brute as well as a grinding one. It was well he died when he did, or I might have killed him."

Mr Crisparkle stopped short in the moonlight and looked at his hopeful pupil in consternation.

"I surprise you, sir?" he said, with a quick change to a submissive manner.

"You shock me; unspeakably shock me."

The pupil hung his head for a little while, as they walked on, and then said: "You never saw him beat your sister. I have seen him beat mine, more than once or twice, and I never forgot it."

—Charles Dickens, *The Mystery of Edwin Drood* (1870), Chapter 7

Men such as Doyle's Dr. Roylott, Dickens's Mr. Murdstone and the stepfather of Neville and Helena Landless in *The Mystery of Edwin Drood*, and Ozias Midwinter's abusive stepfather in Collins's *Armadale* (1866), are extreme examples of bad behavior, at least in the context of their middle-class status. (As we have seen earlier in this chapter, Victorian commentators often expected the worst of stepparents lower down on the social scale.) Other fictional stepfathers, however, sin more by error than by deliberate intent. Elizabeth Gaskell's short fiction contains at least two such men, William Preston in "The Half-Brothers" and Thomas Openshaw in "The Manchester Marriage" (both 1858). Preston favors his biological son over his stepson, Gregory, whom he regards as a dullard until the latter sacrifices his life to save his half-brother. Confronted with Gregory's heroic act, Preston recognizes his own injustice and does what he can to atone for it by burying the young man with the deceased Mrs. Preston; Preston's final resting-place will be at the grave's foot. The story hints that Gregory's intellectual backwardness is in some measure created by Preston, who resents his existence and blames a piece of childish mischief on his part with having brought about Mrs. Preston's premature and fatal labor. As his biological father's stand-in, Gregory thus becomes the object of Preston's feelings of inferiority (the stepfather considers that Gregory is his all-too-successful rival for Mrs. Preston's love) and guilt (Mrs. Preston's death in childbirth might better be laid at her husband's door than at her three-year-old son's).

"The Manchester Marriage" similarly suggests that a husband's sexual jealousy of his rival is a likely source of domestic discord. In this story, Alice Openshaw has first married her sailor cousin, Frank Wilson, son of the sea captain in whose home Alice had lived after being orphaned. Upon the death of Frank's father and the disappearance of Frank's ship, Alice and her stepmother-in-law make ends meet by taking in a lodger, the self-made Openshaw. Captivated by Alice and Frank's disabled daughter, Ailsie, Openshaw marries Alice and does his best to make both mother and daughter happy. But the long absent Frank returns, revealing himself only to Alice's faithful servant Norah. Appalled to learn that her mistress has committed inadvertent bigamy and that her son by Openshaw is illegitimate, Norah seeks to hush Frank by giving him a few minutes' access to the nursery so that he may see the sleeping Ailsie. The maneuver is successful in that Frank departs without encountering his wife, but when it comes out that Norah has admitted a strange man into the household, she is suspected of stealing (or of abetting a thief) and dismissed. Frank, meanwhile, drowns himself. When the truth is revealed to Openshaw, like Preston in "The Half-Brothers" he undergoes a transformation, vowing to "lay [Frank's] head in the grave, as if he were my only brother . . . how he must have hated me! I cannot go home to my wife till all that I can do for him is done." After the burial, he begins "to look upon [Alice] as some one sacred, and to be treated with reverence as well as tenderness"; when Alice dies and Openshaw conducts Ailsie to Frank's grave to tell her the family secret, "for the sad fate of that poor father whom she had never seen, he shed the only tears she ever saw fall from his eyes."[23]

The mistaken identification of Frank as a thief is psychologically appropriate here, since ownership is the central issue in the story: which man properly has title to Alice and Ailsie? Frank has jeopardized his claim by his extended absence and his failure to provide for his womenfolk; the more financially successful stay-at-home Openshaw has fathered Frank's daughter, supported his stepmother, and provided for Alice the vocal and physical expressions of affection that her earlier marriage lacked. Frank's is the legal and biological claim, but Openshaw is the man in possession. And while Openshaw retains his title to both wife and child in the eyes of society, and Frank (whose suicide implies that he finds that title superior to his own) is relegated to a gravestone that identifies him only by his initials, Openshaw's consciousness of his real lack of standing changes his life. The dynamics of this story thus have much to tell us about the ambivalence that middle-class Victorian society apparently felt on the subjects of serial marriage and biological parenting versus nurturance.

Preston and Openshaw are both men whose feelings run strong, which both creates difficulties within their households and helps to secure the reader's ultimate sympathy for these stepfathers. In her final novel, *Wives and Daughters* (1864–1866), Gaskell creates a blended family in which each parent has one biological daughter and one stepdaughter. While the husband, Dr. Gibson, is more interested in his work than in emotion, he is presented as a likeable man and a responsible parent who develops real affection for his stepdaughter, Cynthia Kirkpatrick. In contrast, his wife is held up to narrative ridicule as a woman so self-absorbed that even Cynthia, her biological daughter, is effectively a kind of stepchild. Through her relationship to Cynthia and Cynthia's stepsister, Molly Gibson, Mrs. Gibson is revealed as shallow and hypocritical, incapable of the love that is supposed to be her major domestic function and yet eager to convince everyone within earshot that she is an exceptionally devoted wife and mother.

The Victorian cult of domesticity exalted the middle-class mother as a fount of sympathy. Mrs. Gibson's near-total lack of this quality, though, is typical of many nineteenth-century fictional stepmothers. Collins offers us the stepmother of the title character in *Poor Miss Finch* (1872), who, though busy with her own fourteen children, nevertheless has time to spare for her addiction to romance novels—but none for her blind stepdaughter, with whom she has nothing in common and in whom she takes no interest. Charlotte Yonge creates an exemplary stepmother in *The Young Step-Mother* (1861); although the title character inevitably makes mistakes in handling her husband's three half-grown children, she is sincerely committed to their moral and emotional well-being and to creating a better understanding between them and their father. Yet in *The Castle Builders* (1854), Yonge dissects a mother/stepmother very like Gaskell's Hyacinth Gibson. The three Berners girls are the daughters of a British army officer serving in India, who died soon after the girls (like Rudyard and Trix Kipling) were sent back to England to be fostered by a stranger. Their mother remained in India and married a general, gaining a stepson already in boarding school in England. Some years later the new Lady Willoughby and her husband return to England and assemble their combined children in a single household. While the girls are eager to love their mother, her dismissive attitude toward her stepson, a young man of exceptionally good character, gradually and painfully reveals to them her lack of deep feeling and moral discernment.

Yonge's sense of filial duty was unusually strong even by Victorian standards, and her fiction does not typically encourage its readers (many of whom were middle-class girls and young women) to identify flaws in their parents. Lady Willoughby and her second husband, however, and particularly Lady Willoughby, are among the exceptions to this generalization, as they consistently demonstrate their moral inferiority to young Frank Willoughby and their inability to appreciate or emulate the virtues that he embodies. Similarly, while Collins generally treats mothers kindly and often exempts them from the satire and grotesquerie that mark his approach to other sorts of characters, Mrs. Finch comes across unusually badly. Gaskell, too, usually offers her readers positive visions of motherhood, a role that redeems the fallen title character in *Ruth* (1853), lends interest to the heroine's mother in *Sylvia's Lovers* (1863), and imbues the dour mother of the hero of *North and South* (1854–1855) with whatever attractiveness she may have. Yet Hyacinth Gibson, so eager to use the social clout of Victorian maternity to make herself look good, is a signal failure in the part. For all these authors, the title of stepmother seems to be a way of communicating to readers that these women are not "real" mothers (even though they have biological children as well), and thus not genuine women either.

Given the large number of stepparents included among the Victorian reading public, the presence in Victorian fiction of so many hostile portraits of middle-class members of this group may seem surprising. Surely some readers must have taken offense? Yet in a culture in which etiquette books could take for granted that a stepmother's affection for her husband's children would be lukewarm at best, and child-rearing mores dictated that those who could afford to do so would hire nannies and governesses and the staffs of boarding schools to rear their children, we may discern an awareness that adults may not feel an instinctive liking or sympathy for children. Indeed, that awareness permeates the Victorian approach to constructed families of all kinds. The sponsors of schemes for child emigration, the investigators tracking down suspected baby farmers, and for that matter the members of the National Society for the Prevention of Cruelty to Children (who certainly did not confine themselves to looking at stepfamilies or adoptive parents) all harbored no illusions that adults were uniformly well disposed toward the children in their power. As we have seen throughout this study, the cult of domesticity existed in tandem with what we might see as a counterbalancing cult of realism, in which the snug nests of the idealized middle-class Victorian family might have much darker variants. The nineteenth-century discourse on stepfamilies and foster families was only one convenient forum for these variants' discussion.

EPILOGUE

As this book has sought to demonstrate, understandings of family in Victorian England were complex. On the one hand, many believed it to be the potential salvation of the nation, as the counterbalance to drives that threatened to become destructive when indulged in irresponsibly, such as the sexual urge and the desire for financial profit. On the other hand, others saw family as potentially destructive on its own account, an institution that often demanded endless sacrifice (particularly from women) and sometimes offered few rewards, or that perpetuated a cycle of criminality and destitution among the lower orders of society. Some considered family an intensely conservative and stabilizing force, whether the things that it perpetuated were good or bad; others deemed it the key to reform. Throughout the period, legislators proposed and sometimes adopted bills to ameliorate problems affecting English families on all socioeconomic levels, simultaneously paying homage to the strength and moral beauty of the concept. That a single product of Victorian culture may contain many mutually contradictory messages on the virtues or flaws of domestic existence testifies to the ambivalence with which many people in the nineteenth century regarded this subject, and the degree to which the realities of daily life often conflicted with widely accepted ideals.

The importance assigned to family by both its worshipers and its detractors had practical purposes—clearly, too many to enumerate here, but a brief list may serve to suggest the variety and compass of functions involved. First, unruly individuals might be controlled by establishing that they were not living up to their assigned family roles. Thus, for instance, an Annie Besant could be chastised for continuing to publish birth-control information in defiance of the obscenity laws by losing custody of her daughter; an Evelyn Murray, when her relations decided that she was an unredeemably flawed daughter, could be stripped of her identity and exiled to the Continent; an unemployed and abusive working-class father, who beat his children instead of providing for them, could have his parental rights abrogated. Second, various social causes, including among many others universal education, female suffrage, and the fight against sexually transmitted diseases, could be championed or impeded if one connected them rhetorically to family. A legislator who might be inclined to support married women's property rights on their own merits might withhold that support if he believed that the enactment of such a measure could undermine marriage by sapping husbandly authority, while individuals who considered that a large supply of cheap labor was not in their economic best interests might find that highlighting the negative effects of working mothers on family life was a good way to gain laws limiting women's employment in certain industries. And finally, in the realm of artistic expression, images of family could be manipulated to further the emotional effect that a literary or visual work had on its audience, a circumstance that contributed not only to the popularity of many examples of "high art" but also to the effectiveness of Victorian advertising.

If the importance assigned to family by a wide variety of commentators with a correspondingly wide variety of agendas remained constant over the Victorian period, little else did. Some historians have argued that the Queen's lengthy reign casts a spurious aura of cohesiveness over the era and that it would be less misleading to consider (say) the period from the Reform Bill of 1832 to the Reform Bill of 1867 as one unit, the years from 1867 to the Golden Jubilee of 1887 as another, and the late 1880s and 1890s as culturally part of the pleasure-loving reign of Edward VII. Whether or not we accept this argument, it is useful to bear in mind that in many ways the families of the 1840s did not occupy the same world as those of the 1890s. Changes in the birth and death rates, quality-of-life differences as technology advanced and the economy shifted from an agricultural to an urban-industrial ground, and evolving attitudes on such key subjects as gender roles and religious belief, among other factors, contributed to a transformation of family life on all levels of society. While the speed and extent of social change in the nineteenth century help to explain why so many Victorian commentators saw family as a reassuringly constant presence, something to cling to in an unstable world, in fact the domestic sphere was undergoing metamorphoses comparable to those on display in other realms.

In addition to the changes imposed by modernization, the Victorians experienced the shifts in individual roles that are an inevitable part of growing up. We expect different things of babies than of adolescents, different things of wage-earning adults in their forties than of pensioners in their eighties. These expectations are not always easy to meet. Nor do they remain altogether stable from one generation to the next; consider the extent to which the stereotype of the middle-class American mother has changed between the 1950s and the beginning of the twenty-first century. (When I was growing up in the 1970s, very few mothers of my acquaintance worked outside the home.) Victorian society, like our own, provided countless texts to describe what was appropriate for particular family members at different socioeconomic levels. Proper behavior for a teenaged daughter from the professional classes, a semiskilled workingman with a wife and family to keep, a boy beginning boarding school, and so on were all recorded in detail in genres ranging from advice manuals to fiction to magazine articles.

Naturally, not everyone agreed on the specifics of these roles. Factors such as religious affiliation, membership in a particular political party, educational background, location (rural or urban, for example), wage earners' occupation(s), financial circumstances, and individual personality and family situation influenced the conception of wife/mother/daughter/sister, husband/father/son/brother, from household to household. In some families aunts, uncles, and cousins mattered enormously; in others they were actually or practically nonexistent. In families in which one of the parents had died, the older children might assume considerably more responsibility than was demanded of a child from a similarly situated family with two living parents. A man with no sons might permit his daughters more education and autonomy than would have fallen to their lot if they had possessed brothers. A working-class woman whose husband was disabled would almost certainly have to become her family's breadwinner, whereas her neighbor might stay home while her children were young. That is, however convenient the shorthand, we should be wary of speaking about "the Victorian father," or even about "the upper-middle-class Victorian father in the 1890s," without bearing in mind that such expressions *are* shorthand. Family roles have never been one-size-fits-all, and the wide variation in individual circumstances helps to account for the disparate attitudes toward the emotional healthiness and moral promise of family life.

Definitions of family varied as well—again, as they do today. Upon encountering the scene in which Godfrey Cass reveals himself to his biological daughter and invites her to define him as her father and consider Silas Marner merely a kindly volunteer to whom her rearing has been delegated, many of George Eliot's readers would have found Godfrey's case compelling. After all, contracting out the care of one's children was by no means unusual in the mid-nineteenth century, although surely one reason for writing *Silas Marner* was to persuade the sort of readers who would instinctively have supported Godfrey's claim to rethink their position. Yet England's lack of an adoption law, like the prevalence of cultural suspicion about stepparents, suggests among other things a belief that family ties are above all ties of blood. Conversely, the difficulties encountered by the Deceased Wife's Sister Bill, like the support given to certain reformers' efforts to remove children from their families of origin, indicate that blood was not always the issue; it could be trumped by religion, respectability, or law. Although a man might not be biological kin to his wife's sister or his brother's widow, legally his marriage to either kind of sister-in-law would be a form of incest—whereas first cousins could marry each other even if they were the products of a double marriage involving two sets of siblings.

And under the right circumstances, the family ties of the poor could be set aside at the desire of the governing classes. In any society, "family" is whatever consensus within that society decrees it to be, and as consensus is continually open to negotiation, rules of kinship are subject to change, although change is usually difficult to bring about. The areas of debate where the Victorian family is concerned help to illuminate points about which the culture was particularly doubtful, such as (in the case of child émigrés separated from failed parents) whether heredity or environment was more potent, and whether title to a child should rest ultimately with the parents or the state.

Indeed, studying the Victorian family, whether through historical fact, "life writing" (memoirs, journals, and letters), imaginative literature, or a combination of all of these, can provide today's scholars with unique insights into this fascinating society. Child-rearing practices reveal much about accepted views of human nature in the nineteenth century, for example, just as attitudes toward parenting tell us much not only about approaches to domesticity but also about approaches to realms sometimes taken to be separate from parenting, chief among them the world of work. But in addition to developing a fuller sense of the life of Victorian England, examining Victorian family life offers us an enhanced understanding of our own society—both through what we retain of Victorian culture and what we find most alienating in it.

NOTES

INTRODUCTION

1. T. R. Edmonds, "On the Mortality of Infants in England," *Lancet* 25 (January 30, 1836): 690–694.

2. This courtroom moment is quoted by Karen Offen, "Liberty, Equality and Justice for Women: The Theory and Practice of Feminism in Nineteenth Century Europe," in Renate Bridenthal, Claudia Koonz, and Susan Stuard, eds., *Becoming Visible: Women in European History*, 2nd ed. (Boston: Houghton Mifflin, 1987). Available online at http://www.st-andrews.ac.uk/jfec/cal/suffrage/document/theofemm.htm, p. 13, accessed March 10, 2006.

CHAPTER 1

1. See, for instance, Booth's comments in the "Poverty" section of his first volume on the class that he identifies as consisting of day laborers, porters, factory workers, and the like, in which "the women work a good deal to eke out the men's earnings," and "The comfort of their homes depends, even more than in other classes, on a good wife. Thrift of the 'make-the-most-of-everything' kind is what is needed." These remarks are reprinted in *Charles Booth's London: A Portrait of the Poor at the Turn of the Century, Drawn from His "Life and Labour of the People of London,"* selected and edited by Albert Fried and Richard M. Elman (New York: Pantheon, 1968), p. 18.

2. Harriet Martineau, "Female Industry," *Edinburgh Review* (April 1859), rpt. Susan Hamilton, ed., *"Criminals, Idiots, Women, and Minors": Victorian Writing by Women on Women* (Peterborough, Ontario: Broadview Press, 1995), pp. 29–70.

3. John R. Gillis, *For Better, for Worse: British Marriages, 1600 to the Present* (New York: Oxford University Press, 1985), p. 244.

4. Thomas Wright, *Some Habits and Customs of the Working Classes* (London: Tinsley Bros., 1867), rpt. Lee Jackson, ed., *The Victorian Dictionary: Exploring Victorian*

London. Available online at http://www.victorianlondon.org/publications/habits-11. htm, accessed July 24, 2004.

5. "Hints to Make Home Happy: To Husbands" and "More Hints to Make Home Happy: To Wives," *Punch* (January–June 1844), rpt. Lee Jackson, ed., *The Victorian Dictionary: Exploring Victorian London.* Available online at http://www.victorianlondon. org/women/husbands.htm and http://www.victorianlondon.org/women/wives.htm, accessed July 24, 2004.

6. Pat Jalland, *Women, Marriage and Politics 1860–1914* (Oxford: Clarendon Press, 1986), pp. 66–67.

7. Charles B. Tayler, *Edward, or Almost an Owenite* (London: Religious Tract Society, 1840).

8. Cited in Jeanne MacKenzie, *A Victorian Courtship: The Story of Beatrice Potter and Sidney Webb* (New York: Oxford University Press, 1979), p. 4.

9. Wright, *Some Habits and Customs of the Working Classes,* p. 194.

10. "Good Breeding: Part I," *The Family Economist* 3 (1850): 27–29.

11. Mary Montgomerie Singleton, "Two Moods of a Man: By a Woman," *The Nineteenth Century* 31 (February 1892): 208–223.

12. William Schooling, "Marriage Institutions," *Westminster Review* 135(4) (April 1891): 385–395.

13. Swiney's work is discussed in George Robb, "Race Motherhood: Moral Eugenics vs. Progressive Eugenics, 1880–1920," in Claudia Nelson and Ann Sumner Holmes, eds., *Maternal Instincts: Visions of Motherhood and Sexuality in Britain, 1875–1925* (Houndmills, Basingstoke: Macmillan, 1997), pp. 58–74.

14. Amy Milne-Smith, "A Flight to Domesticity? Making a Home in the Gentlemen's Clubs of London, 1880–1914," *Journal of British Studies* 45(4) (October 2006): 796–818.

15. Lesley Hall, "Eyes Tightly Shut, Lying Rigidly Still, and Thinking of England? British Women and Sex from Marie Stopes to Hite 2000," in Claudia Nelson and Michelle M. Martin, eds., *Sexual Pedagogies: Sex Education in Britain, Australia, and America, 1879–2000* (New York: Palgrave Macmillan, 2004), pp. 53–71.

16. MacKenzie, *A Victorian Courtship,* pp. 95, 118–119.

17. Jalland, *Women, Marriage and Politics 1860–1914,* pp. 83–84 and 92–93.

18. Kathryn Hughes, *George Eliot: The Last Victorian* (New York: Farrar, Straus, Giroux, 1998), pp. 144–149.

19. Geoffrey Robinson, *Hedingham Harvest: Victorian Family Life in Rural England* (London: Century Hutchinson, 1989), pp. 23–28.

CHAPTER 2

1. John Ruskin, "Of Queens' Gardens," *Sesame and Lilies* (Boston: Houghton Mifflin, n.d.), p. 74.

2. Cited in Pat Jalland, *Women, Marriage and Politics 1860–1914* (Oxford: Clarendon Press, 1986), p. 160.

3. Albert Fried and Richard M. Elman, eds., *Charles Booth's London: A Portrait of the Poor at the Turn of the Century, Drawn from His "Life and Labour of the People in London"* (New York: Pantheon, 1968), p. 292.

4. George K. Behlmer, *Friends of the Family: The English Home and Its Guardians, 1850–1940* (Stanford: Stanford University Press, 1998), p. 25.

5. [Walter Austin?], *"One Dinner a Week" and "Travels in the East"* (High Wycombe, Buckinghamshire: Peter Marcan, 1987), p. 27.

6. John Tosh, *A Man's Place: Masculinity and the Middle-Class Home in Victorian England* (New Haven, CT: Yale University Press, 1999), p. 79.

7. Ibid., pp. 79–101.

8. David Newsome, *Godliness & Good Learning* (London: Cassell, 1961), pp. 152–153.

9. Nancy Fix Anderson, "'Not a Fit or Proper Person': Annie Besant's Struggle for Child Custody, 1878–79," in Claudia Nelson and Ann Sumner Holmes, eds., *Maternal Instincts: Visions of Motherhood and Sexuality in Britain, 1875–1925* (Houndmills, Basingstoke: Macmillan, 1997), pp. 13–36.

CHAPTER 3

1. Amy Milne-Smith, "A Flight to Domesticity? Making a Home in the Gentlemen's Clubs of London, 1880–1914," *Journal of British Studies* 45(4) (October 2006): 796–818, 801.

2. Lyndall P. Hopkinson, *Nothing to Forgive: A Daughter's Story of Antonia White* (London: Chatto & Windus, 1988), p. 21.

3. Nigel Nicolson, *Portrait of a Marriage* (New York: Bantam, 1973), pp. 48–52.

4. Pat Jalland, *Women, Marriage and Politics 1860–1914* (Oxford: Clarendon Press, 1986), pp. 276–279.

5. Ibid., pp. 268–272.

6. Julia Courtney, "The *Barnacle*: A Manuscript Magazine of the 1860s," Claudia Nelson and Lynne Vallone, eds., *The Girl's Own: Cultural Histories of the Anglo-American Girl, 1830–1915* (Athens: University of Georgia Press, 1994), pp. 71–97.

7. See Sally Cline, *Radclyffe Hall: A Woman Called John* (New York: Overlook Press, 1998), p. 31.

8. Siân Busby, *The Cruel Mother: A Memoir* (New York: Carroll and Graf, 2005), pp. 61–63.

9. Anna Davin, *Growing Up Poor: Home, School and Street in London 1870–1914* (London: Rivers Oram Press, 1996), pp. 97–112.

10. Carol Dyhouse, *Girls Growing Up in Late Victorian and Edwardian England* (London: Routledge & Kegan Paul, 1981), pp. 84–86.

11. George R. Sims, *How the Poor Live* (London: Chatto, 1883, p. 29), rpt. Lee Jackson, ed., *The Victorian Dictionary: Exploring Victorian London*. Available online at http://www.victorianlondon.org/publications2/howthepoorlive-5.htm, accessed July 24, 2004.

CHAPTER 4

1. Valerie Sanders, *The Brother–Sister Culture in Nineteenth-Century Literature: From Austen to Woolf* (New York: Palgrave, 2002), pp. 34–43.

2. Leonore Davidoff and Catherine Hall, *Family Fortunes: Men and Women of the English Middle Class, 1780–1850* (Chicago: University of Chicago Press, 1987), p. 468.

3. Fred Kaplan, *Dickens: A Biography* (New York: William Morrow, 1988), p. 94.

4. Geoffrey Robinson, *Hedingham Harvest: Victorian Family Life in Rural England* (London: Century, 1989), pp. 41–42.

5. Quoted in Sally Cline, *Radclyffe Hall: A Woman Called John* (Woodstock, NY: Overlook Press, 1998), p. 111.

6. Quoted in Sanders, *The Brother–Sister Culture in Nineteenth-Century Literature,* p. 144.

7. Sanders, *The Brother–Sister Culture in Nineteenth-Century Literature,* passim.

8. Margaret Mare and Alicia C. Percival, *Victorian Best-Seller: The World of Charlotte M. Yonge* (London: Harrap, 1949), pp. 220–222. See also Christabel Coleridge, *Charlotte Mary Yonge: Her Life and Letters* (London: Macmillan, 1903).

9. For further details on Keary and Shaw, see Robert Lee Wolff, ed., *Masterworks of Children's Literature, Vol. 5, Part 2: 1837–1900, The Victorian Age* (New York: Chelsea House, 1985), pp. 201–203 and 429–431.

10. Ellice Hopkins, *The Power of Womanhood, or, Mothers and Sons: A Book for Parents and Those in Loco Parentis* (New York: Dutton, 1899), p. 157.

11. Kathryn Hughes, *George Eliot: The Last Victorian* (New York: Farrar, Straus, Giroux, 1998), p. 26.

12. Quoted in Regenia Gagnier, *Subjectivities: A History of Self-Representation in Britain, 1832–1920* (New York: Oxford University Press, 1991), p. 195.

13. George Eliot, *The Mill on the Floss* (New York: Norton, 1994), p. 121.

14. See Gagnier, *Subjectivities,* pp. 218–219.

15. Quoted in Carol Dyhouse, *Girls Growing Up in Late Victorian and Edwardian England* (London: Routledge & Kegan Paul, 1981), p. 10.

16. Quoted in Alethea Hayter, *Charlotte Yonge* (Plymouth, UK: Northcote House, 1996), p. 57.

17. Harriet Martineau, "Independent Industry for Women," *Daily News* (November 17, 1859), rpt. David J. Bradshaw and Suzanne Ozment, eds., *The Voice of Toil: Nineteenth-Century British Writings about Work* (Athens: Ohio University Press, 2000), p. 301.

18. Quoted in Sanders, *The Brother–Sister Culture in Nineteenth-Century Literature,* p. 73; see also pp. 69–78.

19. Quoted in Davidoff and Hall, *Family Fortunes,* p. 351.

20. Quoted in Hughes, *George Eliot,* pp. 340, 305.

21. Quoted in Louise DeSalvo, *Virginia Woolf: The Impact of Childhood Sexual Abuse on Her Life and Work* (Boston: Beacon Press, 1989), pp. 25–26. Laura was sent to live in the country, apart from the family, at age seventeen; she was permanently institutionalized at twenty-one, when Virginia was nine. DeSalvo suggests that her problems were emotional rather than intellectual, a product of her mother's death, her father's rejection of her, and, perhaps, sexual abuse by her stepbrothers.

22. Drawing on the report of the Parliamentary Commissioners in 1848, Adam Kuper notes, "In five districts in England, there were 1,364 unions within the prohibited degrees between 1835 and 1848. Of these, 90 per cent were with the deceased wife's sister." See "Incest, Cousin Marriage, and the Origin of the Human Sciences in Nineteenth-Century England," *Past and Present* 174(1) (2002): 158–183, 163.

23. Sally Mitchell, *Dinah Mulock Craik* (Boston: Twayne, 1983). Available online at http://www.victorianweb.org/authors/craik/mitchell/4.html, accessed May 16, 2006.

24. Nancy F. Anderson, "The 'Marriage with a Deceased Wife's Sister Bill' Controversy: Incest Anxiety and the Defense of Family Purity in Victorian England," *Journal of British Studies* 21(2) (Spring 1982): 67–86, 69, 73.

CHAPTER 5

1. Leonore Davidoff and Catherine Hall, *Family Fortunes: Men and Women of the English Middle Class, 1780–1850* (Chicago: University of Chicago Press, 1987), p. 388.

2. Di Cooper and Moira Donald, "Households and 'Hidden' Kin in Early Nineteenth-Century England: Four Case Studies in Suburban Exeter, 1821–1861," *Continuity and Change* 10(2) (1995): 257–278.

3. Michael Mason, *The Making of Victorian Sexuality* (New York: Oxford University Press, 1994), p. 71; George K. Behlmer, *Friends of the Family: The English Home and Its Guardians, 1850–1940* (Stanford: Stanford University Press, 1998), p. 275.

4. Dinah Maria Mulock [later Craik], *A Woman's Thoughts about Women* (London: Hurst & Blackett, 1858). Available online at http://www.indiana.edu/~letrs/vwwp/craik/thoughts.html, accessed May 15, 2006.

5. Noel Streatfeild, *A Vicarage Family* (London: Fontana, 1979), p. 91. One of Streatfeild's last books, *Gran-Nannie* (1976), is a biography of the woman who reared her father.

6. Agatha Christie, *Agatha Christie: An Autobiography* (New York: Dodd, Mead, 1977), pp. 15–17.

7. Siân Busby, *The Cruel Mother: A Memoir* (New York: Carroll and Graf, 2005), pp. 120–127.

8. Busby, *ibid.*, p. 163. For a discussion of lodgers, see Leonore Davidoff, Megan Doolittle, Janet Fink, and Katherine Holden, *The Family Story: Blood, Contract and Intimacy 1830–1960* (New York: Longman, 1999), pp. 178–182.

9. Albert Fried and Richard M. Elman, eds., *Charles Booth's London: A Portrait of the Poor at the Turn of the Century, Drawn from His "Life and Labour of the People in London"* (New York: Pantheon, 1968), p. 176.

10. Martha Vicinus, *Independent Women: Work and Community for Single Women, 1850–1920* (Chicago: University of Chicago Press, 1985), p. 23.

11. Eliza Lynn Linton, "Old Maids," *Belgravia* (1876), 478.

12. Teresa Mangum, "Growing Old: Age," in Herbert F. Tucker, ed., *A Companion to Victorian Literature and Culture* (Oxford: Blackwell, 1999), pp. 97–109.

13. Quoted in Alex Shoumatoff, "The Mountain of Names," *New Yorker* (May 13, 1985). Available online at http://www.dispatchesfromthevanishingworld.com/pastdispatches/mountain/mountain_printer.html, accessed May 15, 2006.

14. Geoffrey Robinson, *Hedingham Harvest: Victorian Family Life in Rural England* (London: Century, 1989), pp. 31–32.

15. Thomas Carlyle, *Past and Present* (New York: Charles Scribner's Sons, 1918), p. 173.

16. Cited in Adam Kuper, "Incest, Cousin Marriage, and the Origin of the Human Sciences in Nineteenth-Century England," *Past and Present* 174(1) (2002): 158–183, 171–172.

17. Malcolm T. Smith, "Estimates of Cousin Marriage and Mean Inbreeding in the United Kingdom from 'Birth Briefs,'" *Journal of the Biosocial Sciences* 33 (2001): 55–66, 59.

18. Kuper, "Incest, Cousin Marriage, and the Origin of the Human Sciences in Nineteenth-Century England," p. 173.

19. Davidoff and Hall, *Family Fortunes*, p. 221.

20. Alethea Hayter, *Charlotte Yonge* (Plymouth, UK: Northcote House, 1996), p. 5.

21. Julia Courtney, "The *Barnacle*: A Manuscript Magazine of the 1860s," in Claudia Nelson and Lynne Vallone, eds., *The Girl's Own: Cultural Histories of the Anglo-American Girl, 1830–1915* (Athens: University of Georgia Press, 1994), pp. 71–97, 74.

22. Davidoff and Hall, *Family Fortunes*, p. 354.

23. Davidoff, Doolittle, Fink, and Holden, *The Family Story*, p. 148.

24. Samuel Butler, *The Way of All Flesh* (Garden City: Doubleday, 1944), p. 144.

CHAPTER 6

1. George K. Behlmer, *Friends of the Family: The English Home and Its Guardians, 1850–1940* (Stanford: Stanford University Press, 1998), p. 299.

2. George R. Sims, *How the Poor Live* (London: Chatto & Windus, 1883, p. 24), rpt. Lee Jackson, ed., *The Victorian Dictionary: Exploring Victorian London*. Available online at http://www.victorianlondon.org, accessed July 24, 2004.

3. George R. Sims, quoted in Gertrude Himmelfarb, *Poverty and Compassion: The Moral Imagination of the Late Victorians* (New York: Vintage, 1992), p. 58. Another highly successful exposé of the period was the anonymous pamphlet *The Bitter Cry of Outcast London* (1883), also discussed in Himmelfarb.

4. Henry Mayhew, "Watercress Girl," *London Labour and the London Poor*, Vol. 1 (London: Griffin, Bohn, and Company, 1861), p. 152. Available online at http://etext.lib.virginia.edu/toc/modeng/public/MayLond.html, accessed January 11, 2005.

5. "Murder in Stepney," London *Times* (May 31, 1870), rpt. Lee Jackson, ed., *The Victorian Dictionary: Exploring Victorian London*. Available online at http://www.victorianlondon.org/crime/stepneymurder.htm, accessed May 29, 2006.

6. Thomas Archer, *The Terrible Sights of London, and Labours of Love in the Midst of Them* (London: Stanley Rivers and Co., 1870, p. 17), rpt. Lee Jackson, ed., *The Victorian Dictionary: Exploring Victorian London*. Available online at http://victorianlondon.org/publications/terriblesights-1.htm, accessed May 29, 2006.

7. Siân Busby, *The Cruel Mother: A Memoir* (New York: Carroll and Graf, 2005), pp. 267–269.

8. Albert Fried and Richard M. Elman, eds., *Charles Booth's London: A Portrait of the Poor at the Turn of the Century, Drawn from His "Life and Labour of the People in London"* (New York: Pantheon, 1968), pp. 29–30, 86, 176.

9. D. Rice-Jones, *In the Slums: Pages from the Note-Book of a Diocesan Home Missionary* (London: James Nisbet & Co., 1884, pp. 82–83), rpt. Lee Jackson, ed., *The Victorian Dictionary: Exploring Victorian London*. Available online at http://www.victorianlondon.org/publications6/slums-14.htm, accessed May 29, 2006.

10. Behlmer, *Friends of the Family*, p. 287.

11. John Macpherson, Introduction to *God's Answers: A Record of Miss Annie Macpherson's Work at the Home of Industry, Spitalfields, London, and in Canada*, by Clara M. S. Lowe (London: J. Nisbet, 1882). Available online at http://www.gutenberg.org/dirs/etext04/godsa10.txt, accessed May 30, 2006.

12. Edith Plowden, "Fond Memory," unpublished manuscript, Baldwin Papers, University of Sussex Library, cited in Thomas Pinney, ed., *Rudyard Kipling: Something of Myself and Other Autobiographical Writings* (New York: Cambridge University Press, 1990), p. 223, n.14.

13. Cora L. Díaz de Chumaceiro, "On Rudyard Kipling's Loss of Ayah," *PsyArt: A Hyperlink Journal for the Psychological Study of the Arts*, article 030802 (2003), n.p. Available online at http://www.clas.ufl.edu/ipsa/journal/2003_diaz_de_chumeceiro01. shtml, accessed June 3, 2006.

14. Quoted in Nancy Fix Anderson, *Woman against Women in Victorian England: A Life of Eliza Lynn Linton* (Bloomington: Indiana University Press, 1987), p. 83.

15. Anderson, *Woman against Women in Victorian England*, pp. 81–82.

16. Martha Vicinus, *Independent Women: Work and Community for Single Women, 1850–1920* (Chicago: University of Chicago Press, 1985), p. 44.

17. Behlmer, *Friends of the Family*, p. 295.

18. "The So-Called 'Baby Farming Case' Has Ended," London *Times* (September 24, 1870), p. 9.

19. Quoted in Tamara Silvia Wagner, "'We have orphans . . . in stock': Crime and the Consumption of Sensational Children," in Dennis Denisoff, ed., *Nineteenth-Century Childhood and the Rise of Consumer Culture* (Burlington, VT: Ashgate, 2007).

20. Marianne Novy, *Reading Adoption: Family and Difference in Fiction and Drama* (Ann Arbor: University of Michigan Press, 2005). Novy discusses Victorian fiction in chapters four and five.

21. Tess O'Toole, "Adoption and the 'Improvement of the Estate' in Trollope and Craik," *Nineteenth-Century Literature* 52(1) (June 1997): pp. 58–79, 62.

22. Novy, *Examining Adoption*, pp. 117–118.

23. Elizabeth Gaskell, "The Manchester Marriage," originally published in *Household Words* (Christmas 1858). Available online at http://www.lang.nagoya-u.ac.jp/~matsuoka/EG-Manchester.html, accessed January 30, 2004.

BIBLIOGRAPHY

Anderson, Nancy F. "The 'Marriage with a Deceased Wife's Sister Bill' Controversy: Incest Anxiety and the Defense of Family Purity in Victorian England." *Journal of British Studies* 21(2) (Spring 1982): 67–86.

———. *Woman against Women in Victorian England: A Life of Eliza Lynn Linton.* Bloomington: Indiana University Press, 1987.

Anderson, Robert. "Morality by Act of Parliament." *Contemporary Review* 49 (January 1891): 77–88. An article by a police commissioner urging the passage of legislation to curtail the rights of criminal parents over their offspring.

[Austin, Walter?]. *"One Dinner a Week" and "Travels in the East."* High Wycombe, Buckinghamshire: Peter Marcan, 1987. Sociological commentary reprinted from *All the Year Round*, the Victorian magazine founded by Charles Dickens.

Beeton, Isabella. *The Book of Household Management.* 1859–1861. Available online at http://www.gutenberg.org/etext/10136.

Behlmer, George K. *Friends of the Family: The English Home and Its Guardians, 1850–1940.* Stanford: Stanford University Press, 1998.

Bradshaw, David J., and Suzanne Ozment, eds. *The Voice of Toil: Nineteenth-Century British Writings about Work.* Athens: Ohio University Press, 2000. An excellent compendium of primary sources, with helpful contextualizing headnotes.

Busby, Siân. *The Cruel Mother: A Memoir.* New York: Carroll and Graf, 2005 [2004]. An account of a late-Victorian family situation that culminated in infanticide.

Butler, Samuel. *The Way of All Flesh.* Garden City, NY: Doubleday, 1944 [1903]. A scathing novelistic indictment of middle-class family life.

Carlyle, Thomas. *Past and Present.* New York: Charles Scribner's Sons, 1918 [1843]. Influential commentary on the "condition-of-England question."

Chitty, Susan. *The Beast and the Monk: A Life of Charles Kingsley.* London: Hodder and Stoughton, 1974.

Christie, Agatha. *Agatha Christie: An Autobiography*. New York: Dodd, Mead, 1977. Contains evocative chapters on the author's late-nineteenth-century childhood.

de Chumaceiro, Cora L. Díaz. "On Rudyard Kipling's Loss of Ayah." *PsyArt: A Hyperlink Journal for the Psychological Study of the Arts*, article 030802 (2003), n.p. Available online at http://www.clas.ufl.edu/ipsa/journal/2003_diaz_de_chumeceiro01.shtml.

Cline, Sally. *Radclyffe Hall: A Woman Called John*. Woodstock, NY: Overlook Press, 1998. A study of a major lesbian writer, who was born in 1883.

Coleridge, Christabel. *Charlotte Mary Yonge: Her Life and Letters*. London: Macmillan, 1903. The first biography written of this major domestic novelist, by a close friend.

Cooper, Di, and Moira Donald. "Households and 'Hidden' Kin in Early Nineteenth-Century England: Four Case Studies in Suburban Exeter, 1821–1861." *Continuity and Change* 10.2 (1995): 257–278.

Davidoff, Leonore, Megan Doolittle, Janet Fink, and Katherine Holden. *The Family Story: Blood, Contract and Intimacy 1830–1960*. New York: Longman, 1999.

Davidoff, Leonore, and Catherine Hall. *Family Fortunes: Men and Women of the English Middle Class, 1780–1850*. Chicago: University of Chicago Press, 1997.

Davin, Anna. *Growing Up Poor: Home, School and Street in London 1870–1914*. London: Rivers Oram Press, 1996.

Defining Gender, 1450–1910: Five Centuries of Advice Literature Online. Available online to subscribing libraries at http://www.adam-matthew-publications.co.uk/online/Defining-Gender/index.aspx. A major full-text database of scanned-in primary sources, with accompanying introductory essays by respected scholars.

Denisoff, Dennis, ed. *Nineteenth-Century Childhood and the Rise of Consumer Culture*. Burlington, VT: Ashgate, 2007.

DeSalvo, Louise. *Virginia Woolf: The Impact of Childhood Sexual Abuse on Her Life and Work*. Boston: Beacon, 1989.

Dickens, Charles. "Doctor Marigold." 1865. Available online at http://www.gutenberg.net/etext98/drmrg10.txt. One of a number of "Christmas stories" by Dickens extolling family values.

Dyhouse, Carol. *Girls Growing Up in Late Victorian and Edwardian England*. London: Routledge & Kegan Paul, 1981.

Edmonds, T. R. "On the Mortality of Infants in England." *Lancet* 25 (January 30, 1836): 690–694.

Eliot, George. *The Mill on the Floss*. New York: Norton, 1994 [1860]. The account of the heroine's relationship with her brother was strongly influenced by Eliot's relationship with her brother Isaac.

Fried, Albert, and Richard M. Elman. *Charles Booth's London: A Portrait of the Poor at the Turn of the Century, Drawn from His "Life and Labour of the People in London."* New York: Pantheon, 1968. A substantially shortened version of Booth's landmark sociological survey.

Gagnier, Regenia. *Subjectivities: A History of Self-Representation in Britain, 1832–1920*. New York: Oxford University Press, 1991.

Gaskell, Elizabeth. "The Half-Brothers." 1858. Available online at http://www.lang.nagoya-u.ac.jp/~matsuoka/EG-Brothers.html.

———. "The Manchester Marriage." 1858. Available online at http://www.lang.nagoya-u.ac.jp/~matsuoka/EG-Manchester.html.

———. *Wives and Daughters*. 1864–1866. New York: Penguin, 1977.

Gasson, Andrew. *Wilkie Collins: An Illustrated Guide*. New York: Oxford University Press, 1998.

Gillis, John R. *For Better, for Worse: British Marriages, 1600 to the Present*. New York: Oxford University Press, 1985.

"Good Breeding: Part I." *The Family Economist* 3 (1850): 27–29. An example of the countless nineteenth-century magazine articles calculated to disseminate good family values among the petit bourgeoisie.

Green, Susan. "Making a Marginal Text Central in the Undergraduate Literature Course: The Case of Hannah Cullwick's Diaries." *College Literature* 18(3) (October 1991): 132–137.

Hamilton, Susan, ed. *"Criminals, Idiots, Women, and Minors": Victorian Writing by Women on Women*. Peterborough, Ontario: Broadview Press, 1995.

Hayter, Alethea. *Charlotte Yonge*. Plymouth, UK: Northcote House, 1996.

Hibbert, Christopher, ed. *Queen Victoria in Her Letters and Journals*. New York: Viking, 1985.

Himmelfarb, Gertrude. *Poverty and Compassion: The Moral Imagination of the Late Victorians*. New York: Vintage, 1992.

Hopkins, Ellice. *The Power of Womanhood, or, Mothers and Sons: A Book for Parents and Those in Loco Parentis*. New York: Dutton, 1899. Hopkins was a well-known purity reformer of the late nineteenth century.

Hopkinson, Lyndall P. *Nothing to Forgive: A Daughter's Story of Antonia White*. London: Chatto & Windus, 1988.

Hughes, Kathryn. *George Eliot: The Last Victorian*. New York: Farrar, Straus, Giroux, 1998.

Ittmann, Karl. *Work, Gender and Family in Victorian England*. New York: New York University Press, 1995.

Jackson, Lee, comp. *The Victorian Dictionary: Exploring Victorian London*. Available online at http://www.victorianlondon.org. This enormously useful compendium provides accurately transcribed extracts and full-text scans of a lengthy list of nineteenth-century publications.

Jalland, Pat. *Women, Marriage and Politics 1860–1914*. Oxford: Clarendon, 1986.

Jordan, Thomas E. *Victorian Childhood: Themes and Variations*. Albany: State University of New York Press, 1987.

Kaplan, Fred. *Dickens: A Biography*. New York: William Morrow, 1988.

Kipling, Rudyard. *Rudyard Kipling: Something of Myself and Other Autobiographical Writings*. Ed. Thomas Pinney. New York: Cambridge University Press, 1990.

Kuper, Adam. "Incest, Cousin Marriage, and the Origin of the Human Sciences in Nineteenth-Century England." *Past and Present* 174(1) (2002): 158–183.

Lovell, Mary S. *The Sisters: The Saga of the Mitford Family*. New York: Norton, 2001.

Lowe, Clara M. S. *God's Answers: A Record of Miss Annie Macpherson's Work at the Home of Industry, Spitalfields, London, and in Canada*. London: J. Nisbet, 1882. Available online at http://www.gutenberg.org/dirs/etext04/godsa10.txt. An account of one of the social reformers engaged in child emigration work.

Lynch, Hannah. *Autobiography of a Child*. New York: Dodd, Mead & Company, 1899 [1898].

MacKenzie, Jeanne. *A Victorian Courtship: The Story of Beatrice Potter and Sidney Webb*. New York: Oxford University Press, 1979.

Mare, Margaret, and Alicia C. Percival. *The World of Charlotte M. Yonge, Victorian Best-Seller*. London: Harrap, 1948.

Mason, Michael. *The Making of Victorian Sexuality*. New York: Oxford University Press, 1994.

———. *The Making of Victorian Sexual Attitudes*. New York: Oxford University Press, 1994.

Mayhew, Henry. *London Labour and the London Poor*. London: Griffin, Bohn, and Company, 1851. Available online at http://etext.lib.virginia.edu/toc/modeng/public/MayLond.html. A pioneering series of sociological articles, originally published in the *Morning Chronicle*.

Milne-Smith, Amy. "A Flight to Domesticity? Making a Home in the Gentlemen's Clubs of London, 1880–1914." *Journal of British Studies* 45(4) (October 2006): 796–818.

Mitchell, Sally. *Daily Life in Victorian England*. Westport, CT: Greenwood, 1996.

———. *Dinah Mulock Craik*. Boston: Twayne, 1983.

Mulock, Dinah Maria [later Craik]. *A Woman's Thoughts about Women*. London: Hurst & Blackett, 1858. A best-selling Victorian novelist discusses women's roles in a variety of contexts.

Nelson, Claudia. *Invisible Men: Fatherhood in Victorian Periodicals, 1850–1910*. Athens: University of Georgia Press, 1995.

Nelson, Claudia, and Ann Sumner Holmes, eds. *Maternal Instincts: Visions of Motherhood and Sexuality in Britain, 1875–1925*. Houndmills, Basingstoke: Macmillan, 1997.

Nelson, Claudia, and Lynne Vallone, eds. *The Girl's Own: Cultural Histories of the Anglo-American Girl, 1830–1915*. Athens, GA: University of Georgia Press, 1994.

Nelson, Claudia, and Michelle M. Martin, eds. *Sexual Pedagogies: Sex Education in Britain, Australia, and America, 1879–2000*. New York: Palgrave Macmillan, 2004.

Newsome, David. *Godliness and Good Learning: Four Studies on a Victorian Ideal*. London: Cassell, n.d. [1961].

Nicholson, Nigel. *Portrait of a Marriage*. New York: Bantam, 1974 [1973]. A highly readable account of the marriage of the author's parents, including a lengthy autobiographical fragment by his mother, Vita Sackville-West.

Novy, Marianne. *Reading Adoption: Family and Difference in Fiction and Drama*. Ann Arbor: University of Michigan Press, 2005.

Offen, Karen. "Liberty, Equality and Justice for Women: The Theory and Practice of Feminism in Nineteenth Century Europe." In *Becoming Visible: Women in European History*, 2nd ed., ed. Renate Bridenthal, Claudia Koonz, and Susan Stuard. Boston: Houghton Mifflin, 1987. Available online at http://www.st-andrews.ac.uk/jfec/cal/suffrage/document/theofemm.htm.

O'Toole, Tess. "Adoption and the 'Improvement of the Estate' in Trollope and Craik." *Nineteenth-Century Literature* 52(1) (June 1997): 58–79.

Pawlowski, Merry M. "From the Country of the Colonized: Virginia Woolf on Growing up Female in Victorian England." In *Violence, Silence, and Anger: Women's Writing as Transgression*, ed. Deirdre Lashgari. Charlottesville, VA: University of Virginia Press, 1995, pp. 95–110.

Polhemus, Robert M. *Lot's Daughters: Sex, Redemption, and Women's Quest for Authority*. Stanford: Stanford University Press, 2005.

Poovey, Mary. *Uneven Developments: The Ideological Work of Gender in Mid-Victorian England*. Chicago: University of Chicago Press, 1988.

Robinson, Geoffrey. *Hedingham Harvest: Victorian Family Life in Rural England*. London: Century Hutchinson, 1989 [1977]. Focuses primarily on the author's family history.

Ruskin, John. *Sesame and Lilies*. Boston: Houghton Mifflin, n.d. [1865].

Sanders, Valerie. *The Brother-Sister Culture in Nineteenth-Century Literature: From Austen to Woolf*. New York: Palgrave, 2002.

Schooling, William. "Marriage Institutions." *Westminster Review* 135(4) (April 1891): 385–395.

Singleton, Mary Montgomerie. "Two Moods of a Man: By a Woman." *The Nineteenth Century* 31 (February 1892): 208–223.

Skene, Felicia. *The Inheritance of Evil; or, The Consequences of Marrying a Deceased Wife's Sister*. 1849. Available online at http://anglicanhistory.org/fiction/skene/inheritance1849.02.html.

Smelser, Neil. "The Victorian Family." In *Families in Britain*, ed. R. N. Rapoport, M. P. Fogarty, and R. Rapoport. London: Routledge and Kegan Paul, 1982, pp. 59–74.

Smith, Malcolm T. "Estimates of Cousin Marriage and Mean Inbreeding in the United Kingdom from 'Birth Briefs.'" *Journal of the Biosocial Sciences* 33 (2001): 55–66.

"The So-Called 'Baby Farming Case' Has Ended." London *Times* (September 24, 1870): 9.

Streatfeild, Noel. *A Vicarage Family*. London: Fontana, 1979 [1963]. A fictionalized autobiography by a well-known children's writer.

Tayler, Charles B. *Edward, or Almost an Owenite*. London: Religious Tract Society, 1840. One of the many RTS publications designed to inculcate "right morals" in the Victorian reading public.

Tosh, John. *A Man's Place: Masculinity and the Middle-Class Home in Victorian England*. New Haven: Yale University Press, 1999.

Tucker, Herbert F., ed. *A Companion to Victorian Literature and Culture*. Oxford: Blackwell, 1999.

Vicinus, Martha. *Independent Women: Work and Community for Single Women 1850–1920*. Women in Culture and Society. Chicago: University of Chicago Press, 1985.

Wolff, Robert Lee, ed. *Masterworks of Children's Literature, Vol. 5, Part 2: 1837–1900, The Victorian Age*. New York: Chelsea House, 1985. Contains the texts of six significant Victorian children's novels (by Frederic Farrar, Annie Keary, Charlotte Yonge, "Hesba Stretton," Flora Shaw, and Juliana Ewing), with helpful biographical commentary.

Yonge, Charlotte M. *The Castle Builders; or, The Deferred Confirmation*. New York: Garland, 1976 [1854].

———. *The Young Step-Mother*. London: Macmillan, 1889 [1861]. Like *The Castle Builders*, a novel about a blended family.

INDEX

About the Author

CLAUDIA NELSON is Professor of English and director of Women's Studies at Texas A&M University. In addition to coediting three anthologies of essays, she is the author of *Boys Will Be Girls: The Feminine Ethic and British Children's Fiction, 1857–1917*, *Invisible Men: Fatherhood in Victorian Periodicals, 1850–1910*, and *Little Strangers: Portrayals of Adoption in America, 1850–1929*, which won the Children's Literature Association award for the best scholarly book of 2003 in the field of children's studies.